KT-473-759

SHAKESPEARE AND THE
AMERICAN NATION

Why do so many Americans celebrate Shakespeare, a long-dead English poet and playwright? By the nineteenth century newly independent America had chosen to reject the British monarchy and Parliament, class structure and traditions, yet their citizens still made William Shakespeare a naturalised American hero. Today the largest group of overseas visitors to Stratford-upon-Avon, the Royal Shakespeare Company and Bankside's Shakespeare's Globe Theatre come from America. Why? Is there more to Shakespeare's American popularity than just a love of men in doublet and hose speaking soliloquies?

This book tells the story of America's relationship with Shakespeare. The story of how and why Shakespeare became a hero within American popular culture. Kim C. Sturgess provides evidence of a comprehensive nineteenth-century appropriation of Shakespeare to the cause of the American nation, and shows that as America entered the twentieth century a new world power, for many Americans Shakespeare had become as American as George Washington.

KIM C. STURGESS has studied in America and currently teaches Shakespeare and comparative literature courses at American universities in London.

SHAKESPEARE AND THE AMERICAN NATION

KIM C. STURGESS

CAMBRIDGE
UNIVERSITY PRESS

PUBLISHED BY THE PRESS SYNDICATE OF THE UNIVERSITY OF CAMBRIDGE
The Pitt Building, Trumpington Street, Cambridge, United Kingdom

CAMBRIDGE UNIVERSITY PRESS
The Edinburgh Building, Cambridge, CB2 2RU, UK
40 West 20th Street, New York, NY 10011–4211, USA
477 Williamstown Road, Port Melbourne, VIC 3207, Australia
Ruiz de Alarcón 13, 28014 Madrid, Spain
Dock House, The Waterfront, Cape Town 8001, South Africa

http://www.cambridge.org

First published 2004

Printed in the United Kingdom at the University Press, Cambridge

Typeface Adobe Garamond 11/12.5 pt.   *System* LATEX 2_ε [TB]

A catalogue record for this book is available from the British Library

ISBN 0 521 83585 2 hardback

Contents

vi   *Contents*

Acknowledgements

I would like to thank a number of people and acknowledge all the kind and expert help I received during both the research and the writing of this book.

Kate Bateman, American Embassy, London; Robert Bearman, Shakespeare Birthplace Trust, Stratford-upon-Avon; Christopher Bigsby, University of East Anglia, together with the Arthur Miller Centre, UEA, for a research travel grant; Michael D. Bristol, McGill University; Andrew Carroll, Legacy Project, Washington DC; Eric Homberger, University of East Anglia; Rachel Howell, Dallas Public Library; Kimberly Kline; Mary E. Kramer, Library of Congress; C. Lynn Mathieu, Johns Hopkins University; Hilda Molesky, Cornell University; Peter Rawlings, University of the West of England; Geoff Ridden, King Alfred's, Winchester; Barbara Willis, Central Rappahannock Regional Library, Fredericksburg; Georgianna Ziegler, Folger Shakespeare Library.

I would also like to thank the staff of libraries at the University of California, Santa Barbara, Cornell University, the Folger Shakespeare Library, William and Mary College, Williamsburg, the Library of Congress and the British Library for kindly allowing me access to their collections.

How many ages hence
Shall this our lofty scene be acted over
In states unborn and accents yet unknown!

Julius Caesar, Act 3, Scene 1

Prologue

In 1996 the chairman of the US House Policy Committee, Congressman Christopher Cox, stated that 'English, our common language, provides a shared foundation which . . . allowed people from every corner of the world to come together to build the American nation.'[1] More recently, James Crawford suggested that Californians could explain their support for Proposition 227 (dismantling the state's bilingual education programme) by saying, 'If you live in America, you need to speak English.'[2] For some Americans there is 'a patriotic subtext: one flag, one language'.[3]

These opinions reflect one side of the growing public debate about multilingualism and the changing ethnic make-up of the population of the United States. There is in America today an 'English Only' movement that is campaigning to have an amendment added to the United States Constitution that would, for the first time, make English the national language. While this proposal has, to date, been defeated, at least twenty-six states have declared English their official language.

Few people, either inside or outside of US politics, can ignore the changing ethnic mix of the population of the United States. On 18 September 2000, *Newsweek* magazine reported that in at least four US states, most notably California, ethnically 'white' Americans were now a minority and the suggested trend means that by the end of this decade two more states will record similar census results.[4]

Former president Bill Clinton affirmed the 'right' to bilingualism in Executive Order 13166. Today, US federal law ensures that funds are available to support education in languages other than English and for the production of multilingual government publications. While many Americans welcome this potential for greater cultural diversity, others are not so sure. What appears to concern Christopher Cox is that 'national policies [might] undermine the important role of a common language of national understanding'.[5] The fear is that English, the language of cultural conditioning for the United States, might become marginalised, and with it, any single unifying national culture be lost.

The concerns now expressed in the twenty-first century on the floor of Congress, in the media and on the Internet are not new in American history. What today some fear for the future was reality during the nineteenth century, with politicians and newspaper editors frequently expressing the very same anxiety about 'foreign' values and the dilution of what some regarded as American tradition. Then, just as today, census data revealed what many Americans had observed for themselves on the streets of New York, Cincinnati or San Francisco. In 1850 the 'decennial' US population census clearly showed the increasing number of 'foreign-born' Americans and that for the majority of US residents (if not all of them actually US citizens) English was not a 'mother tongue'.[6] Members of the then American Establishment regarded the growing numbers of immigrants, together with their 'imported' language and culture, a threat to the American nation. Their response was to promote the identification and usage of cultural symbols and traditions thought to represent Anglo-American monoculture. The key component to this promotion of the monoculture of national unity was to be the English language. Appropriated to this political and cultural project was the most recognised and respected playwright in America, an Englishman, one William Shakespeare.

NOTES

1. Christopher Cox, 'Welcoming Immigrants to a Diverse America: English as Our Common Language of Mutual Understanding', http://policy.house.gov/documents/statements/english.html.
2. James Crawford, 'A Nation Divided by One Language', *Guardian*, 8 March 2001.
3. Ibid.
4. Jon Meacham, 'The New Face of Race', *Newsweek*, 18 September 2000, pp. 38–48.
5. Cox, 'Welcoming Immigrants to a Diverse America'.
6. Campbell J. Gibson and Emily Lennon, 'Historical Census Statistics on the Foreign-Born Population of the United States: 1850–1990', Population Division Working Paper no. 29, US Bureau of the Census, http://www.census.gov/population/www/documentation/twps0029/twps0029.html. Based upon data found in *Historical Statistics of the United States: Colonial Times to 1970* (Washington DC: US Government Printing Office, 1975).

Introduction

The works of William Shakespeare and the cultural phenomenon that has materialised around the playwright's name now appear to be nowhere more at home or unconsciously accepted than in the United States of America. As Shakespeare is considered the pre-eminent writer in the English language, for many people it has been easy to accept his reception in America without question. However, there is much to suggest that if citizens of the United States in the nineteenth century had followed the rhetoric of the original leaders of the Revolution, Americans might have been expected to reject Shakespeare as an unwanted English anachronism. After all, for most native-born Americans, the plays and poetry of Shakespeare were theoretically a product of a foreign culture. Shakespeare utilised seemingly archaic elaborate language to tell the story of pre-American, European class-based society and hereditary aristocracy.

The thirteen original states had been unified by their rejection of the 'old world'. In the words of writer Thomas Paine, independence was to mean 'England to Europe: America to itself'.[1] The leaders of the colonists appeared to preach a doctrine of rebellion against 'old world' politics and values. The traditional European social hierarchy, a key component in many of Shakespeare's plays, was seen as a manifestation of tyranny, and the leaders of the colonists, now proclaiming themselves Americans, united their people behind the twin slogans of Freedom and Equality. America was an idea conceived in binary opposition to the dominant monarchist British culture of the seventeenth and eighteenth centuries, and, as Michael D. Bristol has suggested, 'In a sense America can be understood as a deliberate historical refusal of tradition.'[2]

Moreover, to better promote this American crusade for a 'new beginning' free from European influence, there was a need for, and indeed substantial evidence of, considerable anti-English fervour in American nationalist texts. This is clear from the tone and content of the Declaration of Independence,[3] and again, though more subtly, in the lyrics of the American national anthem, *The Star-Spangled Banner*.[4] It echoed in public orations every Fourth of July practically unabated until America entered the First World War in 1917.

Yet despite all the above, the works of William Shakespeare, an English playwright, were embraced by citizens throughout the United States and the stories contained within the plays are today accepted as part of American cultural heritage. During the nineteenth century Americans learnt to use the possessive pronoun 'our' when referring to Shakespeare, something not done with other foreign writers. James Fenimore Cooper famously said that William Shakespeare was 'the great author of America',[5] and there is indeed evidence that Shakespeare dominated the American stage while the numerous American editions of his plays became required reading for many patriotic Americans. The name Shakespeare could be found on almanacs, patent medicines, saloon signs and the deeds to gold mines. He was a subject to be found in American journals, poems, literature, burlesques, paintings and dime novels.

Many scholars have acknowledged the extent of Shakespeare's popularity in the USA. As early as 1927, Ashley Thorndike went so far as to suggest that 'Washington, Lincoln, Shakespeare . . . are the three whom Americans universally worship'.[6] For Lawrence Levine, 'Shakespeare *was* popular entertainment in nineteenth-century America',[7] while Simon Williams has insisted that 'Shakespeare was even more part of popular culture in the United States than he was in Britain.'[8] Howsoever the extent of Shakespeare's popularity is emphasised, as Michael D. Bristol has acknowledged, this popularity was 'a kind of anomaly'.[9] Sanford E. Marovitz has suggested that 'when treated focally rather than incidentally . . . Shakespeare may seem to constitute one of the most remarkable paradoxes in the social and intellectual history of the United States'.[10] And as Frank Mott wrote, almost as a footnote to a book on American publishing,

Absurd as some of the efforts to make Shakespeare a full-fledged Yankee may seem, they must be recognised as a phase of the militant nationalism of a period which lasted for many years after political independence was won . . . Shakespeare was adopted by America, and that in spite of his British origins.[11]

Such comments about the cultural history of the United States, the world's only 'superpower' and perhaps 'superculture', need further explanation.

SCHOLARSHIP ON SHAKESPEARE AND AMERICA

While over many years writers have recognised America's keen appetite for Shakespeare, two key studies focused attention on Shakespeare's position within American culture. Lawrence Levine, in *Highbrow/Lowbrow: The Emergence of Cultural Hierarchy in America*, explored how Shakespeare and other expressions of what is now often considered to be 'high art' were accepted by a nation that espoused equality and democracy. Levine maintained that the 'nineteenth century had harboured two Shakespeares; the humble, everyday poet who sprang from the people . . . and towering genius', but that ultimately Shakespeare was moved from 'popular culture to polite culture'.[12] Levine suggested that although Shakespeare was a key part of American popular culture throughout much of the nineteenth century, by the start of the twentieth century America's 'elite' had claimed him for their own.

Michael D. Bristol, in *Shakespeare's America, America's Shakespeare*, suggested that Shakespeare served the 'interests of class domination' but admitted that this was not the whole story. Bristol maintained that the 'institution of Shakespeare has a quite specific history in Britain [but] a substantially different history as an institution in North America'.[13] It is this 'different history' I will explore in this book. Bristol's work also first highlighted the political and cultural significance of the 'symbolic geography of the Folger building' and brought to far greater prominence the important oration of Joseph Quincy Adams.[14] The valuable work of both Levine and Bristol should be recognised as central to my book. However, while Levine and Bristol (and others publishing on the subject at about the same time) would appear to have been affected by a media-driven political controversy over issues of the literary canon and education curriculum, hopefully it has now become possible to explore these issues in a freer or perhaps more judicious fashion. This has been my aim.

While many other eminent scholars have contributed to the current critical understanding of Shakespeare, it is significant that some Americans have chosen to go beyond literary criticism to overtly politicise the issue, proclaiming links between the plays and the founding and development of the American republic. In 1877 Joseph Watson did just this with an article 'Shakespeare in America' published in the *New York Herald*, informing the American readership of the importance of Shakespeare to American ethnogenesis.[15] Several years later the politics of nation were again emphasised as Frank M. Bristol searched Shakespeare for quotations relevant to the 'New World'. In *Shakespeare and America* (1898) Bristol claimed that 'In no less than twelve plays does Shakespeare use expressions . . . inspired by America.'[16] Other attempts to directly associate American ethnogenesis with Shakespeare were to follow.

In the period immediately preceding America's entry to the First World War, Charles Mills Gayley expressed patriotic sentiments together with his appreciation of Shakespeare. In *Shakespeare and the Founders of Liberty in America* (1917) Gayley maintained that William Shakespeare was a believer in the kind of political system later to be established in the American republic.[17] The book ended with an appeal to America to join the European conflict on the side of the country that, along with America, shared the language and culture of Shakespeare. More than twenty years later, at the time of the American entry to the Second World War, Alwin Thaler presented similar arguments in *Shakespeare and Democracy* (1941), again speculating on the possible 'democratic sympathies' of a politically motivated playwright.[18]

American authors providing commentaries on America and Shakespeare have also, in varying ways, helped institutionalise the process of appropriation. In *Shakespeare in America* (1939) Esther Cloudman Dunn provided a very readable history of America's relationship with Shakespeare.[19] Dunn's adoption of a journalistic style allowed her to freely interpret the evidence and express her belief in a longstanding widespread appreciation of Shakespeare as literature, seemingly by all American patriots whatever their cultural background.

Other writers have freely created links between the myth and symbol of America and the playwright. Helene Wickham Koon chose an evocative title for her *How Shakespeare Won the West* (1925), a book narrating the way Shakespeare's plays were embraced as popular culture in the West by pioneers, cowboys and miners.[20] This 'Wild West' motif reappeared in 1998 when, writing for the *Smithsonian*, Jennifer Lee Carrell described 'How the Bard Won the West'.[21]

These are just a few of the many notable writings that over the years have helped confirm America's adoption of Shakespeare. However, within a few years of each other and by means of public oration rather than more orthodox academic activity, three American scholars publicly proclaimed America's nineteenth-century appropriation of Shakespeare. These orations became part of the very process of appropriation that they sought to describe. The first, Ashley Horace Thorndike, in an address before an invited audience at the British Academy in London in 1927, proclaimed that in the nineteenth century, during the process of American nation building, 'Shakespeare has been a symbol of unity, a moving force, almost a directing deity'.[22] Four years later, William Adams Slade, speaking in his official capacity as librarian of the Library of Congress, delivered a eulogy for Henry Clay Folger and in the process reviewed America's relationship with Shakespeare, providing a similar message to that of Thorndike.[23] Subsequently, Slade was to utilise much of the same text for a report presented to the elected members of the United States Seventieth Congress.

On an even more prominent stage and state occasion, Joseph Quincy Adams delivered an oration before the president of the United States and assembled dignitaries in 1932. In his address, Adams recounted the history of Shakespeare's appropriation to the cause of E Pluribus Unum. Adams's strong rhetoric was to clearly proclaim the significance of Washington DC as the chosen site for a Shakespeare memorial:

In its capital city a nation is accustomed to rear monuments to the persons who most have contributed to its well-being. And hence Washington has become a city of monuments. Varied in kind, and almost countless in number, they proclaim from every street, park and circle the affection of a grateful American people. Yet amid them all, three memorials stand out, in size, dignity and beauty, conspicuous above the rest: the memorials to Washington, Lincoln, Shakespeare.[24]

The pronouncements made by Thorndike, Slade and Adams, three American scholars, are similar in tone, and given their manifestly political nature I have considered all three part of a formal conclusion to the nineteenth-century appropriation process.

While it is clear that library shelves are well supplied with books on Shakespeare, the more recent orthodox hypothesis on America's nineteenth-century relationship with the plays has largely consisted of three broad generalisations. It has been frequently inferred that Americans, as civilised people, quite naturally recognised Shakespeare's universal appeal. It is reasoned that while Shakespeare constituted a significant part of American stage drama, the plays were performed primarily as a result of the presence in America of British actors and theatre managers. And finally, it has even been assumed that Americans celebrated Shakespeare because they were generally Anglophiles. The results of my own research, presented in this book, suggest that these orthodox assumptions are too simplistic and also, more importantly, misleading. Key questions have remained unanswered; for example, does American acceptance of Shakespeare during the nineteenth century really represent a paradox, and, if it does, how did acceptance occur and why? I will provide answers.

The results of my research, together with the reinterpretation of so much earlier work, offer an alternative, fuller commentary on America's energetic consumption of Shakespeare. With this book I confirm and explain the paradox of the appropriation of Shakespeare and its powerful presence within American popular culture during the nineteenth century. I highlight the importance of Fourth of July orations for the commonly expressed hostility to England and how the attendant popularity of oratory helped boost consumption of Shakespeare. I explain the broad American context, highlighting the importance of the twin concepts of manifest destiny and Anglo-Saxonism, which together facilitated increased consumption of Shakespeare by the populace. I reveal the presence and emphasise the significance of political elements within the preface to the 'First American Edition' of Shakespeare published in 1795, aspects that were to be mimicked in later publications. While revisiting the scholarship of previous writers on America and Shakespeare, this book supplies new material and creates a connection between the now familiar stories of the African Grove Theatre, the Astor Place riot, the actor Edwin Forrest and the establishment of Shakespeare libraries in America. I link nineteenth-century American interest in the Shakespeare authorship controversy with a wider objective of 'republicanising' the plays. Lastly, I reconnect the important pronouncements of Ashley Thorndike, William Adams Slade and Joseph Quincy Adams.

METHODOLOGY AND SCOPE

In preparing this cultural history I have embraced the philosophy of Joseph Hopkinson and his preface to the 1795 'First American Edition' of Shakespeare, in which he condemned British academics for attacking their predecessors (he appeared to regard this as largely a matter of 'point scoring').[25] This is not a book about books; with the words of Hopkinson in mind, I have therefore chosen not to directly refute or challenge named former commentators in the field.

The subject of Shakespeare and nineteenth-century America provided a myriad of different academic issues. To avoid what could be termed 'mission creep', it has been necessary for me to be judicious and maintain a sharp focus on the book topic. I have concentrated on the apparent paradox of popular consumption and appropriation of Shakespeare to the cause of the American nation rather than on any appreciation of his plays by American literati. Equally, as this is a book on Shakespeare and America, I have chosen not to repeat familiar arguments about the possible universality of Shakespeare's plays.

I have resolved not to stray from the American topic to address the question of Shakespeare's reception and appreciation in England, Germany or any other country. While Shakespeare was, of course, embraced by non-English-speaking cultures, in such cases the plays were read and performed in another language, sometimes translated by a major literary figure. For example, when translated by Goethe, Schiller or Schlegel in Germany,[26] Shakespeare not surprisingly became something rather different from the English original (as did the work of Edgar Allan Poe when translated by Baudelaire in France). It is also worth recalling that a number of European countries effectively came into existence only in the mid-nineteenth century, and, unlike America, did not owe their existence to a war against England, the essential paradox behind the American appropriation of Shakespeare.

This book represents an attempt to tell one story among many in relation to the construction of an American identity, problematic as that in turn is. America is hardly explained by the appropriation of Shakespeare any more than it is by emphasis on its immigrant nature, its frontier experience, its urban centres, its liberal constitution. But the slow and essentially unending business of cultural definition is not without its fascination and the appropriation of Shakespeare played a role, modest or otherwise, in that process.

I am aware that in recent years the question of American exceptionalism has been actively debated. In terms of this book, however, I am concerned precisely with a time when American politicians and writers and a heteroglot people were themselves declaring their exceptionalism and seeking both to find justification for that belief and mechanisms for facilitating it. The irony is that while calling for native writers with the capacity to create a literature commensurate with the country they also turned to a foreign author and, by accommodating him to their own necessities, claimed him as their own. There were those who opposed this process, including some of the more significant writers of the age, but in the end those voices did not prevail.

Key to my narrative is the fact that only in the city of Washington DC, symbolically sited close to the Capitol building housing the US Congress, is there a memorial library dedicated to the study of Shakespeare's texts, and I have included a detailed account of how this memorial came to be established. No comparable building or collection exists adjacent to the Houses of Parliament in London or the Reichstag in Berlin. The siting of the Washington DC library and its unprecedented collection of seventy-nine copies of the important First Folio help to confirm the special position of Shakespeare within the tradition of the American nation.

CHAPTER ORGANISATION AND CONTENTS

The book is divided into two main sections. In part 1 I explore the paradox of the American consumption of Shakespeare, the evidence that Americans did not simply watch and read but actively 'consumed' Shakespeare, and that this level of consumption was greater than that enjoyed by any native writer. Within this section I argue that the American state was conceived in direct opposition to England and that, throughout the following century, Americans created and celebrated an image of the 'English enemy' that helped to unite the population and, in the process, to define the American nation. Prior to the threats posed in the twentieth century by Communism and more recently 'terrorism', England, with her trade empire, was considered to be the primary danger to the continued success of the American 'revolution'. This is the paradox of the American consumption of Shakespeare.

In part 2 I comprehensively explore how and why Shakespeare was appropriated to the cause of creating a unifying American heritage. Finally, I include an account of the establishment of the Folger Shakespeare Memorial Library, a symbolic 'national monument' to Shakespeare on Capitol Hill, Washington DC. In appendices 1 and 2, I reproduce the full text of the rare 1795 preface to the 'First American Edition' and provide a location map for the Folger Shakespeare Memorial Library.

NOTES

1. Thomas Paine, *Common Sense*, ed. Isaac Kramnick (Harmondsworth: Penguin, 1976), p. 91. First published 1776.
2. Michael D. Bristol, *Shakespeare's America, America's Shakespeare* (New York: Routledge, 1990), p. 51.
3. Thomas Jefferson, 'The Declaration of Independence', in *Cornerstones of American Democracy* (Washington DC: National Archives Trust Fund Board, 1995).
4. Stephanie St. Pierre, *Our National Anthem* (Brookfield: Millbrock Press, 1992), p. 28.
5. James Fenimore Cooper, 'Notions of the Americans: Picked up by a Travelling Bachelor', in Robert E. Spiller, *James Fenimore Cooper* (New York: American Book Co., 1936), p. 20.

6. Ashley Horace Thorndike, *Shakespeare in America* (London: Oxford University Press, 1927), pp. 20 and 10.

7. Lawrence W. Levine, *Highbrow/Lowbrow: The Emergence of Cultural Hierarchy in America* (Cambridge MA: Harvard University Press, 1988), p. 21.

8. Simon Williams, 'European Actors and the Star System, 1752–1870', in Don B. Wilmeth and Christopher Bigsby, eds., *The Cambridge History of American Theatre* (Cambridge: Cambridge University Press, 1998), p. 310.

9. Bristol, *Shakespeare's America*, p. 2.

10. Sanford E. Marovitz, 'America vs Shakespeare: From the Monroe Doctrine to the Civil War', *Zeitschrift für Anglistik und Amerikanistik*, 34 (1986), pp. 33–46.

11. Frank Luther Mott, *Golden Multitudes: The Story of Best Sellers in the United States* (New York: Macmillan Co., 1947), p. 55.

12. Levine, *Highbrow/Lowbrow*, pp. 69 and 56.

13. Bristol, *Shakespeare's America*, p. 10.

14. Ibid., p. 75. For more on Henry Clay Folger and Joseph Quincy Adams, see ibid., chapter 3, 'The Function of the Archive'. See also Stephen J. Brown, 'The Uses of Shakespeare in America: A Study in Class Domination', in David Bevington and Jay L. Halio, eds., *Shakespeare, Pattern of Excelling Nature* (London: Associated University Press, 1978), pp. 230–1, and Alan Sinfield, 'Heritage and the Market, Regulation and Desublimation', in Jonathan Dollimore and Alan Sinfield, eds., *Political Shakespeare: Essays in Cultural Materialism* (Manchester: Manchester University Press, 1994), p. 256.

15. Joseph Watson, 'Shakespeare in America', *New York Herald*, 26 February 1877, p. 6.

16. Frank M. Bristol, *Shakespeare and America* (Chicago: Hollister & Bros., 1898), p. 8.

17. Charles Mills Gayley, *Shakespeare and the Founders of Liberty in America* (New York: Macmillan, 1917).

18. Alwin Thaler, *Shakespeare and Democracy* (Knoxville TN: University of Tennessee Press, 1941).

19. Esther Cloudman Dunn, *Shakespeare in America* (New York: Benjamin Blom, 1939).

20. Helene Wickham Koon, *How Shakespeare Won the West* (Jefferson WI: McFarland & Co., 1925).

21. Jennifer Lee Carrell, 'How the Bard Won the West', *Smithsonian*, 19/5 (August 1998), pp. 99–107.

22. Thorndike, *Shakespeare in America*, p. 10.

23. William Adams Slade, 'The Significance of the Folger Shakespeare Memorial: An Essay toward an Interpretation', in *Henry C. Folger: 18 June 1857–11 June 1930* (New Haven, 1931).

24. Joseph Quincy Adams, 'The Folger Shakespeare Memorial Dedicated April 23, 1932, Shakespeare and American Culture', *Spinning Wheel*, 12/9–10 (June–July, 1932), p. 212.

25. *The Plays and Poems of William Shakespeare: Corrected from the Latest and Best London Editions, with Notes, by Samuel Johnson, L.L.D. To Which Are Added,*

a Glossary and the Life of the Author . . . First American Edition (Philadelphia: Bioren & Madan, 1795). See appendix 1 below.

26. For more on German translations and adaptations of Shakespeare, see Roy Pascal, *Shakespeare in Germany 1740–1815* (Cambridge: Cambridge University Press, 1937). Pascal suggests that 'German critics of Shakespeare [were] only a small section of the German people' and that 'the German theatre-going public appreciated the plays of Shakespeare as middle-class tragedies, i.e. as something non-Shakespearean' (p. 1).

PART ONE

The paradox

CHAPTER I

Manifest consumption of Shakespeare

Shakespeare has got to be a kind of deity.

Herman Melville

Before television, film and professional sport were developed to satisfy American needs for mass entertainment, there was just theatre. It has been said that in the nineteenth century every new American town had to have a church and a theatre and sometimes the theatre arrived first.[1] While in the 'old world' of Europe innumerable stage plays had by then been written and were performed, the work of just one single playwright, William Shakespeare, can be seen to have attracted a mass American audience. Americans did not passively watch the plays; they actively consumed Shakespeare and everything that carried his name.

ON STAGE

As new cities prospered and their populations increased, '*Macbeth* was performed at Lexington, Kentucky in 1810, *Richard III* in Cincinnati in 1815; and *Othello* in Louisville in 1817.'[2] In Pittsburgh, in 1818, the theatre audience was offered both *Hamlet* and the *Hamlet Travestie* within a few days.[3] On the east coast between 1800 and 1860, the population of Charleston had the opportunity to see '600 performances of twenty-three of Shakespeare's plays'.[4] Theatre records show that *Othello* was performed forty-one times in Mobile, Alabama, between 1832 and 1860, twenty times in Memphis between 1837 and 1858, and twenty-two times in Louisville between 1846 and 1860.[5]

By 1857, theatre had become a key element in the social life of San Francisco, the important 'gateway city' to California and the territories of the West.[6] A newspaper article captured the extent to which Shakespeare had already entered the lives of the fortune seekers: 'There is hardly a butcher or a newspaper boy in the city who does not understand "like a book", the majority of the playable plays of Shakespeare, so often have they seen them acted, ranted, or slaughtered upon our boards.'[7] The writer then added that in the seven years since the theatres in San Francisco first opened, audiences had seen '86 Hamlets, 63 Richards and 57 Macbeths'.

In the longer-established cities of the East, Shakespeare entertained the energetic masses of American citizens. In Philadelphia, in just six years between 1835 and 1841, audiences watched eighty-three performances of *Richard III*, fifty-seven of *Othello* and fifty-three of *Hamlet*.[8] In New York, Shakespeare was consumed by the contrasting audiences of the elegant Astor Place Opera House and the Bowery Theatre, the latter a favourite of the rising classes. So popular were the plays that on 10 May 1849, during a single evening, there were three separate audiences in the city watching *Macbeth* (something unlikely to occur today, despite a much larger metropolitan population). Shakespeare was such a box-office attraction that, several years later, the American actor Edwin Booth performed *Hamlet* for 100 consecutive nights at the Winter Garden Theatre. This remarkable season began on 26 November 1864 and ended 22 March 1865, a record broken only by yet another season of *Hamlet* in 1923.[9] Plays by Shakespeare were so clearly dominant on the American stage that it is generally accepted they 'accounted for one-fifth to one-quarter of performances'.[10]

The empirical evidence is supported by a statistical study of theatrical entertainment in five Middle Western cities, namely Cincinnati, St. Louis, Detroit, Louisville and Lexington, between 1800 and 1840. In all, Ralph Leslie Rusk recorded 7,594 separate 'theatrical performances'.[11] This data, while representing only five cities, provides an indication of the rapid increase in the popularity of theatre as America moved towards mid-century. Rusk records the number of performances occurring in each decade as follows:

	all performances	Shakespeare
1801–10	51	2
1811–20	451	37
1821–30	1400	73
1831–40	5692	321

As it was usual in American theatres to have two performances per day, these statistics would suggest that by 1840 a sizable proportion of the population was attending theatrical entertainment. Given the number of performances and absence of other forms of mass recreation it can be concluded that theatregoing formed a significant part of the social life of western cities.

Of the 7,594 'entertainments' recorded, Rusk and Ashley Thorndike, his supervising professor at Columbia University and the man soon to make his *Shakespeare in America* address, adjudged 1,800 to be 'legitimate drama'. Of these, 433, or nearly 25 per cent, were plays by Shakespeare and this was the most significant contribution of any single playwright. Unfortunately, Rusk did not regard the numerous burlesques based on Shakespeare as a separate category and these appear to be included within the 2,647 farces. As Shakespeare was a popular subject for parody within 'theatrical farce', it is likely that Shakespeare's presence on the American stage was even more prominent. This aside, the 433 performances of 'serious' drama provide us with an indication of how popular Shakespeare had already become.

Performance of Shakespeare cannot be attributed to a lack of alternative material. In his study Rusk counted 967 different plays then in performance, only nineteen of which were by Shakespeare.[12] An alternative study covering New Orleans only (which also confirms Shakespeare as the most performed playwright) identified 1,141 different plays performed in the city over the thirty-six years between 1806 and 1842.[13] That plays by Shakespeare were performed more often than the others would seem to suggest they were more popular with audiences.

Rusk also recorded the number of times each of Shakespeare's plays was performed. The three with the highest number of performances were as follows:

Richard III	68
Othello	62
Hamlet	60

Rusk's study is supported by other published data. David Grimsted also collated material on theatre performances.[14] Grimsted's data, when retabulated, shows the number of performances between 1800 and 1851 for three additional cities:

	Philadelphia	Charleston	New Orleans
all performances	3593	1242	2086
Shakespeare	819	276	417
% Shakespeare	23	22	20

To highlight the growth in theatre attendance over this period of fifty-one years, 77 per cent of the performances recorded in Philadelphia occurred during the twenty years ending 1851. For New Orleans the figure is 85 per cent. The data also indicates that the most frequently performed full-length play over the entire period was *Richard III*. Three of Shakespeare's plays have the highest number of performances:

Richard III	410
The Lady of Lyons[15]	362
Pizarro[16]	340
Hamlet	331
Macbeth	304

Data such as this helps to confirm the written accounts left by travellers to the western states, as it does the observations of contemporary American writers and the anecdotes that appeared in the American press. As a source of entertainment and a stamp of civilised society, Shakespeare was ubiquitous both in the long-established eastern cities and in the booming frontier towns. There was a demonstrable and marked rise in his popularity at mid-century, with his most performed plays featuring strong soldier-aristocrats reacting with violence to any perception of threat.

A DEMAND FOR SHAKESPEARE

While it may be clear that Shakespeare made up a disproportionate amount of theatre entertainment, it has been suggested that nineteenth-century American audiences watched Shakespeare simply because many of the managers and actors of touring companies were British and therefore performed the material with which they felt most familiar, namely Shakespeare. While this theory may at first appear to account for Shakespeare's predominance, closer consideration suggests that it ignores the wider cultural context and market economics. The suggestion that a significant portion of the American population paid to see Shakespeare's plays primarily because British actors and their managers were familiar with Shakespeare is speculative and, I suggest, unsound. Any assertion that Americans, known for exercising their individual will, paid to see Shakespeare simply because it was convenient for touring companies implies Americans were passive and subservient to the will of British actors, a situation I will demonstrate to be very far from the truth.

Considered by some a cliché, 'supply and demand' is a basic law accepted by marketing professionals. Without consumer demand, supply cannot be viable or sustained. Additionally, it must be stated that while consumer demand can be stimulated it cannot wholly be created. For American theatres and stock companies to be financially successful performing so much Shakespeare, there had to be audience demand for the type of entertainment that was provided by his plays and not by other playwrights. The performance data and anecdotal evidence already presented suggests that American audiences repeatedly paid to watch a relatively small number of Shakespeare's plays in repertory, and it is probable that something within the context of nineteenth-century America stimulated this audience demand.

While it should not be denied that theatre managers and actors from Britain made up a proportion of those who catered for the entertainment needs of Americans, the professionals who visited America did not travel as theatrical 'missionaries'. They went to earn dollars and, with more than a thousand different plays then in performance, they preferred to present those likely to attract a large paying audience. The evidence shows that throughout the nineteenth century American audiences proved themselves willing to pay to watch Shakespeare. They made their preference clear by ticket purchase, and, as I will demonstrate, they were to become well known for very forcibly expressing their views to theatre managers and actors alike.

SHAKESPEARE IN PRINT

While Shakespeare's rise in popularity on the American stage was part of the wider phenomenon of nineteenth-century public theatre, the growth in sales of Shakespeare in print was directly attributable to the process of appropriation. The purchase of an American book of play scripts for home reading represents an act of individual choice untainted by foreign publishers.

The first American-produced copies of Shakespeare's complete works were sold in Philadelphia in 1795. American publishers recognised the potential market for Shakespeare and the public were soon offered a variety of new editions. In *American Shakespearean Criticism* (1939), Alfred Van Rensselaer Westfall provided a list of single and complete editions published in America between 1790 and 1866.[17] This list, when presented in a retabulated form based on the date of issue, reveals that the frequency of publication of new editions increased after the year 1800 to average five per decade until 1849. The retabulated data also demonstrates that at the start of the next decade there was a sixfold increase:

	number of editions
1790–9	1
1800–9	3
1810–19	5
1820–9	4
1830–9	5
1840–9	5
1850–9	29
1860–6	5

This retabulation of Westfall's data includes only 'complete' editions of Shakespeare, ignoring the relatively few (seven) publications of single plays during the same period. Westfall's list utilised earlier work by Philadelphia lawyer Henry N. Paul, who was to present his collection of American editions to the Folger Shakespeare Library in Washington DC. Allowing for the fact that in a very few cases the Paul-Westfall list is unable to offer an exact publishing date, the huge rise in the number of editions issued during the decade commencing 1850 must be considered significant.

The rise is confirmed by another publication, William Jaggard's *Shakespeare Bibliography* of 1911, which shows thirty-nine American editions for the same period.[18] This dramatic rise in the publishing and consumption of Shakespeare by Americans is further confirmed by Westfall's estimation that by 1865 the total number of new and reprinted American editions had reached 'one hundred and fifty'.[19]

An alternative published bibliography for American Shakespeare editions, which predates Westfall but appears to have been unknown to him, confirms the dramatic growth in Shakespeare publishing in America from the year 1850. In December 1889, the librarian of the Shakespeare Memorial Library, Stratford-upon-Avon, published a pamphlet detailing 138 American editions of the works published between 1795 and 1889, no fewer than 108 of them published in the thirty-nine years from 1850.[20] After reviewing data of this type, it is clear that American publishers regarded the market for Shakespeare as substantial, and that each in turn repackaged and re-presented the text to meet the needs of book buyers.

It is possible to suggest, however, that the large number of editions issued does not prove the number of copies sold. To precisely quantify the sales for any particular book title it would be necessary to physically access the account records of each and every individual publisher. In the case of Shakespeare the sheer number of publishers and booksellers who were marketing their own versions unfortunately makes this task impractical at present.[21] Despite the absence of proven sales data, however, there is sufficient evidence of other kinds to confirm that commercially minded American booksellers were responding to real consumer demand. The widespread availability of Shakespeare editions suggests volume sales. In 1834, just one advertisement placed by Truman, Smith & Co. of Cincinnati offered Shakespeare's 'dramatic works for sale in seven different forms'.[22] Frank Mott, in his chapter 'Shakespeare: American Best Seller', suggested that the 'number of editions . . . continuously available in the United States is amazing'.[23] He reported that Leypoldt's *American Catalogue* for the year 1876 'lists no less than sixty-five edition[s] of the complete plays then in print'.[24]

Nineteenth-century Americans consumed the plays of an Elizabethan English playwright. While the literati might have been occupied with the type of issues comprehensively explored by Francis Otto Matthiessen in his *American Renaissance*,[25] there was a more significant populist consumption of Shakespeare consistent with the mass culture described by Lawrence Levine. While Shakespeare's popularity in America has been acknowledged in many cultural studies, what has often been evaded is that this high level of consumption represents a real paradox. Enthusiastically patriotic and hostile to the then English hegemony, Americans could have been expected to generally reject Shakespeare as an unwanted symbol of continued cultural dominance. However, while a few voices were raised in ineffectual protest, all the evidence available suggests that the majority did the exact opposite.

The following chapter will demonstrate the depth of anti-English sentiment that developed at the time of the War of Independence and continued throughout the period in which Shakespeare was generally embraced as a popular playwright and appropriated to serve the American nation.

NOTES

1. Joe Cowell, *Thirty Years Passed among the Players: Interspersed with Anecdotes and Reminiscences of a Variety of Persons, Directly or Indirectly Connected with the Drama during the Theatrical Life of Joe Cowell, Comedian* (New York: Harper & Bros., 1844), p. 87.
2. Alfred Van Rensselaer Westfall, *American Shakespearean Criticism 1607–1865* (New York: H. W. Wilson, 1939), p. 59.
3. Henry Bradshaw Fearon, *Sketches of America. A Narrative of a Journey of Five Thousand Miles through the Eastern and Western States of America* (London: Longman, Hurst, Rees, Orner & Brown, 1818), pp. 209–10.
4. Woodrow L. Holbein, 'Shakespeare in Charleston, 1800–1860', in Philip C. Kolin, ed., *Shakespeare in the South: Essays on Performance* (Jackson MS: University Press of Mississippi, 1983), p. 88.

5. Charles B. Lower, 'Othello as Black on Southern Stages', in Kolin, ed., *Shakespeare in the South*, p. 201.
6. Koon, *How Shakespeare Won the West*, p. 13.
7. *Golden Era* (San Francisco), 15 February 1857. Quoted here from Koon, *How Shakespeare Won the West*, pp. 88–9.
8. Raoul Granqvist, *Imitiation as Resistance: Appropriations of English Literature in Nineteenth-Century America* (Madison NJ: Fairleigh Dickenson University Press, 1995), p. 256, n. 208. See also Arthur Wilson, *A History of the Philadelphia Theatre* (New York: Greenwood Press, 1935), pp. 18–19.
9. Louis Marder, *His Exits and His Entrances: The Story of Shakespeare's Reputation* (Philadelphia: J. B. Lippincott & Co., 1963), p. 312.
10. Gary Taylor, *Reinventing Shakespeare: A Cultural History from the Restoration to the Present* (London: Vintage, 1991), pp. 196–7.
11. Ralph Leslie Rusk, *The Literature of the Middle Western Frontier*, 2 vols. (New York: Columbia University Press, 1925), vol. i, pp. 411–14. Rusk collated his data from published announcements in newspapers from five cities.
12. Ibid., pp. 412–14.
13. Nelle Smither, *A History of the English Theatre in New Orleans* (New York: Benjamin Blom, 1944). After Shakespeare, the second most popular playwright was John Baldwin Buckstone, with 340 performances of his thirty-six plays.
14. David Grimsted, *Melodrama Unveiled: American Theater and Culture, 1800–1850* (Los Angeles: University of California Press, 1968), pp. 250–5.
15. Edward Bulwer-Lytton, *The Lady of Lyons or, Love and Pride* (New York: T. H. French, 1838).
16. Richard Brinsley Sheridan, *Pizarro* (New York: Thomas Longworth, 1819). An adaptation of a play by August von Kotzebue.
17. Westfall, *American Shakespearean Criticism*, pp. 168–84.
18. William Jaggard, *Shakespeare Bibliography* (Stratford-upon-Avon, 1911), pp. 527–34. Unfortunately, the city of publication is not indicated for many entries. It would be possible to conclude that an even greater number of American editions were published over this ten-year period.
19. Westfall, *American Shakespearean Criticism*, p. 77.
20. A. H. Wall, *A List of the Editions of Shakespeare's Works Published in America* (Stratford-upon-Avon: Shakespeare Memorial Association, 1889). Of the 138 editions listed, the Stratford library had only fifteen within their collection. Wall made an appeal to Americans to 'inspect their book shelves', and on finding any edition required by the Shakespeare Memorial Library to 'place their names and addresses on the fly leaves, and send them on to the Librarian' (p. 6).
21. For an example of the general rise in book sales during the mid-nineteenth-century period, brought about by cultural influences rather than economic reasons, one can refer to data from the American Bible Society. The society records show that the number of Bibles issued for the year 1846 was 161,974 Bibles and 321,899 New Testaments. For 1856 the number rose to 240,776

Bibles and 427,489 New Testaments. See Carl Bode, *The Anatomy of American Popular Culture 1840–1861* (Berkeley: University of California Press, 1959), p. 142. For a study of publishing in the USA, see Michael Winship, *American Literary Publishing in the Mid-Nineteenth Century: The Business of Ticknor and Fields* (Cambridge: Cambridge University Press, 1995).

22. *Cincinnati Daily Gazette*, 7 May 1834. Quoted here from Rusk, *The Literature of the Middle Western Frontier*, vol. II. p. 6.
23. Mott, *Golden Multitudes*, p. 58.
24. Ibid.
25. Francis Otto Matthiessen, *American Renaissance: Art and Expression in the Age of Emerson and Whitman* (New York: Oxford University Press, 1941).

CHAPTER 2

America: a proudly anti-English 'idea'

I HATE England; though I love some Englishmen.

Nathaniel Hawthorne[1]

From the Declaration of Independence in 1776, anti-English sentiment was expressed by many Americans, paradoxically at the same time as Shakespeare was celebrated and enjoyed. Hans Kohn, referring to the early nineteenth century, wrote of the 'bitter opposition in America to England', amounting to a 'venomous hatred'.[2] Gustave de Beaumont, writing in 1830, observed that Americans generally 'detested the English'.[3] According to another scholar, Edward P. Crapol, 'Anti-British nationalism, running like a red skein through American history, apparently served a negative but nonetheless essential role in the development of an American patriotism.'[4]

That there was hostility to England and the English during the early period of the republic is not surprising and following the War of Independence can perhaps be considered natural. What I will demonstrate in this chapter, however, is the full extent to which this strong anti-English sentiment became institutionalised and an expression of American nationalism while simultaneously Shakespeare gradually became subsumed into national consciousness.

An essay by Jürgen Heideking described the process by which England became the important 'other' both at the time of the Revolution and 'during the first 125 years of American independence'.[5] This essay and others within the collection *Enemy Images in American History* demonstrated how the creation of a separate American identity for the nation relied upon a process of recording first the English, and then other groups as 'the enemy'. The argument can be made that anti-English sentiment was a necessary precursor to maintaining America as a political binary to England and also that hostility to the English constituted a defining part of early American republicanism.

This promotion of England as the American enemy can be observed throughout the nineteenth century. Specific events such as trade disputes, the 1812–14 war, territorial conflicts over Oregon and Maine in the 1840s and the Lincoln administration's fear of England's intervention on the side of the South in the war of secession all constitute specific periods when America formally expressed its hostility to England.

NEITHER ANGLOPHOBIA NOR ANGLOPHILIA

In a quest for greater clarity I will not use the more common term 'Anglophobia' to refer to this widespread sentiment, as the word 'phobia' implies a type of fear or dread that is quite different from the prejudice and animosity that was directed towards England following the Declaration of Independence. Furthermore, for many nineteenth-century Americans the prefix 'Anglo-' carried with it a suggestion of racial and cultural affiliation to a period of history that predated the emergence of the people of England from their pre-eleventh-century collection of regional identities and allegiances to become a recognisable nation. The prefix 'Anglo-' was associated by Americans with a 'Saxon' pre-English idyll, rather than with the imperial nation of the nineteenth century.[6] While today scholars may differ as to when exactly England as a nation came into being, Americans in the eighteenth and nineteenth centuries were clear. The expressed opinion of Thomas Jefferson, perhaps influenced by Rapin de Thoyras's *Histoire d'Angleterre*, his preferred historical study,[7] was that the period before the Norman Conquest of 1066 was 'pre-England' and therefore, for nineteenth-century Americans, Anglo-Saxon.[8] What I wish to emphasise is that America was not anti-Anglo-Saxon; America was anti-English. The American cult of Anglo-Saxonism will be dealt with in a later chapter.

To correctly identify the existence of anti-English sentiment it is also necessary to acknowledge the confusion caused by the common use of the term 'British'. 'British' refers to the people of a unified political state that came into being with the Act of Union of 1707, yet the term is often used when Americans specifically mean 'English' and vice versa. The effect of this almost random application of national signifier can sometimes obscure the intended target for prejudice or hostility. It can be quickly recognised, however, that when in American cultural history there appears to have been criticism of the British, it has in fact been criticism of the nation of England and not of the citizens of Scotland, Wales or Northern Ireland. Throughout

American history there has been a strong suspicion, if not belief, that the United Kingdom of Great Britain was in fact a political union created for and dominated by the English, and it has therefore been the English who have been regarded as the oppressor. The truth of this belief is thankfully beyond the scope of this book.

EVIDENCE OF EARLY ANTI-ENGLISH SENTIMENT

The popularity of the American tradition of the heroic Puritan 'pilgrim fathers' helped reinforce the suggestion that colonists of New England came to the 'new world' to escape the cultural corruption and decadence of an England dominated by the British monarchy and Established Church. The seventeenth-century Puritans sought to remove the 'impurities' that had oppressed their spiritual and physical wellbeing. The New England colonists, while mainly English in ancestry, felt the need to distance themselves from what in their perception England had become. The seeds of future anti-English prejudice arrived in the 'new world' with the Puritans, and while relatively repressed for the first century of colonisation, it remained a potent force beneath the surface.

There were many others who had no natural amity towards England. The many colonists in America whose culture and country of birth were non-English, such as the Dutch, Germans, Scandinavians and French, naturally felt a growing antagonism towards the British king and British influence on the American continent. One estimate as to the family origins of colonists suggests that in 1790 only 58 per cent of Americans originated from the British Isles and can therefore be known to have had English as their 'mother tongue'. For the remaining 42 per cent, either their linguistic origins were unknown or English was a foreign language. For this sizable minority at least, there was no natural loyalty to English culture.[9]

A very early example of the way the colonists in New England demonstrated their anti-English hostility can be seen in the response to fugitives from English justice. Three of the signatories to the death warrant of King Charles I were later to flee the restoration of the monarchy by escaping to New England. The English parliament issued arrest warrants for Edward Whalley, William Goffe and John Dixwell, but 'over and over, God-fearing and law-abiding Puritans hid the regicides, fed and clothed them, and helped them to find new havens'.[10] Despite substantial rewards of £100 per man and a twenty-one-year hunt, neither redcoats nor colonial officers could shake the solidarity of anti-monarchist New England.

THE PRELUDE TO REVOLUTION

Pamphleteers and newspaper editors skilfully utilised inflammatory language both to express and to encourage anti-English sentiment. A newspaper article from June 1775 by 'Coriolanus' demonised the British army with a type of imagery that would encourage an enduring hatred amongst colonists. The British soldiers were described as

Base Wretches, who fight for Pay and Plunder; Caitiffs devoid of Principles of Tenderness, Humanity and Honour! . . . What may we not expect from such merciless Ravagers? – Alas! Must we see our flourishing Country pillaged and laid waste, our Houses fired, our Fathers massacred, our Wives, our Mothers, our Sisters, and our Daughters, fall Prey to brutal and inhuman Ravishers; our tender Infants torn from the Breasts, the Walls and Fences sprinkled with their Blood, whilst Cries and Groans transpierce the yielding Air! . . . Forbid it Heaven![11]

It would be easy to speculate that the writer of this piece, using the name of a character popularised in one of Shakespeare's plays, was also influenced by a speech made to the citizens of Harfleur in Shakespeare's *Henry V*.[12] Whether or not this was so, the piece was clearly considered to have captured the emotion of the moment, as it was later reprinted in at least four other New England publications.

Later the same year, Philip Freneau published a poem designed to boost American patriotism, which included the following lines:

> Our city ravag'd and our towns on fire,
> Troops pour'd on troops to Britain's lasting shame,
> That threaten all with universal flame:
> These are the Kings, the monarchs of the sea,
> Exerting power in lawless tyranny.[13]

While the poem clearly identified the British monarchy as the enemy, both the advertisement promoting its sale and its title page featured five evocative lines from Shakespeare's *Henry V*.[14] The speech beginning 'In peace there's nothing so becomes a man' (Act 3, Scene 1), originally written to encourage patriotic feeling in Elizabethan England, was ironically appropriated by Freneau to increase hostility to Britain and the British military during America's war for independence. Shakespeare had already become a useful tool for American republican propaganda.

Prior to his famous treatise *Common Sense*, Thomas Paine wrote under various pseudonyms as a journalist and pamphleteer, accusing English 'Kings, Commons, and Lords' of 'horrid cruelties'.[15] Later, in January 1776, when Paine finally published the hugely influential *Common Sense*, he argued against the English system of government and its aristocracy. Paine informed his readers that since the bloodshed of Lexington he had personally rejected George III for being a 'hardened, sullen tempered Pharaoh of [England]'. Paine went on to call the king a 'wretch', who despite his 'pretended title of FATHER OF HIS PEOPLE can unfeelingly hear of their slaughter, and composedly sleep with their blood upon his soul'.[16] It was with anti-English journalism such as this that the citizens of the British colonies gradually became inspired to take their momentous step towards revolution.

THE DECLARATION OF INDEPENDENCE

While perhaps all political revolutions commence with anti-Establishment rhetoric, there was a unique feature in the revolt of the thirteen American colonies. The American War of Independence (1776–83) was supported by many in the wealthy ruling elite, declaring a popular revolt against a system of government and economic order that had allowed this elite to secure its comfortable lifestyle. This revolution was not the action of an oppressed impoverished proletariat, but rather the calculated process of a people who saw the economic benefits that would result from the promotion of 'life, liberty and the pursuit of happiness'.[17] Perhaps because of this fact, the fifty-six signatories to the Declaration of Independence felt the need to strongly emphasise the differences between themselves and the British monarchy, and in so doing helped to create an identifiable anti-English fervour that can be traced from this document to several important symbols of the American nation.

The Declaration of Independence was the key document in the establishment of the American state and became the rallying point for George Washington's Continental Army, as it has been for American patriots ever since. However, this document consists mainly of a list of complaints made by the colonists against the king of England and the British government. Of the document's forty-three lines, thirty-three can be considered as largely devoted to communicating the many injustices that had been suffered under British 'tyranny'. Rather than a declaration of what the new nation of the 'united States of America'[18] stood for, the Declaration of Independence can be interpreted as a statement of what America stood against. Above all, the ideology in the document indicated that the newly independent nation was not going to be another England. This revolution had no manifesto, just a declaration of all the injustices the populace had suffered under a tyrannical monarchy.

The Declaration of Independence has become a sacred icon to Americans not so much for what it actually says as for what it has come to symbolise. In 1776 the thirteen 'States of America' clearly stated that the basis for their future ideology was to be opposition to England. As Heideking suggests,

> The hostility towards England was primarily motivated by ideological beliefs and convictions; one could even argue that the American image of an English enemy was the first ideological enemy image in modern history . . . By constructing and disseminating this enemy image, the American patriots in a way anticipated the formation of a separate American nation. In that sense, the enemy image helped to create and construct a separate national identity, because it acted as a unifying force in the face of all the existing diversity and fragmentation in and between the states.[19]

The positioning of England as the enemy marked the first step in the process of 'inventing a tradition' for the new nation of America. America, from the outset, was anti-English and any celebration of American values was made easier by having an identifiable binary opposite. Eric Hobsbawm defined this nineteenth-century process of 'invention' in the following way: 'Invention of Tradition is taken to mean a set of practices, normally governed by overtly or tacitly accepted rules and of a ritual or symbolic nature, which seek to inculcate certain values and norms of behaviour by repetition.'[20] From 1783, as America created an annual celebration for its recent victory over Britain, the symbolic importance of the existence of a foreign enemy was affirmed by repetition during the annual Fourth of July celebrations.

FOURTH OF JULY ORATIONS

A key institutionalised cultural event in the nineteenth-century American calendar was the annual celebration of the Fourth of July, the 'Sabbath of the nation'.[21] Beyond the light-hearted festivities, however, there was, each year, prior to the customary parade, an almost ritualised public reading of the Declaration of Independence, complete with its vilification of the British monarchy and state. After this reading it was considered fitting to have a formal oration, 'Emphasizing the virtues of freedom, democracy, patriotism, the sacrifices of the heroes of the Revolution (and later wars) in defending American soil'.[22] This annual oration established English 'tyranny' as the point from which Americans could measure their collective virtue and developing national glory. One could not celebrate American independence without consciously recognising what America had become independent from. If American citizens post-1776 considered themselves 'free', then prior to 1776 these same citizens were plainly 'enslaved'. Since independence, for many millions of Americans each year the United States has been presented as 'heroic' and England, at least subconsciously, as 'villainous'. Fanny Trollope, writing in 1832, perhaps not surprisingly regarded this ceremony as containing 'bad feeling [and] unvarying abuse of the mother country', and described the Declaration of Independence itself as a 'warlike manifesto'.[23]

Nineteenth-century Fourth of July orations followed a formula. They began with a ritual demonisation of the English, together with stories of how American patriots threw off the yoke of tyranny. This was followed by a glorification of the American State and the American people. The third component of the oration was usually a discourse on a contemporary political issue of concern to the orator. Traditionally, the orations lasted from one to two hours and many notable Americans, such as John Quincy Adams, Daniel Webster, Charles Sumner and Shakespearean actor Edwin Forrest, were given the honour of making the address. The significance of the orations to nineteenth-century Americans can be judged by the fact that many speakers, or the sponsoring civic authorities, chose to publish the texts, and one assumes that these 'souvenirs' were bought by the American public.

The New York State Library currently has a collection of 1,345 orations published between 1777 and 1954. When tabulated by date and analysed, it becomes clear that 1,091 or 81 per cent of these chauvinistic tributes to America were published between 1800 and 1879. This period of seventy-nine years, when the orations were considered so much a part of the annual celebrations, include all the years in which England was the recognised 'public enemy' and the years most important to the formation of American national symbols. These years also represent the period in which Shakespeare became popularised as an appropriated playwright of the USA.

ORATIONS AND RHETORICAL SKILLS

The orations of the nineteenth century were part of a process by which Americans learned the collective tradition and myth that helped sustain the belief that the United States was created through a heroic struggle against a tyrannous enemy. The orations, while apparently a celebration of American achievement, were through necessity in part anti-English. 'Patriotism and nationalism formed oratory's ideological background.'[24] The Fourth of July, while reinforcing the commonly felt hostility to England, ironically helped popularise oration and public speaking as a form of 'art' and entertainment. Shakespeare provided convenient texts that clearly demonstrated the art of rhetoric and public speaking. Declamation of the monologues from Shakespeare became an important part of every nineteenth-century American schoolchild's experience, and this symbiotic association with the annual Fourth of July orations helped link Shakespeare with American nationalism. While these orations were founded on an opposition to England, 'the popular affiliation between Shakespeare and the patriotic discourse on liberty . . . seemed implicitly to nationalize part of the English poetic heritage'.[25]

Some orations were charged with personal hostility and seem to have been designed to influence future generations. An oration by Archibald Buchanan offers evidence of the ritualised form that the Fourth of July was to take as Americans celebrated their Independence Day. Buchanan told his Baltimore audience that it was their patriotic duty to

Train up our children to contemplate with horror, the British name! . . . and that while I live, I will remember the injuries of Britain! I will annually, read over the catalogue of her iniquities; I will declaim against them; I will admonish mankind of them; and when death shall, at length, draw his cold hands over the eyes forever, my last dying words to the spectators round shall be 'Friends remember Britain'.[26]

Other orators, such as Samuel Berrian before the Tammany Society in New York (the regional political machine of the emerging Democratic Party), used the occasion to express support for those they considered to be victims of English oppression. Berrian, in 1815, appealed to the American audience to support the Irish people in a revolution against their English oppressor.[27]

South of New York in Charleston, firemen gathered to hear their speaker mount a vitriolic attack on English actions in America. During this oration, Joseph H. Dukes referred to the Scots and the Welsh as kindred spirits, people who, like Americans, had suffered for the cause of freedom.[28] He invoked the names of 'Wallace at Stirling' and 'Bruce at Bannockburn'. Duke told his audience that he felt 'they were fighting for their firesides – for their children – for the institutions of their country, and the altars of their religion'. The Charleston firemen were encouraged to 'echo back the song of the Welsh from their native fastnesses' and continue the struggle against the English enemy.

In the 1819 Salem oration, Andrew Dunlap, a Massachusetts lawyer, reiterated the popular belief that America was now free from the pollution of Europe. The audience, with their strong Puritan heritage, heard that 'America, in the innocence of her youth, and disengaged from the pollution of European Connexions, is the pride and promise of the world.'[29] Dunlap also highlighted the importance of the defeat of the British at the battle of New Orleans for American tradition. After recounting the names of the recent battles fought in the war of 1812–14, he concluded by saying, 'it was for the battle of New Orleans to complete the circle of the glories of America, and to fill the world with the splendours of her fame . . . this victory, the most remarkable which history can record'.[30]

Several published orations demonstrate that some speakers, while personally appreciative of Shakespeare, celebrated American independence at the same time as reinforcing the negative image of England. Charles Sprague, a banker and poet, delivered the Boston Fourth of July oration in 1825. The symbolism of the American state and its historical fight with England was combined with Sprague's personal affinity with the English language. His description of the Fourth of July as the 'Sabbath Day of Freedom', combined with references to England's 'intolerance and tyranny [that] had for ages leagued to keep their victim down',[31] affirmed the continued binary opposition of the two nation states.

Sprague's nationalism, however, was balanced by a respect for the language shared by the two nations. Sprague informed his fellow citizens, 'We owe England much. Nothing for her martyrdoms, nothing for her proscriptions; nothing for the innocent blood with which she stained the white robes of religion and liberty.' But he followed this by asking the rhetorical question, 'Who that speaks, and reads, and thinks her language, will be slow to own his obligation?'[32] While Sprague emphasised the importance of the shared language, he went on to suggest that England had deserved what he implied was divine retribution. Sprague celebrated the three living signatories to the independence document, stating that their ' "alliance" was, indeed, a "holy" one, for it met the approving smile of a Holy God!'.[33]

John Quincy Adams was another orator who chose to link Shakespeare with his text in praise of America. When he delivered the Fourth of July oration in 1831, to an audience in the town that now bore his name, Adams quoted from a number of European writers, such as Tacitus, Gibbon and Smollett, to support his argument, each time identifying the author. However, as a demonstration of his confidence that his fellow citizens were already well acquainted with the plays of Shakespeare, he felt his quotations from *Julius Caesar* needed no explanatory reference.[34]

In 1845, Senator Charles Sumner repeated the now accepted term 'Sabbath of the nation' to affirm the seemingly sacred status of the Fourth of July celebrations. His public oration of over eighty pages, directed to an audience larger than the one then seated in the hall, argued that America should be above resorting to the 'animal spirit' of war.[35] Delivered in 1845, when America was on the point of conflict with Mexico over the territory of Texas and with the old enemy England over the territory of Oregon, Sumner appropriated Shakespeare both to increase national consensus and to advance the cause of peace. His quotation from *Henry V*, chosen to illustrate the danger of acting like a 'tiger', was from 'Our own Shakspeare' (*sic*), and this use of the possessive pronoun, together with the later quotation from *Hamlet*, emphasised the extent to which Shakespeare was becoming a naturalised American poet.

While the Fourth of July oration was known to all American citizens, few appeared to be critical of the form or content of this theatrical event. However, the words of ex-slave and political activist Frederick Douglass, while carefully considered, suggest how much a part of nineteenth-century tradition the story of English tyranny was, though, as an abolitionist, his remarks were also intended to demonstrate the irony of the Fourth of July orations for African-Americans:

The causes which led to the separation of the colonies from the British crown have never lacked for a tongue. They have all been taught in your common schools, narrated at your firesides, unfolded from your pulpits, and thundered from your legislative halls, and are as familiar to you as household words. They form the staple of your national poetry and eloquence.[36]

Another rare contemporary critique of the Fourth of July orations appeared in a history of the USA published in 1849. The author, Richard Hildreth, wrote of the orations, 'there are more than enough', and insisted that his version of American history would be 'unbedaubed with patriotic rouge'.[37] In a published review of Hildreth's book, the *United States Democratic Review* suggested that the orations were part of an American ' "Mutual Admiration Society," [indulged] in the vain hope of compensating ourselves for the contempt of England, the only country for whose respect we really care a straw'.[38]

The importance of the annual Fourth of July celebration in reinforcing England's position as America's traditional enemy should not be underestimated. As Eric Hobsbawm has observed, 'Americans had to be made. The invented traditions of the USA in this period were primarily designed to achieve this object.'[39] The orations became the text of national consciousness.

Throughout the nineteenth century, citizens in cities across America listened each year to a formal oration in which England was positioned as the enemy and the United States glorified as the heroic crusader for freedom.

While the original orations were basically spontaneous expressions, in succeeding years they served to reflect and reinforce public consciousness of the symbols and myths of the American Nation.[40]

IMAGERY AND ANTHEMS THAT POSITIONED ENGLAND
AS THE ENEMY

In 1793 Congressman Elias Boudinot delivered a Fourth of July oration that linked the story of American independence with the biblical imagery of the Children of Israel. Boudinot told his audience that God had instructed the Children of Israel to 'remember this day, in which ye came out of Egypt, out of the house of bondage'.[41] He then went on to suggest that the American people should regard themselves and their enemy in similar terms:

Let us then, my friends and fellow citizens, unite all our endeavors this day, to remember, with reverential gratitude to our supreme benefactor, all the wonderful things he has done for us, in our miraculous deliverance from a second Egypt – another house of bondage.[42]

There then followed a prayer and a newly written patriotic song that pointedly appropriated the tune of a popular British anthem, *Rule Britannia*.[43] In all six stanzas the chorus resounded with 'Hail Columbia' in place of 'Rule Britannia':

> When exil'd Freedom, forc'd to roam,
> Sought refuge on Columbia's shores,
> The lovely wand'rer found a home,
> And this day that made her ours.
> Hail Columbia! Columbia Hail to thee
> The praise is due, that MAN IS FREE![44]

In a Fourth of July oration for 1797, this time before the General Society of Mechanics and Tradesman, the speaker told his audience that they were now collectively 'gloriously triumphant over the proud legions of despotic Britain'.[45] George James Warner called upon them to 'Teach [their children] to love their country; to contend for liberty; to despise monarchy.'[46] According to Warner, American citizens had freed themselves from 'slavery' and tyranny. Within this text there was an almost biblical 'set my people free' tone, with Britain substituted for the symbolic Pharaoh and his forces.

The 1812–14 war between the United States and Britain was marked by the burning of Washington DC by British forces and the victory of General Andrew Jackson at the Battle of New Orleans. Both events can be seen to have provided permanent monuments to the anti-English nature of the American state in the nineteenth century. Following Andrew Jackson's victory against the British army on 8 January 1815, and as an act of celebration to announce the news, 'newspapers across America printed two lines from *Henry VI*':[47]

> Advance our waving colors on the walls,
> Rescued is Orleans from the English wolves.

However, while the English were seen as defeated 'wolves', the nationality of Shakespeare was ignored by newspaper editors. Shakespeare unwittingly provided the words that were used to promote the important cause of American nationalism, the Battle of New Orleans coming to be regarded as far more important psychologically for generations of Americans than Wellington's triumph at Waterloo was for the English.

The burning of Washington DC in September 1814 and the attack on the nearby port of Baltimore provided an even more enduring and all-pervading statement of anti-English feeling. The unsuccessful naval bombardment of Fort McHenry, Baltimore, by the British navy was witnessed by American lawyer Francis Scott Key while 'confined' to a British warship. After the battle, Key wrote a poem called 'The Defence of Fort McHenry' that would come to be known by all Americans as 'The Star-Spangled Banner'.[48] While the first stanza is now well known, the second and third stanzas of Francis Scott Key's poem more clearly reinforce the suggestion that England was America's threatening enemy:

> On the shore dimly seen through the mists of the deep,
> Where the foe's haughty host in dead silence reposes,
> What is that which the breeze, o'er the towering steep,
> As it fitfully blows, half conceals, half discloses?
> Now it catches the gleam of the morning's first beam
> In full glory reflected now shines in the stream
> 'Tis the star-spangled banner – O long may it wave
> O'er the land of the free and the home of the brave!
>
> And where is that band who so vauntingly swore,
> That the havoc of war and the battle's confusion
> A home and a country should leave us no more?
> Their blood has wash'd out their foul footstep's pollution.
> No Refuge could save their hireling and slave
> From the terror of flight or the gloom of the grave,
> And the star-spangled banner in triumph doth wave
> O'er the land of the free and the home of the brave.

In the words of 'The Star-Spangled Banner', the 'land of the free and the home of the brave' is only such because its citizens rejected and repulsed British 'tyranny'. The 'foe's haughty host' are the British military, whose 'foul footstep's pollution' was 'wash'd out' with blood. As with the Declaration of Independence, this icon of American nationalism was created as a direct response to the American fear of England's political and economic dominance.

The powerful imagery of this poem was utilised in the climax to the 1998 'State of the Union' address, when then president Bill Clinton invoked for his audience the 'smoke of a fierce battle' clearing to reveal the American flag.[49] The battle in question was that between America and Britain. While the television audience was unlikely to have felt any hostility to England when considering the words of the poem by Francis Scott Key, for nineteenth-century Americans the English enemy were rarely far from their thoughts.

Yet another patriotic song, this time composed for the 1832 Fourth of July celebrations, was to repeat this anti-English message. The manuscript draft of *America*, by Samuel F. Smith, carries a verse not published in later versions:

> No more shall Tyrants here
> With haughty steps appear and soldier bands.
> No more shall Tyrants tread
> Above the Patriots dead.
> No more our blood be shed by Alien hands.[50]

Given this high level of anti-English sentiment, it is perhaps not surprising that even when America was drifting towards civil war over the secession of the Confederacy, many people chose to link England with the internal divisions that threatened the Union. In 1848, one newspaper responded to claims made by a 'Mr Bayly of Virginia', during a debate in the United States Congress, that England was behind the American abolition movement and that this was evidence of England's 'organised effort to dissolve the Union'.[51] The writer went on to use two quotations from Shakespeare to argue that slavery was 'doomed' irrespective of any 'plots' or motives of the abolitionists themselves. The congressman's opinion was shared and several years later repeated by another more famous American. In 1862, Samuel Morse, a respected Massachusetts-born painter and inventor of the telegraph and Morse code, published a pamphlet directly accusing England of being behind the conflict and of a conspiracy by the British aristocracy to break the Union.[52]

In addition to the patriotic anthems and Fourth-of-July orations there was another element of nineteenth-century culture that helped reaffirm the position of England as America's enemy. This element was battle site memorials.

HISTORIC SITES AFFIRM THE THREAT OF THE ENGLISH

It is natural for any nation to celebrate battle sites and commemorate the sacrifice of its soldiers. In the case of America, however, the only 'foreign' army that has ever fought on the soil of the United States was British. Given this fact, any annual remembrance of historic battles carries with it a subtle anti-English message. During the nineteenth century, for example, the citizens of New York celebrated 'Evacuation Day' on 26 November, the date on which the British military left the city in 1783. In Vermont, the Battle of Bennington has been commemorated annually on 16 August; in Louisiana, the Battle of New Orleans is still marked on 8 January; while throughout the USA, 19 April is formally celebrated as Patriots' Day, marking the date of the first battle in the war for independence from Britain. While these military anniversaries still remain part of the American calendar today, one can imagine how much more emotionally charged such occasions must have been in the nineteenth century. Though battle memorials confirm that England was at first a literal enemy, long after political independence was achieved England's position as the spiritual enemy functioned within the mechanism that consolidated American national identity.

THE ENEMY IN THE THEATRE

The American theatre had, since the days of the Revolution, been an important platform to express and encourage American patriotism while paradoxically presenting many plays fresh from London. To meet the demands of their audience, playwrights and theatre managers supplied a stream of plays and songs that celebrated the glory of America while reinforcing anti-English prejudice. It was common practice to incorporate caricatures of the English in American stage entertainment. Such figures were presented as effete, arrogant and tyrannical. Royall Tyler wrote a play entitled *The Contrast* that reflected contemporary public sentiment.[53] In this play, first performed in 1787, 'Tyler adopts the techniques of Sheridan's "comedy of manners" to produce a nationalistic play that juxtaposes the innate decency of American society with the corrupting influence of the British.'[54] Other plays, such as John Leacock's *The Fall of British Tyranny; or, American Liberty*

Triumphant of 1776, William Dunlap's *André* of 1798, a dramatised story of an English spy during the War of Independence, his *Yankee Chronology* of 1812 and his *Glory of Columbia: Her Yeomanry!* of 1817, can be seen both to feed and to encourage the latent anti-English sentiments of the audience.

The institutionalised repetition of negative representations of England and the English, linked with chauvinistic expressions of American pride, created a powerful force of social conditioning. There was a populist response. Wherever Americans gathered together to enjoy the bene-fits of independence there were populist demonstrations that echoed the anti-English sentiment so much a part of early post-independence ideology.

POPULIST HOSTILITY TO ENGLAND

The American theatre audience came to expect some form of patriotic enter-tainment whatever the particular play or playwright. Even as Shakespeare's plays were finding a larger audience in the newly independent America, ridicule of England and the English was considered a fixture on any the-atre programme. As part of the entertainment that accompanied the first recorded performance of Shakespeare in New Orleans, on the evening of 2 June 1817, the audience were treated to 'the favourite of the American Soldier, or [the] Battle of New Orleans', with theatre manager A. Cargill as the enthusiastic vocalist.[55] The fact that Shakespeare could share the pro-gramme with expressions of anti-English sentiment implies that there was already a separation of the playwright, together with his artistic output, from any negative association with the political and cultural construct of England.

Lawrence Levine highlighted the hypersensitivity of the American audi-ence to anything that implied glorification of England or its people, even if this 'glorification' occurred while the audience were attending a play by Shakespeare. Levine mentions the fact that during a very rare American performance of *Henry V* several lines had to be 'censored' to avoid violent reaction from the American audience. It appears that the king's declara-tion that he ' "thought [that] upon one pair of English legs did march three Frenchmen" was interpreted as propaganda in favour of aristocratic England against revolutionary France'.[56] An earlier performance of the play at the Philadelphia Chestnut Street Theatre in 1808 had to be sus-pended on account of the ensuing 'riot', and the theatre manager William

Wood considered removing the line from further performances. This action proved to be unnecessary, however, as it appears that *Henry V*, with its heroic images of a victorious English king, was considered to be too provocative for American audiences and significantly the play seems not to have been performed again.

Studying the contemporary press it would appear that, other than Shakespeare and his plays, anything associated with England was considered a legitimate target for nationalistic zeal. Almost any positive symbol of English achievement, or suggestion of English arrogance, could provoke a hostile reaction from the American public. While Shakespeare was embraced as popular entertainment, and touring companies from London met the increasing demand for theatre performers, English actors and theatre managers were the targets of at least 'seven major disturbances [and] many more threats and protests between 1825 and 1849' by people who regarded themselves as 'defenders of national pride'.[57]

One such threat occurred when English actress Fanny Kemble and her father Charles toured east-coast theatres between 1832 and 1834, primarily performing Shakespeare. In her published journal of the 'tour' Fanny recounts an occasion when she was threatened by the spectre of an audience protest in Washington DC. On 19 January 1833, during a horse ride, she had been indiscreet and made several comments which were interpreted as being critical of America. Prior to her performance at a Washington theatre that evening her father received a written warning that if Fanny did not make 'a public apology' she would be hissed off the stage. By the time she arrived in Philadelphia on 30 January, the accusations had been printed on handbills and circulated to the theatre audience. Charles Kemble made the necessary conciliatory gestures to the audience and the play was performed without further problems.[58]

It is important to note that while English actors were considered welcome additions to the American stage this welcome was conditional on there being a clear understanding that the English visited the United States in recognition of its exceptional achievement. Deference had to be shown and any implied criticism was unacceptable and regarded as an offence against the whole nation.

Very little was needed to provoke demonstrations of American resentment towards the English. The period around the Fourth of July orations was fraught with danger for English people making their living in the United States. In New York, on 9 July 1834, a mob that had formed with the intention of disrupting an interracial marriage demonstrated their 'patriotism' by moving on to attack the nearby Bowery Theatre. Gustave de Beaumont wrote that the crowd believed that an 'English actor named Farren [had] spoken ill of the American people', and therefore, while their other 'activity' was suspended, the mob moved to the Bowery to vent their pent-up fury.[59] A report of this riot in the *New York American* suggested that 'Mr Farren, stage manager of the Bowery Theatre had been represented as having cursed the Yankees, called them jack asses and said that he would gull them whenever he could.'[60] This unsubstantiated accusation, made by a New York butcher, led to George F. Farren's arrest by the New York police.

The newspaper report stated that, following Farren's release, a crowd of '1000 persons' had broken into the theatre, occupied the stage and demanded that he be immediately dismissed. Included on the programme of entertainment at the theatre that evening was American actor Edwin Forrest. Thomas S. Hamblin, the theatre manager, went onto the stage waving an American flag to appeal to the crowd but, despite this conciliatory symbol, was pelted with missiles. A diary entry by Philip Hone reported 'this they disregarded, because the hand which held [the flag] was that of an Englishman, and they would listen to nobody but "American Forrest" '.[61] Forrest, the Philadelphia-born son of a Scottish immigrant, addressed the crowd and announced that the Englishman Farren was now 'sacked' and the crowd, then satisfied, left the theatre.[62] What had started (and was later to finish) as a 'race riot', had widened to include an attack on the person and property that had suggested English arrogance towards the American people.

The widespread and frequent occurrence of this type of disturbance caught the attention of a newspaper editor in Philadelphia. Under the headline 'The Philosophy of Theatrical Riots', the editor criticised the actions of the crowds and those persons who exploited American hostility to England:

We recollect many theatrical riots. One occurred in Boston, some years ago against the elder Kean, or Kean the First. Another occurred in New York against Wood. Another occurred afterwards in New York, against Anderson. And one lately occurred in this city against Macready and another more recently against the same personage in New York.[63]

The writer then went on to condemn those persons who, for reasons of personal or political enmity, encouraged riots against visiting English actors. For the writer it was clear that American–English rivalry and political enmity lay behind the riots, rather than any quarrel with the quality of actors. The writer accused other newspapers of encouraging the violence and branded other editors as 'traitors to the profession'. News of these theatre riots, together with the implied popular expressions of anti-English hostility, were widely reported across the United States, newspapers merely reprinting what was now an 'old' story from other publications.

The most significant demonstration of public anger directed against symbols perceived to demonstrate English arrogance occurred in New York the night before the Philadelphia-based editor had felt the need to comment on the growing problem. On 10 May 1849 the infamous Astor Place riot took place. While prior to this night there had been a long-running trivial dispute between two actors about their respective performance style, it was popular hostility to the English that led to violence and bloodshed on a scale not seen before on the streets of New York. While the final statistics are still a matter of debate, it is thought that as many as thirty-one people died and 150 were injured following a truncated performance of *Macbeth* at the Astor Place Opera House by the British actor William Macready. Such was the popularity of Shakespeare that there were three separate theatres presenting *Macbeth* to audiences that night. In addition to Macready, Thomas Hamblin was at the Bowery Theatre and Edwin Forrest at the Broadway Theatre.

While some in the audience may have known that Forrest and Macready had disagreed over acting styles, it was the anti-English element of the dispute that was to inspire their riotous involvement. On the night of 7 May, 'when Forrest spoke Macbeth's lines, "What rhubarb, senna or what purgative drug will sour these English hence?" the entire audience . . . rose and cheered for several minutes'.[64] Forrest, with his previous experience of the 'Farren' theatre riot of 1834, was well aware that American nationalism had the potential to unleash a mob with violent and dangerous results, yet it appears he did nothing to defuse the situation.[65]

It is clear that any personal enmity between the two actors was far from the minds of New Yorkers and the riot that occurred three nights later involving up to ten thousand people was not about the staging of Shakespeare. The violent protest was provoked by the presence of non-deferential English actors on the American stage and the widespread belief that the presence of Macready represented an insult to the quality of American actors and to their admirers. Handbills distributed in New York on the day of the riot identify the clear anti-English motivation of the crowd:

Workingmen
Shall
Americans or English Rule
IN THIS CITY
The crew of the English steamer has threatened all
Americans who shall dare to express their opinion this
night at the English aristocratic Opera House!!
We advocate no violence, but a free expression of opinion
to all public men!
Workingmen! Freemen!!
Stand by your
Lawful Rights.
American Committee[66]

The rioters, inspired by this type of handbill, were prevented from storm-
ing the opera house only by a detachment of the New York militia firing
point-blank into the crowd. The 'American Committee' has been identified
as associated with nativist groups who were actively campaigning against
further immigration and any behaviour they regarded as 'un-American'.
Dime-novel author Ned Buntline was one person involved with both the
Astor Place riot and the nativist movement, and he was later convicted
and imprisoned for one year for his actions in leading elements of the
mob.

When a full report of the riots appeared in a Washington newspaper, the
editor commented, 'One cannot help observing that the two abominable
elements that made this mob formidable, were hatred of the rich, and
hatred of the English.'[67] Seven days later the same newspaper demanded
that the political 'demagogues' who put the 'god of party' before the 'blood
of the innocent' to inflame the 'haters of England' be held responsible for
the riot.[68]

The Astor Place riot has featured in many studies on the history of
the American stage. However, while commentators have accepted that a
public argument between two actors had very little to do with the ensuing
violence, most have seen class conflict as the principal cause of the riot.
Though it is reasonable to suggest that the majority of rioters were the
'workingmen' of New York, I would suggest that any class-based hostility
was directed towards 'the class' of American that appeared to celebrate
the symbols thought to embody English culture and English 'aristocratic'
gentility. The context in which the Astor Place riot took place suggests
that, despite hostility to these symbols, the 'workingmen' did not regard
Shakespeare as a representative of either. The latent hostility that led to the
deaths of thirty-one people was a product of the anti-English sentiment

that had been encouraged to unify the American nation and maintain the ideology of the revolution.

In addition to the numerous examples of anti-English journalism that can be found in the American press of the nineteenth century, there is anecdotal evidence that many visitors from Europe were struck by the extent of hostility to England displayed by the American public. Such visitors included Henry Fearon, Tyrone Power, Henry Tudor, Isabella Lucy Bird, Harriet Martineau, Frederick Marryat and Gustave de Beaumont, as well as the more famous Alexis de Tocqueville, Francis Trollope and Charles Dickens, all of whom published books based on their impressions of the United States. While their views of Americans and American democracy varied, they all observed how quick Americans were to celebrate their fellow citizens' and their country's achievements while enthusiastically demonstrating their hostility towards England.

One of the earliest traveller tales to highlight chauvinistic animosity towards England also hinted at the paradox of the phenomenon. In 1818 Henry Fearon pointed to the complex relationship between English heritage and post-independence attitudes, observing, 'In spite of all these various ties of connection with England, and with Englishmen, [Americans] appear generally to regard both with jealousy and hatred.'[69] However, while 'The nation at large dislike England . . . both individually and collectively, [they] would be offended should a hint be expressed that they were of Irish or of Dutch, and not of English descent.'[70] It is this apparent desire to simultaneously claim Anglo-Saxon ancestry while, at the slightest provocation, broadly condemn many if not all aspects of the English state and English mannerisms that may have hindered some observers in recognising the almost institutionalised anti-English sentiment.

As a Frenchman living during a period of war between England and his homeland, it might be supposed that Alexis de Tocqueville was unlikely to be Anglophile. Yet he entitled one chapter of his renowned study of America in the early 1830s 'Why the National Vanity of the Americans Is More Restless and Captious Than That of the English', and went on to observe, 'It is impossible to conceive a more troublesome or more garrulous patriotism.'[71] Tocqueville's travelling companion Gustave de Beaumont stated, 'To say that the Americans hate the English is to render their feeling imperfectly', clarifying his assertion by suggesting that behind the patriotism there was also a suspicion of jealousy.[72] As a writer in the *United States Democratic*

Review expressed it, 'The United States and the United Kingdom . . . must be rivals, and rivals are never friends.'[73]

The institution of the Fourth of July celebration had played a role in creating this element of 'national character' that was now observable in many American citizens. However, the co-existence of patriotism and anti-English sentiment, noted by both Tocqueville and Beaumont, was real enough and potentially threatening to anyone who hoped either to visit America or to market their literary output there. Charles Dickens, well known for his social critiques of Victorian England, acknowledged the risks involved when anyone, but particularly someone from England, chose to write comments that offered anything other than unrestrained praise for America. In an introduction to *American Notes*, published in 1842, he revealed his concern as to the likely response from American readers:

I can scarcely be supposed to be ignorant of the hazard I run in writing of America at all. I know perfectly well that there is, in that country, a numerous class of well-intentioned persons prone to be dissatisfied with all accounts of the Republic whose citizens they are, which are not couched in terms of exalted praise.[74]

What Dickens most feared, of course, occurred, and the American press savaged him for what they regarded as ill-considered opinions from the 'Englishest of Englishman'. Generally book reviewers praised the first two chapters, which recounted the trials of a transatlantic crossing, but attacked Dickens's account of his travels in America. As one reviewer wrote, America was

a subject respecting which, he knows nothing, and we cannot receive his fancies for facts; moreover, he is not, individually, responsible for his sentiments, they belong to every Englishman, from the chained naked wretches of the coal mines, and work-worn, white factory slaves, to the sovereign, who, not personally, but whose pageantry, crushes down the whole nation.[75]

The language and tone of this review demonstrate how a simple travelogue became merely the latest skirmish in the long-running war between America and England. Although the reviewer claimed that 'we are not one of those who care what Dickens, or any other foreigner "thinks of us"; nor do we suppose that his opinion will have aught to do with our national destinies',[76] the barely concealed anger of the review suggested otherwise.

A reviewer in the *New Englander* highlighted as one of the key elements of anti-English sentiment a perception of England as a nation riddled by aristocratic arrogance and snobbery. The accusation was that 'Mr. Dickens . . . puts on airs as if he belonged by birth and breeding to those higher classes which constitute the "Corinthian capital" of English society.' After reading *American Notes* the self-declared former Dickens enthusiast stated, 'The perusal of [the book] has served chiefly to lower our estimate of the man, and to fill us with contempt for such a compound of egotism, coxcombry, and cockneyism.'[77]

Dickens further offended American pride when his personal experiences of travelling were later fictionalised in the novel *Martin Chuzzlewit*. Despite his popularity as an author, he was unable to defuse or calm the nationalist sentiments that had been engendered by the declaration of 1776 and the subsequent 'cultural' war that had been fought metaphorically each Fourth of July.

In addition to the well-documented clashes over literary representations of the American state, there are other accounts of life in the early nineteenth century that offer evidence of the widespread anti-English sentiment. The British comedian and actor Joe Cowell, who managed a number of theatres in the USA from 1821 to 1844, published an account of his life in America.[78] Having lived twenty-three years in the country, Cowell can be assumed to have felt positive or at least neutral towards America and his book was broadly positive about American society. As he had met Fanny Trollope, and was in the United States when her book was published to such public furore, it could be argued that he was unlikely to repeat her 'mistakes'. He did, however, provide additional first-hand accounts of various aspects of American life that loosely confirm statements made by Tocqueville, Trollope and Dickens.

Cowell had arrived on the quayside in New York on the evening of 24 October 1821. In his book he describes his first few hours spent on Wall Street and Broadway and the manner in which he was received. The first question he records being asked by an American, following his return from a brief walk, is indicative of the combative approach to visitors from England. The American asked, 'Wasn't [New York] very superior to London?'[79] After recounting several other assertions of American supremacy, Cowell concluded, 'The feeling created by the war with England, then long since over, was still rankling in the minds of the lower order of American, as if it were yet raging, and their hatred of an Englishman they took a pride in showing whenever in their power.'[80]

The general antipathy to the English, commented on by Cowell, still existed in 1850. In an instruction manual for prospective English emigrants to the United States, published in London, George Nettle advised his readers that 'the conceit and boosting of the Yankees is quite absurd and ridiculous, and their notions of the English manners and constitution rather amusing to an Englishman: but it will be prudent, however, for the emigrant to listen to remarks'.[81] Nettle concluded by observing that 'Of all nations on the face of the earth, the English is the most disliked by Yankees.'[82]

Towards the close of the century there was an appeal to the cause of American self-interest that in itself managed to highlight several aspects of the anti-English sentiment that had been so much a feature of American nationalism. Goldwin Smith, as an Englishman, was perhaps always likely to provoke anger more easily than he was to facilitate positive reflection. As Professor of English Literature and Constitutional History at Cornell University, New York State, however, he perhaps felt able to comment on what had by then become part of American tradition. In the *North American Review* he wrote a critique of 'the hatred of England' and the romanticised American view of the heroic struggle against English tyranny.[83] Smith argued that this 'patriotic' hostility to England should finish.

According to Smith, hatred of England did 'mischief in more ways than one. It drives British emigration from American shores to Australia at a time when the self-governing element in this country is in danger of being swamped by alien elements.'[84] Smith voiced his perhaps optimistic hope that 'The Fourth-of-July treatment of history is now visibly going out of fashion among the higher class of American writers.'[85] He went on to argue that there were three different forms of anti-English sentiment expressed. One was used to win the Irish-American vote and another as a means of trade protectionism. The third, in his view the only genuine hatred, originated from a romanticised view of the hostility between the two nations. Smith wrote that it was 'strange to hear people reviling British character while in their book-cases and in the hands of their children are books which . . . must cast character in the British mould'.[86]

Smith's opinions provoked a broad defensive reaction in the next issue. No fewer than seven articles were published in direct response to his suggestion (referred to as an accusation) that Americans hated the English. Writer after writer rebutted the suggestion that Americans could collectively feel an emotion as irrational as hatred. As each writer in turn passionately justified American resentment of the English, however, Smith's original suggestion of the existence of hatred appeared to become more tenable. According to one James Harrison Wilson,

Americans do not hate England, the home of their race. They hate the insulting, domineering, aggressive policy of the British government. They hate the supercilious and patronizing airs, the intolerance and self-sufficiency, and the arrogance and superiority of the class which controls and represents that government.[87]

In this rebuttal can be seen the fundamental separation that many Americans had made. England as 'home of their race' had been divorced from the 'supercilious . . . superiority of the class' contemporary England was thought to embody. Anglo-Saxon antecedents were admired but England as a rival and critic was generally denigrated.

Smith's article did, however, anticipate a softening in attitude towards England. As the nineteenth century drew towards its close and American ascendancy was more clearly confirmed, there was a gradual change in the relationship. As Jürgen Heideking has suggested,

From the days of the Declaration of Independence on, Americans saw their nation as the rightful heir and successor to the British Empire. The recurrent attacks on British Imperialism during the mid-nineteenth century seem to conceal, at least to a certain extent, their desire for economic domination and political leadership. It is certainly no accident that the improvement of Anglo–American relations and the fading away of the image of an English enemy went hand in hand with the decline of British power, the dissolution of the British Empire, and the rise of the United States to superpower status.[88]

The important role of a threatening foreign 'other' for America, previously fulfilled by England, was, early in the twentieth century, to be transferred, via events such the 'Red Scare', to the political philosophy of Communism.

CONCLUSION TO PART I

Eighteenth-century American colonists responded to what they regarded as intolerable tyranny. Their desire for freedom found its most articulate expression in the Declaration of Independence. Once that independence had been secured, the idea of an external enemy retained its utility. Patriotic zeal and anti-English sentiment fostered unity and created a sense of camaraderie amongst the diverse peoples who now were to constitute the fledgling nation. What is singular, however, and marks the nineteenth-century period, is that at the same time that America declared its cultural independence, and many things English were often considered symbols of 'the enemy' of freedom, liberty and democracy, Shakespeare was embraced and consumed by the citizens of the young republic. Shakespeare, of all the elements of cultural conditioning, somehow avoided the contempt felt by Americans for England and the English. This is the 'anomaly'; this is the 'paradox' that deserves greater attention.

Acknowledging but, for this book, discounting the suggestion that Shakespeare may embody some form of universal transcendental human experience, the following chapters will highlight the various factors that encouraged the appropriation and naturalisation of an Elizabethan English writer.

NOTES

1. Letter to William D. Ticknor, 9 November 1855, in Nathaniel Hawthorne, *The Letters, 1853–1856*, ed. Thomas Woodson et al. (Columbus OH: Ohio State University Press, 1987), p. 401.

2. Hans Kohn, *American Nationalism: An Interpretive Essay* (New York: Macmillan, 1957), pp. 26–7.

3. Gustave de Beaumont, *Marie or Slavery in the United States*, trans. Barbara Chapman (Baltimore: Johns Hopkins University Press, 1999), p. 31 and appendix C, pp. 217–19. First published 1835. This book was intended as a 'companion piece' to Tocqueville's *Democracy in America*.

4. Edward P. Crapol, *America for Americans: Economic Nationalism and Anglophobia in the Late Nineteenth Century* (Westport CT: Greenwood Press, 1973), p. 4.

5. Jürgen Heideking, 'The Image of an English Enemy', in Ragnhild Fiebig-von Hase and Ursula Lehmkuhl, eds., *Enemy Images in American History* (Providence RI: Berghahn Books, 1997), p. 93.

6. Sharon Turner, *The History of the Anglo-Saxons, from Their First Appearance above the Elbe, to the Death of Egbert: with a Map of Their Ancient Territory* (London: T. Cadwell & W. Davies, 1799).

7. Paul Rapin de Thoyras, *Histoire d'Angleterre* (n.p., 1727).

8. Thomas Jefferson, 'A Summary View of the Rights of British America', in Jefferson, *Writings*, ed. Merrill D. Peterson (New York: Library of America, 1984), pp. 104–22. Jefferson repeatedly referred to his Saxon ancestors being conquered by 'William the Norman' (p. 118). He also expressed the belief that 'the Whig deduces his rights from the Anglo-Saxon source, and the Tory from the Normans'. See letter to Major John Cartwright, 5 June 1824 (p. 1491).

9. The first US census of 1790 did not require any indication as to a person's country of birth or ethnicity. It was not until 1850 that a citizen's ancestory became part of recorded data. However, work at the University of Michigan has provided a useful estimate. See 'Historical Demographic, Economic, and Social Data: U.S., 1790–1970', Inter-University Consortium for Political and Social Research, University of Michigan Study 00003, http://www.icpsr.umich.edu/cgi/archive.prl?study=3&path=ICPSR.

10. Webb Garrison, *Lost Pages from American History* (Harrisburg PA: Stackpole Books, 1976), p. 60.

11. Coriolanus, *Providence Gazette*, 24 June 1775. Misspelt 'Cariolanus' in the *Gazette*. See Arthur M. Schlesinger, *Prelude to Independence: The Newspaper War on Britain 1764–1776* (New York: Alfred A. Knopf, 1966), pp. 246–7.

12. Act 3, Scene 3.

13. Philip Morin Freneau, *A Voyage to Boston. A Poem* (New York, 1775), p. 21.

14. The advertisement appeared in the *Pennsylvania Gazette*, 15 November 1775.

15. Schlesinger, *Prelude to Independence*, pp. 250–2.
16. Paine, *Common Sense*, p. 92.
17. Jefferson, 'The Declaration of Independence'.
18. Ibid.
19. Heideking, 'The Image of an English Enemy', p. 95.
20. Eric Hobsbawm and Terence Ranger, eds., *The Invention of Tradition* (Cambridge: Cambridge University Press, 1983), p. 1.
21. Charles Sprague, *The Poetical and Prose Writings of Charles Sprague* (Boston MA: Ticknor, Reed, & Fields, 1849), p. 3. From an oration delivered in Boston in 1825.
22. See New York State Library, Special Collection, Fourth of July Orations, http://www.nysl.nysed.gov/library/features/july4/index.html.
23. Fanny Trollope, *Domestic Manners of the Americans*, ed. Pamela Neville-Sington (London: Penguin, 1997), p. 67. First published 1832.
24. Granqvist, *Imitation as Resistance*, p. 125.
25. Gary A. Richardson, 'In the Shadow of the Bard', in Judith L. Fisher and Stephen Watt, eds., *When They Weren't Doing Shakespeare: Essays on Nineteenth-Century British and American Theatre* (Athens GA: University of Georgia Press, 1989), p. 126.
26. Archibald Buchanan, *An Oration Composed and Delivered at the Request of the Republican Society of Baltimore, on the Fourth of July, One Thousand Seven Hundred and Ninety-Four* (Baltimore: Clayland Dobbin & Co., 1794), pp. 8–9.
27. Samuel Berrian, *An Oration Delivered before the Tammany Society or Columbian Order . . . in the City of New-York, on the Fourth Day of July, 1815* (New York: John Low, 1815).
28. Joseph H. Dukes, *An Oration Delivered before the Firemen of Charleston, on the Fourth of July, 1844* (Charleston: Walker & Burke, 1844), p. 8.
29. Andrew Dunlap, *An Oration Delivered at Salem on Monday July 5, 1819* (Salem MA: Warwick Palfray Jr, 1819), p. 4.
30. Ibid., p. 11.
31. Sprague, *The Poetical and Prose Writings*, pp. 3 and 15.
32. Ibid., p. 19.
33. Ibid., p. 29.
34. John Quincy Adams, *An Oration Addressed to the Citizens of the Town of Quincy, on the Fourth of July, 1831, the Fifty-Fifth Anniversary of the Independence of the United States of America* (Boston MA: Richardson, Lord & Holbrook, 1831), pp. 30 and 36.
35. Charles Sumner, *The True Grandeur of Nations, Mr Sumner's Oration. July 4, 1845* (Boston MA: American Peace Society, 1845).
36. Frederick Douglass, 'What to the Slave is the Fourth of July?', oration of 5 July 1852, in James M. Gregory, *Frederick Douglass, the Orator* (New York, 1893), pp. 103–6.
37. Richard Hildreth, *History of the United States of America, from the Discovery of the Continent to the Organization of Government under the Federal Constitution* (New York: Harper & Bros., 1849).

38. 'History of the United States', *United States Democratic Review*, 26/139 (January 1850), pp. 44–9.
39. Hobsbawm and Ranger, eds., *The Invention of Tradition*, p. 279.
40. I use the terms 'symbol' and 'myth' in the same manner as Henry Nash Smith, who defined them as 'an intellectual construction that fuses concept and emotion into an image. The myths and symbols with which I deal have the further characteristic of being collective representations rather than the work of a single mind'. See Henry Nash Smith, *Virgin Land: The American West in Symbol and Myth* (Cambridge MA: Harvard University Press, 1950), p. vii.
41. Elias Boudinot, *An Oration, Delivered at Elizabeth-Town, New Jersey, Agreeably to a Resolution of the State Society of Cincinnati, on the Fourth of July, 1793* (Elizabeth-Town NJ, 1793), p. 6.
42. Ibid., pp. 6–7.
43. *Rule Britannia* was written in 1740 by Thomas Arne.
44. Boudinot, *An Oration*, pp. 29–30.
45. George James Warner, *Means for the Preservation of Public Liberty, an Oration Delivered in the New Dutch Church, on the Fourth of July, 1797: Being the Twenty-First Anniversary of Our Independence, 'Ode Composed for the Occasion, by P. Freneau'* (New York, 1797), p. 9.
46. Ibid., p. 16.
47. Robert V. Remini, *Andrew Jackson* (New York: Harper & Row, 1969), p. 74. The two lines are from *Henry VI, Part 1*, Act 1, Scene 6.
48. St. Pierre, *Our National Anthem*, p. 25. This poem was set to music, increased in popularity during the nineteenth century, and was finally accepted as America's national anthem by Act of Congress in 1931.
49. William Clinton, 'State of the Union' address, US Congress, 26 January 1998. http://abcnews.go.com/sections/us/DailyNews/SOU98_990118.html.
50. Oscar George Theodore Sonneck, *Report on The Star-Spangled Banner, Hail Columbia, America, Yankee Doodle* (Washington DC: Government Printing Office, 1909), p. 74.
51. *North Star* (Rochester NY), 19 May 1848.
52. Samuel Morse, *The Present Attempt to Dissolve the American Union, a British Aristocratic Plot* (New York: John Trow, 1862). The accusation was originally publicised in a letter written by Morse's brother, Sidney E. Morse, that was published in *Harper's Weekly*, 15 December 1860.
53. Royall Tyler, *The Contrast* (Philadelphia: Prichard & Hall, 1790).
54. Peter A. Davis, 'The Plays and Playwrights', in Wilmeth and Bigsby, eds., *The Cambridge History of American Theatre*, p. 244.
55. Joseph Patrick Roppolo, 'Shakespeare in New Orleans, 1817–1865', in Kolin, ed., *Shakespeare in the South*, p. 115.
56. Levine, *Highbrow/Lowbrow*, p. 60. Levine quotes from William B. Wood, *Personal Recollections of the Stage* (Philadelphia, 1855), pp. 118–19.
57. Bruce A. McConachie, 'American Theatre in Context', in Wilmeth and Bigsby, eds., *The Cambridge History of American Theatre*, p. 151.

58. Fanny Kemble, *Journal of a Young Actress*, ed. Monica Gough (New York: Columbia University Press, 1990), p. 145.

59. Beaumont, *Marie*, p. 246.

60. *New York American*, 10 July 1834.

61. Philip Hone, *The Diary of Philip Hone 1828–1851*, ed. Baynard Tuckerman, 2 vols. (New York: Dodd, Mead & Co., 1889), vol. 1, p. 109.

62. The rioters, reported to number ten thousand, moved on to Rose Street to attack and destroy property owned by African-Americans and their abolitionist supporters. This was the fifth successive night of rioting by New Yorkers over issues of miscegenation and race.

63. *Public Ledger and Daily Transcript* (Philadelphia), 11 May 1849, Philadelphia. For an account of the Anderson riots, see Hone, *Diary*, vol. 1, pp. 39–40.

64. Levine, *Highbrow/Lowbrow*, p. 63.

65. Philip Hone considered Forrest to be largely responsible for the Astor Place riot, describing him as 'a vulgar, arrogant loafer, with a pack of kindred rowdies at his heels'. See Hone, *Diary*, vol. 11, p. 360.

66. Richard Moody, *The Astor Place Riot* (Bloomington IN: Indiana University Press, 1958), p. 130.

67. 'Riots and Loss of Life in New York', *National Era* (Washington DC), 17 May 1849.

68. 'New York Riots – Law – Liberty – Order', *National Era* (Washington DC), 24 May 1849.

69. Fearon, *Sketches of America*, p. 366. Fearon travelled on behalf of thirty-nine English families who were then considering the prospect for emigration. His book is thus a detailed report of living conditions as would concern those seeking a new life far from Europe. He arrived 6 August 1817 and departed 10 May 1818.

70. Ibid., p. 368.

71. Alexis de Tocqueville, *Democracy in America*, ed. Phillips Bradley, 2 vols. (New York: Vintage Books, 1945), vol. 11, p. 236. Tocqueville travelled over seven thousand miles in the USA and Canada in 1832 making notes for this book. Vol. 1 first published 1835, vol. 11, 1840.

72. Beaumont, *Marie*, p. 217.

73. 'The United States and the United Kingdom', *United States Democratic Review*, 1/5 (May 1853), p. 25.

74. Charles Dickens, *American Notes for General Circulation*, ed. F. S. Schwarzbach (London: Everyman, 1997), p. 275. This introduction was later 'suppressed' on the advice of the publisher John Foster.

75. *Southern Literary Messenger*, 9/1 (January 1843), p. 59.

76. Ibid.

77. Anon (J. T. Thompson), *New Englander*, 1/1 (January 1843), pp. 64–84. Despite the controversy or perhaps because of it, *American Notes* sold between 50,000 and 60,000 copies within the first few days of its publication in America. See Mott, *Golden Multitudes*, pp. 79–84.

78. Cowell, *Thirty Years Passed among the Players*.
79. Ibid., p. 55.
80. Ibid., p. 56.
81. George Nettle, *A Practical Guide for Emigrants to North America by a Seven Years Resident in North America* (London: Simpkin, Marshall & Co., 1850), p. 53.
82. Ibid.
83. Goldwin Smith, 'The Hatred of England', *North American Review*, 150/402 (May 1890), pp. 547–63.
84. Ibid., p. 548.
85. Ibid., p. 554.
86. Ibid., p. 557.
87. T. W. Higginson, Andrew Carnegie et al., 'Do Americans Hate England?', *North American Review*, 150/403 (June 1890), pp. 740–79. For Wilson, see p. 772.
88. Heideking, 'The Image of an English Enemy', p. 107.

PART TWO

The appropriation

CHAPTER 3

Beginning the appropriation of Shakespeare and the 'First American Edition' of his works

> Which of our statesmen, our divines, our poets, our philosophers, has
> not learned from him?
>
> Delia Bacon

During the eighteenth century learned and wealthy colonials gradually became more aware of Shakespeare's plays. Reflecting this interest, a number of amateur actors informally performed Shakespeare in several American cities. However, the first professional performance recorded was of *Richard III* in New York on 5 March 1750. It is from this date and this performance that the gradual process of appropriation can be traced, assimilating the man and the plays into the myths and traditions of the American nation.

It is not the purpose of this book to provide a detailed history of Shakespeare on the American stage, as this has been offered by many other publications.[1] While theatre was central to the development of popular culture in the nineteenth century, it is the aspect of presentation or publication of Shakespeare directly associated with the social and political development of an American national consciousness that concerns this book, the process by which Shakespeare was appropriated to the cause of nation building.

The process of appropriation has been defined by Jean I. Marsden as 'to take possession of for one's own'.[2] For this book, 'appropriation' denotes the process whereby American society can be seen as 'imprinting [its own] ideology on the plays and the mythological construct of Shakespeare'.[3] As Marsden conceded, 'Scrutinised dispassionately, every act of interpretation can be seen as an act of appropriation – making sense of a literary artefact by fitting it into our own parameters.'[4] However, while the appropriation of Shakespeare came about by the action of independent American citizens, this action, identifiable in so many individuals and institutions over a relatively short period, suggests that the appropriation was a response to a collective felt need. It is the process of 'fitting [Shakespeare] into [America's] own parameters' and the existence of a collective need that constitutes the cultural paradox of the popularity of Shakespeare in nineteenth-century America.

RICHARD III, A TYRANT FIT FOR A REBELLIOUS POPULATION

Taken in isolation the performance of *Richard III* in 1750 might seem to have little significance. Even at this early point in American history, however, the choice of this play out of the thirty-seven by Shakespeare highlights one particular aspect that would later have increasing significance. Shakespeare, and *Richard III* in particular, was appropriated to serve political needs rather than those of mere entertainment.

The choice of *Richard III* for the first professional performance is worthy of attention, as this play, more than any other work by Shakespeare, concentrated on the apparently arrogant, corrupt and immoral nature of the English monarchy. The murderous villainy of Richard, formerly duke of Gloucester, which was emphasised in the shortened Colley Cibber adaptation of the play then performed, must have served to underscore the potential benefits of a republican system of government.[5] When towards the close of the play the actor playing Richmond, standing over the dying king, spoke the lines 'Farewell, Richard, and from thy dreadful end / May future Kings from tyranny be warn'd', it seems likely that the audience would have felt a flush of republican zeal.

As the editor of the 'Edwin Booth' edition would later comment, the version of *Richard III* performed on the American stage 'lowers Shakespeare's ideal of Gloster – making him a coarse monster of cruelty, devoid of the finer strain of innate royalty'.[6] Kings behaving badly, it seems, was exactly what the audience wanted to see, and this factor ensured that the play, above all others, would dominate the American stage and popular consciousness.

During the seven years of the War of Independence, perhaps surprisingly given civic opposition to public theatre, the Continental Army and their supporters still managed to find time to enjoy Shakespeare's plays. Less surprisingly, while twenty-one performances are recorded for the period, the most performed play was *Richard III*.[7] While Americans were fighting to break political and trade ties with Britain, Shakespeare was considered an ally in the fight rather than a symbol of English cultural influence.

Richard III constituted a powerful portable 'oral' essay against the excesses of the English monarchy. With *Richard III*, Shakespeare unknowingly provided a tool for any American propagandist. It was the anti-monarchist sentiment present within the play, rather than its dramatic quality as the conclusion to the *Henry VI* English history cycle, that made *Richard III* the ideal choice for American audiences.[8] Just as *Richard II* was once appropriated, it has been argued, by the followers of the earl of Essex to promote an uprising against Queen Elizabeth I, so Shakespeare was appropriated by members of the new American Establishment to disseminate a political message that reinforced the ideology of republicanism. This political agenda that lay behind the choice of *Richard III* seems to go largely unrecognised by many scholars and teachers and by the millions of American children still required to study the play as part of school courses.[9]

While *Richard III* can be considered an early example of appropriation, other plays were also helpful to the republican cause. Shakespeare's tragedies abound with representations of the villainy and folly of monarchs. Plays in which monarchs or aristocratic leaders are portrayed as riddled with fatal flaws were popular with republican audiences, who perhaps readily identified with a writer who they chose to assume shared their anti-monarchist beliefs. Confirming the ideological importance of Shakespeare, Walt Whitman, late in his career, publicly linked the history plays, complete with their portrayal of 'wolfish earls', to the process by which American republican ideals had been so successfully communicated.[10]

EARLY APPROPRIATION IN POLITICAL WRITINGS

Between 1750 and 1776 there were a total of 166 performances of fifteen of Shakespeare's plays in six American cities.[11] While an increasing number of Americans watched Shakespeare on the stage, however, texts were available only in expensive editions published in England and brought by ship across the Atlantic. In *American Shakespearean Criticism*, Alfred Van Rensselaer Westfall observed that by the middle of the eighteenth century 'eight editions of Shakespeare had appeared in England', and he suggested not unreasonably, that a number of copies could have found their way to America.[12] However, while Americans would have 'had the opportunity to read Shakespeare before the Revolution [and] to know his plays . . . any knowledge of his works was limited to a few intellectual leaders favoured in scholarly and cultural advantages'.[13] Despite the rarity of Shakespeare in book form, quotations from plays, learnt from these few copies, were appropriated for use in the early debates that concerned the dispute with Britain and the form of republican democracy that future independence might bring.

The use of Shakespeare in speeches and pamphlets provided gravitas and, by association, implied intellectual accomplishment. Shakespeare supplied a lexicon of quotations that could be used to support or undermine many arguments that would increasingly become part of American life and shared American tradition.

In 1775, Charles Lee published a pamphlet in Philadelphia that argued against the impending rebellion, utilising quotations from Shakespeare to call on colonists to support the loyalist cause.[14] Other writers drew freely on Shakespeare using parodical form. In a creative response to Thomas Paine's then recent publication *Common Sense*, a writer in the *Philadelphia Gazette* used a lengthy parody of Hamlet's famous soliloquy.[15] The piece began,

To write, or not to write; that is the question – Whether 'tis nobler in the mind to bear Th'unlicenswrongs of furious party-zeal, Or dip the pen into a nest of hornets, And still, by teazing, wake them?[16]

The writer continued in this vein for ten lines until the question was posed, 'Who would endure this Pain?', the word 'Pain' marking the point where the writer reverted to more 'normal' journalistic prose. The text that followed argued against the ideas of *Common Sense* and for the continuance of the colonial status quo.

Other issues important to Americans were also to be debated by the use of Shakespeare. The institution of slavery, contentious from as early as the eighteenth century, was in 1773 supported in a pamphlet by Richard Nisbet by use of selective quotations from Shakespeare, while several years later precisely the opposite argument was presented by Noah Webster, again appropriating quotations from Shakespeare.[17] While Shakespeare was still relatively unknown, the increasing political awareness of the population allowed more Americans to be introduced to his plays and to what would be seen as a source of philosophy and affirmation of cultural values.

APPROPRIATION AND THE COMMON FELT NEED

Following the end of the War of Independence the pace of appropriation increased. During the late eighteenth and the early part of the nineteenth century, when America expanded its territory and its citizens assumed the existence of 'American destiny', Shakespeare's plays and characters became part of popular culture and a common idiom. For most citizens it appears to have been a natural and uncontroversial process that did not require any official Act of Congress or Presidential Executive Order. As the English language had been used by the founding fathers for the codification of two primary statements of nationhood, namely the Declaration of Independence and the Constitution of the United States, perhaps its position within the American state was manifest. English, while not specified as the national language by the US Constitution or any Act of Congress, had become 'American'. Perhaps it was primarily for this reason that America's naturalisation of Shakespeare, the most respected English poet and playwright, went largely unnoticed. While for many citizens the appropriation was unconscious, however, it was not accidental.

In April 1786, John Adams, soon to be the second president of the United States, in the company of Thomas Jefferson, travelled to Warwickshire to visit Shakespeare's birthplace. In his journal, Adams commented on the state of the house, 'as small and as mean as you can conceive'.[18] In *Shakespeare's America, America's Shakespeare*, Michael D. Bristol described the noteworthy journal entries and suggested that they reveal that Adams was shocked to observe that the 'English fail to display proper reverence and care for their own traditions', and that there was 'little real appreciation for Shakespeare's cultural and historical significance'.[19] For Adams, on what was for him a kind of pilgrimage, the lack of interest in Shakespeare demonstrated by the civic authorities and the wider populace was somehow disturbing.

It is significant that just three years after the peace treaty that confirmed American independence, two men who would become the influential second and third presidents of America chose to make the arduous journey into rural England to visit Shakespeare's birthplace. It is also interesting that Adams noted the extent to which the English public (untouched by any intellectual musings by the minority literati) undervalued Shakespeare. It is easy to speculate that perhaps two future presidents of America subconsciously considered Shakespeare available for adoption by a fledging nation then more in need of national exemplars than England.

It was Adams and Jefferson, together with Benjamin Franklin, who agreed to the use of the motto E Pluribus Unum, 'from many one', on the Great Seal of the United States and on the US dollar bill.[20] The motto was selected to symbolise the goal of the new nation, which was to find or construct common bonds that would ensure that the initial 42 per cent of ex-colonists for whom English was not the 'mother tongue' would unite with the dominant property owners to create a stable society where business could prosper. E Pluribus Unum can be considered to have been the driving motivation behind the increasing fervour of American nationalism and can be shown to be indirectly linked to the appropriation of Shakespeare to the cause of promoting what Tocqueville later described as an 'Anglo-American' culture.[21]

While Shakespeare may have been considered available for adoption, there were several problems to be overcome if the author and the plays were to be accepted by the greater American population. In addition to the cost of purchasing and transporting editions published in England, there was another barrier to a wider acceptance of the text. While some Americans saw Shakespeare as part of their inheritance, English editions of his works were too easily associated with the taint of English arrogance. American citizens might want the plays, 'but they wanted them free from obligations to English scholars'.[22] As demonstrated below, editions of Shakespeare that arrived in America bearing the names of editors such as Johnson, Steevens, Reed and Malone featured extensive notes that claimed to supply explanations and information not otherwise understood by the 'unlearned' reader. For many Americans, who regarded themselves equal if not superior to Europeans, this help from English scholars was neither welcome nor acceptable.

It was not until American publishers started to print and market Shakespeare that this problem could be solved, the cost of access reduced and a wider appreciation of Shakespeare become possible. This connection between the marketing of Shakespeare and a wide acceptance of the appropriation amongst Americans could be said to have less to do with literary aesthetics than with the economic system favoured by the property owners and merchants.

Michael D. Bristol has suggested that 'Marxists . . . frequently described the age in which Shakespeare lived as the moment of the heroic emergence of the bourgeoisie',[23] and it could perhaps be argued that post-independence Americans unconsciously acted as enthusiastic inheritors of this now 'heroic' middle-class tradition. In addition to holding the potential to assist E Pluribus Unum, Shakespeare represented a business opportunity. As Shakespeare was valued by American citizens privileged enough to be able to afford English editions, it was time that a wider readership 'profited'. Increasingly, any obvious association with England's scholars was removed from Shakespeare and the text was marketed to American citizens as a homegrown product.

THE 'FIRST AMERICAN EDITION'

The first complete American edition of Shakespeare was published in Philadelphia in 1795, only twelve years after the end of the War of

Independence, but 172 years after the First Folio appeared in London. Shakespeare was offered to American citizens in eight duodecimo volumes for the price of one dollar each. While the title page maintained that the edition was 'Corrected from the Latest and Best London Éditions',[24] the 'Preface' and 'The Life of the Author' were both written by an American living in Philadelphia and dated 1 July 1795.

In his study of American Shakespeare criticism, Alfred Van Rensselaer Westfall acknowledged the importance of this 'First American Edition'. However, his interest was confined to discovering the name of the unaccredited American editor and identifying the British edition/s that may have been used for the text of the plays. Westfall's conclusion as to the editor's identity is that it was a Joseph Hopkinson, and that 'the American editor built his text on Ayscough's 1791 Dublin edition, took his glossary probably from Gordon's 1792 Edinburgh edition, [and] most of his end notes from some source which contained Johnson's'.[25] If Westfall was correct, this first edition was not American scholarship, the edition not having been produced from 'original' source material or 'edited' in the academic sense.

It was perhaps for this reason that nineteenth-century American Shakespearean scholars chose to ignore this edition and Hopkinson's candidacy for the title of 'First American Editor'. This symbolic 'laurel' was awarded to Joseph Dennie, a personal friend of Hopkinson, fellow Philadelphia lawyer, a 'recognised scholar'[26] and the editor of the later Shakespeare variorum edition of 1805. The importance of Hopkinson's 1795 American edition is that it was the 'first' example of the way the demands of the American market and the national sentiment were going to influence the prefaces and the style of future Shakespeare publications.

JOSEPH HOPKINSON, AMERICAN NATIONALIST

The name of Joseph Hopkinson as the American 'editor' and writer of the preface reinforces the impression of nationalism strongly suggested by the tone of this edition. Hopkinson was a young Philadelphia lawyer who had excellent American nationalist credentials. His father, Francis Hopkinson, later described as a 'jurist, wit and dilettante', was one of the signatories to the Declaration of Independence on behalf of the state of New Jersey,[27] and subsequently claimed to have helped design the American flag. Hopkinson senior was a person of substance and reputation in the new republic and someone who, at his graduation ceremony in Philadelphia in 1757, had listened to the charge delivered by the Reverend Mr Smith, including both

Christian teachings and the secular words of advice given by Polonius to his son in *Hamlet*.[28]

Joseph Hopkinson appears to have benefited from his father's influence as, in addition to writing the preface to the 'First American Edition', he became a federal judge and congressman. Committed to American issues, Hopkinson junior was also an occasional contributor to the Philadelphia magazine *Port Folio*, and is credited with the composition of the words of the popular patriotic song *Hail Columbia*. This song, first performed on 25 April 1798, was sung enthusiastically by theatre audiences across America throughout the next century. The lyrics of *Hail Columbia* captured the essence of nationalism, so much a part of nineteenth-century America, and of course hinted at the spectre of England, the ever-present natural enemy:

> Hail Columbia! Happy land!
> Hail ye heroes, heav'n born band,
> Who fought and bled in Freedom's cause
> . . .
> And when the storm of war was gone,
> Enjoy'd the peace your valour won.
> Let Independence be our boast;
> Ever mindful what it cost;
> Ever grateful for the prize,
> Let its altar reach the skies.[29]

As if to confirm the patriotic status of this song, Philip Hone later described it as 'the nation's anthem',[30] and Charles Dickens was to remark that, in an article highly critical of the English, an American newspaper journalist had suggested that if a third war with England were to be fought, the victorious Americans would sing 'Hail Columbia in the scarlet courts of Westminster'.[31] Hopkinson was later to explain why he had become a songwriter for popular theatre. His 'object . . . was to get up an American spirit, which should be independent [. . .] and look and feel exclusively for our own honour and rights'.[32]

Hopkinson was also responsible for political pamphlets such as *What Is Our Situation and What Our Prospects?*, a chauvinistic and 'sabre-rattling' treatise written around 1798. Hopkinson called to his countrymen, 'let us, at once lift the shield of defence, and swear to stand or fall by our sacred rights . . . Let the American spirit stand forth in its native dignity and strength, and let it be seen that it "is not dead but sleepeth".'[33]

It is interesting to note that in this same pamphlet Hopkinson attacked the arrival of post-independence 'immigrants', and accused a group of 'fifteen or twenty thousand naturalised Frenchmen' of not sharing 'American values'. This type of language, invoking ideas of American purity under threat from immigrants, was to become a major feature of nationalist rhetoric throughout the nineteenth century. It was from the pen of the author of such a variety of nationalist texts that the preface of the 'First American Edition' of Shakespeare was to flow.

The political pedigree of Hopkinson suggests that the issue of American nationalism partly motivated his assistance in the production of the 'First American Edition' of Shakespeare. The style and content of the fifteen pages of criticism that introduced Shakespeare to the American reader adds more weight to this speculation. The nationalist 'tone' of the preface, and the ambiguity as to the precise source of the text, provides additional evidence that the promotion of Shakespeare in the first half of the nineteenth century was less about furthering literary scholarship than about promoting Shakespeare to the newly independent citizens.

THE PREFACE TO THE 'FIRST AMERICAN EDITION' (1795)

The title page signalled the edition's part in the process of appropriating Shakespeare for the American nation. The page clearly proclaims itself the 'First American Edition', with the following 'Preface . . . offered to the citizens of the United States'.[34] The intention of both editor and publisher appears to have been to ensure that readers remained fully conscious of their adopted national identity while reading the words of this famous dramatist and poet. A significant link was already being forged between the American reader and William Shakespeare the writer.

The preface was used to explain to the reader why this American edition was published and what there was of value in Shakespeare. The reader was informed that William Shakespeare was 'the greatest theatrical writer in the English language'.[35] Shakespeare's value was underlined by the fact that copies of his works had hitherto sold in London for 'about an hundred guineas' and that the poet was held in the highest esteem, 'so tumultuous [was] the admiration of his talents'.[36]

Having credited Hopkinson, the Philadelphia lawyer, with this preface, it is perhaps easy to recognise a style of writing that contains the essence of 'marketing copy' that would not be out of place on the rear cover of a modern paperback. With this unique preface, Shakespeare was being promoted as a founding father of the American language. After many years of anti-English sentiment, American readers unfamiliar with Shakespeare perhaps understandably needed to be persuaded that he was important and that his work was something of literary value. In his preface, Hopkinson presented the argument that would best suit the sensibilities of an aspiring American public.

While writing in appreciation of Shakespeare, however, Hopkinson felt the need to acknowledge and challenge the often-voiced prejudice against one aspect of stage drama. He wrote, 'The most popular and formidable objection to theatrical exhibitions appears to be, that they have an immoral tendency.'[37] Having repeated the accusation, Hopkinson the lawyer prepared to set out his rebuttal by first comprehensively condemning the 'great immorality of the British stage' together with its dramatists.[38] This done, he then made it clear that Shakespeare was altogether different. He informed the American reader that 'the fools of Shakspeare are always despised, and his villains are always hated', and that 'his works indeed abound with exquisite maxims of morality'.[39] The English stage was immoral but Shakespeare and his work were not. Hopkinson was insistent that 'the reproaches which have been thundered from the pulpit against the stage, cannot reasonably be applied to the stage of Shakspeare'.[40]

This 'First American Edition' now offered a wider public the opportunity to read and enjoy Shakespeare, and Hopkinson, with his preface, encouraged both the old elite and a new readership to accept Shakespeare as exceptional, being both moral and instructional.

Having dismissed the immorality charge, Hopkinson then set out to flatter the cause of American nationalism by highlighting the arrogant manner in which British editors had ridiculed each other's textual analysis. It had been common practice for editors in Britain to openly discredit the work of their predecessors, challenge their capabilities and indulge in public quarrels. Hopkinson derided both Alexander Pope and Dr Samuel Johnson for their self-promotion and their use of public insults to denigrate other editors. He concluded, 'If the western continent shall ever have the glory to produce a Shakspeare, it is to be hoped that his commentators will not rake for distinction through the kennels of Billingsgate.'[41]

While linking this comment on the possible motives of early British editors to the issue of their expansive editorial notes, Hopkinson introduced a characteristically American view of how Shakespeare should be read by an American public. According to Hopkinson,

[The] American reader is seldom disposed to wander through the wilderness of verbal criticism. An immense tract of excellent land uncultivated and even unexplored, presents an object more interesting to every mind than those ingenious literary trifles that in Europe are able to command so much attention.[42]

This clear reference to the American experience of taming the wilderness suggested that American readers were quite able to explore Shakespeare on their own without the interference of any pretentious English literary 'aristocracy'. The implication was that the American citizen was superior to his/her English counterpart. This 'First American Edition' was therefore offered to the American public without the kind of notes that, according to Hopkinson, 'clogged [London editions] with . . . successive explanations, each of which accompanied by the name of its inventor'.[43]

Hopkinson then emphasised what he appears to have regarded as evidence of the depravity and stupidity of the English, fully aware that this type of rhetoric would encourage an enthusiastic response from his American readers. He commented on the low level of civilisation in Elizabethan and early Jacobean England:

How wretched must have been the state of English literature in the days of Shakspeare, when six years elapsed after his decease, before his friends found it worth their trouble to print his plays! This did not arise from poverty, but the total want of taste in the English nation, for Queen Elizabeth alone . . . bestowed three hundred thousand pounds sterling upon a single paramour.[44]

Hopkinson wanted Americans to consider themselves better than the English, and he gave them the opportunity to show their nation's superiority by acknowledging Shakespeare's pre-eminence ahead of a country that suffered such a 'total want of taste'. Shakespeare was thus already being distanced from the English nation and the British monarchy. If Shakespeare was largely undervalued and misunderstood by what, for Americans, were the tyrannical kings and queens of Britain, then he could be considered to have something in common with the American people. Shakespeare was available for adoption. The writings of this 'son of a Yeoman', this common-born man, who, through individual talent, had excelled in his chosen art and profession, were now available to English-speaking Americans ready to embrace new exemplars. Americans could now demonstrate their superiority over the old English rulers by appreciating and appropriating the man and the plays that together, in essence, shared their experience and what they regarded as their Anglo-Saxon heritage.

This preface of ten pages represented the first published American literary criticism on the subject of Shakespeare, and it reflected many elements that were of concern to Americans in the closing part of the eighteenth century. The Americanisation of the discourse and the style of presentation within this edition influenced subsequent editions and provide evidence of the

To shield fair virtue, and to shame her foes.
Time bowed before him, Death resigned his trust,
Kingdoms come back, and Monarchs left the dust:
All, at his bidding, burst Oblivion's grave,
To warn, to win, to chasten, and to save.
Proud was the lyre beneath its master's hand,
And rapt the listeners of our father-land.
Soon from the Old the New World caught the strain,
And hailed on Freedom's shores the Drama's reign;
From spot to spot the inspiration flew,
And reared at last this vaulted dome – for you![49]

The audience was offered an 'anointed Bard', who, through his plays, had fulfilled a central purpose, 'To warn, to win, to chasten, and to save . . . And rapt the listeners of our father-land'. The suggestion was that, like early Americans, Shakespeare was involved in the fight against tyranny and was therefore a fitting hero to inspire the 'New World'. This same theme was later to be developed by Delia Bacon when she argued that Shakespeare was a 'prophet' of the coming American nation.[50] The idea that Shakespeare, in some way, shared the dreams of the leaders of the American Revolution was particularly attractive to a people seeking confirmation of their exceptionalism. For Americans, Shakespeare was more than just entertainment. Like the works of Adams, Franklin and Jefferson, his plays were to be read, studied and revered.

AMERICANISATION OF LATER EDITIONS OF SHAKESPEARE

Editors and publishers began to suggest to prospective book buyers the patriotic imperative for Americans to acquire personal copies of Shakespeare. Forms of textual identification with the American nation were to feature in many editions that, via booksellers and mail order, found their way into homes across America. The Americanisation was in some cases very subtle, but links between Shakespeare and the topic of American nationalism were nevertheless still recognisable.

Four years after the Astor Place riot, an edition of Shakespeare edited by Charles Knight included a dedication to the British actor William Macready, in recognition of his visit to the USA 'upon [his] noble task of presenting at our then national theatres, the text of Shakspere'.[51] Macready had fled the United States after the riot in fear of his life, but for Charles Knight the act of presenting Shakespeare was 'noble' and a service to the American nation.

In Richard Grant White's edition of 1865, the preface, addressed to the American people, linked the work of editing Shakespeare to the American War of Secession, symbolically offering the now completed edition to the American public on Shakespeare's birthday:

Begun when our country was strong and happy in long-continued peace and prosperity, it was interrupted, near its close, by a bloody struggle which has tried or proved, to shake that prosperity to its foundations, and which, involving us all in its excitement, absorbed the best energies of every generous soul; – it is finished as that strength seems to be renewed and established more firmly than before, and under glad auguries of peace and a prosperity which we may reasonably hope will never again be so interrupted. Here is my peace-offering.[52]

The connection between the American nation and Shakespeare was made repeatedly, the 1878 William T. Amies 'illustrated' Shakespeare declaring itself the 'American Standard Edition'. The preface, symbolically 'offered to the American public', also carried the chauvinistic claim that 'the publisher can not but believe that he has supplied a want long felt in a country where the productions of him who has been justly said to possess the greatest name in all literature, receive even wider and more intelligent admiration than in England itself'.[53] As with the 'First American Edition' of 1795, American pride was boosted by the suggestion that national collective 'intelligence' was confirmed by a greater appreciation of Shakespeare than was afforded to the playwright in England.

Even copies of Shakespeare that had not been formally associated by the editor or publishers to the American nation were likely to be linked 'informally' by a proud purchaser. A copy that once belonged to Henry Clay Folger, the president of Standard Oil of New York and later the benefactor of the Folger Shakespeare Library, received such an inscription. On the title page of an edition by Lippincott & Co. of Philadelphia, Folger wrote quotations from two major influences on American national thought, Ralph Waldo Emerson and Abraham Lincoln. The words of Lincoln that Folger used to 'Americanise' his personal copy of Shakespeare were 'it matters not to me whether Shakspeare be well or indeed ill acted, with him, the thought suffices'.[54]

Walt Whitman also personalised a copy of Shakespeare in a manner that linked the text to the American nation. Three months prior to his death in 1891, Whitman gave a copy of Shakespeare to a friend as a keepsake. Before the title page Whitman pasted an autographed picture of himself, followed by what appears to be a newspaper 'proof' of his article 'What Lurks behind Shakspeare's Historical Plays?' In this article, Whitman made the argument that Shakespeare was spiritually an American. Whitman asked the reader,

Will it not indeed be strange if the author of 'Othello' and 'Hamlet' is destined to live in America, in a generation or two, less as the cunning draughtsman of the passions, and more as putting on record the first full exposé – and by far the most vivid one, immeasurably ahead of doctrinaires and economists – of the political theory and results . . . which America has come on earth to abnegate and replace?[55]

Even an American such as Whitman, who had for so many years proclaimed his independence from symbols of 'old world' influence, formally appropriated Shakespeare for the American nation.

Shakespeare was also sufficiently 'American' to be given to war heroes in recognition of their service and as a means to prepare for and recover from the trials of patriotic duty. Shakespeare was the gift regarded as being sufficiently 'American' to present to a heroine of the War of Secession, Clara Barton, the founder of the American Red Cross. The presentation was made in recognition of her 'many valuable services rendered to the sick and wounded at the Flying Hospital, 10th Army Corp in front of Richmond V. A., Stockport Feb, 1865'.[56] Some years later, in 1892, the War Service Library was supplying copies of Shakespeare, courtesy of the 'people of the United States through the American Library Association for the use of Soldiers and Sailors'.[57] Shakespeare was now truly fit for heroes and considered to be an inspiration and comfort for those about to fight for the continuance of the ideals that, from 1776, had been the cornerstone of the very idea of America.

The process of appropriation took many forms, but transformation of a collection of play scripts into an inspirational secular 'bible' for the American nation is something significant and unique. Hopkinson and the other 'early' editors of Shakespeare, rather than just confirming their own intellectual standing in society, seem to have regarded their editorial task as an act of patriotic duty and civic service. The task of editing and presenting Shakespeare was in part, it seemed, the act of claiming ownership for the American people. American citizens were superior to those of England, and that superiority was to be reinforced and further encouraged by the democratic appreciation of the pre-eminent philosophical and cultural text in the 'American' language. For American citizens, whatever their ancestral background, Shakespeare was offered as an integral part of their national inheritance. Identifiably American editions offered the means by which this national ownership could be affirmed.

NOTES

1. For a history of the American theatre, see Wilmeth and Bigsby, eds., *The Cambridge History of American Theatre.*
2. Jean I. Marsden, ed., *The Appropriation of Shakespeare* (New York: Harvester Wheatsheaf, 1991), p. 1.
3. Ibid.
4. Ibid.
5. See Westfall, *American Shakespearean Criticism*, pp. 46–7. See also *The Tragic History of King Richard III, Altered from Shakespear by Colley Cibber* (London: J. & R. Tonson, 1766). The play was cut from 3,403 to 2,380 lines with about half the original characters omitted.
6. Preface to *King Richard III, as Presented by Edwin Booth*, ed. William Winter (New York: Francis Hart & Co., 1881). Adapted from Colly Cibber.
7. Jared Brown, *The Theatre in America during the Revolution* (Cambridge: Cambridge University Press, 1995).
8. Shakespeare is believed to have written *Henry VI, Parts 1–3*, and *Richard III* between 1589 and 1592, as a 'series'. All the chief characters in *Richard III* had been introduced and, importantly, developed in the preceding three plays.
9. See the comments of Al Pacino as director and star of the film *Looking for Richard* (USA, 1996). Pacino describes *Richard III* as a 'difficult play' and comments, 'I don't know why we even bother to do this at all.'
10. Walt Whitman, 'What Lurks behind Shakspere's Historical Plays?', *Prose Works 1892*, vol. II, *Collect and Other Prose*, ed. Floyd Stovall (New York: New York University Press, 1964), p. 554.
11. Westfall, *American Shakespearean Criticism*, p. 55.
12. Ibid., p. 38.
13. Ibid.
14. Charles Lee, *Strictures on a Pamphlet Entitled a 'Friendly Address to All Reasonable Americans, on the Subject of Our Political Confusions,' Addressed to the People of America* (Philadelphia: T. Green, 1775).
15. 'To the People of Pennsylvania', *Pennsylvania Gazette*, 27 March 1776.
16. Ibid. For another early example of the use of Shakespeare in parody, see the *Kentucke Gazette* of 25 August 1787. See also Rusk, *The Literature of the Middle Western Frontier*, vol. II, p. 4.
17. Richard Nisbet, *Slavery Not Forbidden by Scripture. Or, A Defence of the West-India Planters, from the Aspersions Thrown out against Them* (Philadelphia, 1773). Noah Webster, *Effects of Slavery on Morals and Industry* (Hartford CT: Hudson & Goodwin, 1793).
18. John Adams, *The Works of John Adams, Second President of the United States*, 10 vols. (Boston MA: Little, Brown & Co., 1856), vol. III, p. 394.
19. Bristol, *Shakespeare's America*, pp. 53–5.
20. While the precise origin of this motto is uncertain, *E Pluribus Unum* appeared in the crest of the *Gentleman's Magazine* from its first edition published in

London in 1731. This magazine is known to have been popular with many influential figures in pre-Revolution America.

21. Tocqueville, *Democracy in America*, vol. ii.
22. Westfall, *American Shakespearean Criticism*, p. 79.
23. Bristol, *Shakespeare's America*, p. 86.
24. *The Plays and Poems of William Shakespeare: Corrected from the Latest and Best London editions, with Notes, by Samuel Johnson, L.L.D. To Which Are Added, a Glossary and the Life of the Author . . . First American Edition* (Philadelphia: Bioren & Madan, 1795).
25. Westfall, *American Shakespearean Criticism*, p. 89. The same conclusion as to the editor's name was reached by Buton Alva Konkle, *Joseph Hopkinson, 1770–1842: Jurist, Scholar, Inspirer of the Arts* (Philadelphia: University of Pennsylvania Press, 1931).
26. Westfall, *American Shakespearean Criticism*, pp. 84–95.
27. Annie Russell Marble, *Heralds of American Literature* (Chicago: University of Chicago Press, 1907), p. 19.
28. 'Gentlemen', *Pennsylvania Gazette*, 11 August 1757.
29. Joseph Hopkinson, *Hail Columbia* (Philadelphia: J. Ormrod, 1798).
30. Hone, *Diary*, vol. i, pp. 125–6.
31. Dickens, *American Notes*, p. 202.
32. Letter from Hopkinson to a resident of Wilkes-Barre PA, 24 August 1840. Quoted here from Konkle, *Joseph Hopkinson*, p. 83–4.
33. Joseph Hopkinson, *What Is Our Situation and What Our Prospects?* (Philadelphia, 1798), p. 38. For a biography of Hopkinson, see Konkle, *Joseph Hopkinson*.
34. *The Plays and Poems of William Shakespeare . . . First American Edition*, pp. ii–iii.
35. Ibid., p. 3.
36. Ibid.
37. Ibid., p. iv.
38. Ibid.
39. Ibid., pp. vi and viii.
40. Ibid., p. vii.
41. Ibid., p. x.
42. Ibid.
43. Ibid.
44. Ibid., pp. xvi–xvii.
45. *Liberty Hall* (Cincinnati), 21 March 1820. Quoted here from Rusk, *The Literature of the Middle Western Frontier*, vol. ii, p. 6.
46. Ibid., p. 5.
47. Charles Sprague, 'Shakspeare Ode – Delivered at the Boston Theatre in 1823, at the Exhibition of a Pageant in Honor of Shakspeare', in Sprague, *The Poetical and Prose Writings*, p. 43. This poem was to reappear at a formal ceremony held in Stratford-upon-Avon in 1887.

48. Charles Sprague, *The Prize Ode, Recited at the Representation of the Shakspeare Jubilee, Boston, Feb. 13, 1824* (Boston, 1824).

49. Sprague, *The Poetical and Prose Writings*, pp. 93–4.

50. Delia Bacon, *The Philosophy of the Plays of Shakspere Unfolded* (London: Groombridge & Sons, 1857).

51. *The Comedies, Histories, Tragedies and Poems of William Shakspere*, ed. Charles Knight (Boston MA: Little, Brown & Co., 1853). In the same year, another edition introduced Shakespeare to readers with the now common 'American Preface'. See *The Works of Shakespeare*, ed. J. Payne Collier (New York: Redfield, 1853).

52. *The Works of William Shakespeare*, ed. Richard Grant White (Boston MA: Little, Brown & Co., 1865).

53. *The Complete Works of William Shakespeare: American Standard Edition, Carefully Collated and Compared with the Editions of Halliwell, Knight, Collier, and Others, with a Comprehensive Life of the Great Dramatist, by Charles Knight; Beautifully Illustrated with Numerous Steel Engravings, from Original Drawings, Chiefly Portraits in Character of the Most Distinguished American Actors* (Philadelphia: William T. Amies, 1878).

54. *The Complete Works of William Shakespeare* (Philadelphia: J. P. Lippincott & Co., 1875). Part of the Folger collection: PR2752 1875k As. Col.

55. Walt Whitman, *Critic*, 27 September 1884. This piece was later to be included in *Democratic Vistas and Other Papers* and *November Boughs*. See Whitman, *Prose Works 1892*, vol. II, *Collect and Other Prose*, pp. 554–6 In the *Critic*, 'Shakspeare' is the spelling used, while in Whitman's own later publications, 'Shakspere' is preferred. The edition of Shakespeare formerly owned by Whitman is *The Complete Works of William Shakespeare: from the Text of Johnson, Steevens, & Reed: with Biographical Sketch by Mary Cowden Clarke* (Edinburgh: William P. Nimmo, 1866). This copy is held by the Folger Shakespeare Library: PR2754 1K1 copy2 Sh. Col.

56. *The Complete Works of Shakspeare* (Cincinnati: Rickey & Carroll, 1864). This copy is held by the Folger Shakespeare Library: PR2752 1864h Sh. Col.

57. *The Complete Works of William Shakespeare* (Chicago: Morrill, Higgins & Co., 1892). See the copy held by the Folger Shakespeare Library: PR2752 1892c.

CHAPTER 4

Jacksonian energy – Shakespearean imagery

Art thou base, common, and popular?

Henry V, Act 4, Scene 1

As Americans continued to celebrate their two military victories over England, their western frontier advanced towards the Pacific Ocean. An explosive period of growth energised the population. There were new immigrants, a greater market for manufactured goods, new states, but political power remained largely with the 'old' east-coast elite. The ideology of the Revolution survived in the political rhetoric but it was the coming of the Jacksonian era (1830–50) that ensured that a greater proportion of the population began to feel empowered.

While wealth and a sense of nation increased, Shakespeare can be seen to have touched the diverse lives of Americans occupying all strata of society. Lawrence Levine put forward the following reason for this apparent omnipresence:

Shakespeare was popular, first and foremost, because he was integrated into the culture and presented within its context. Nineteenth-century Americans were able to fit Shakespeare into their culture so easily because he *seemed* to fit – because so many of his values and tastes were, or at least appeared to be, close to their own, and were presented through figures that seemed real and came to matter to the audience.[1]

The shared 'values and tastes' suggested here by Levine, key to this chapter, imply that there was an element in Shakespearean imagery that in some way matched the Jacksonian energy of the audience and became part of an expression of their transition to sustainable nationhood.

74

NATION OF MANY NATIONS

Any suggestion that Americans of the early nineteenth century were of one mind or character is likely to be resisted. In addition to disparate ancestry, the citizens who populated the United States and benefited from the success of the Revolution and Constitution now occupied lands with very different climatic and topographical conditions. Walt Whitman, who by 1855 symbolised the period in many ways, recognised and celebrated the diversity of this America in many poems of the collection *Leaves of Grass*. Whitman wrote that he himself was 'One of the Nation of many nations'.[2] Years later, in a book about the Jacksonian era, Frederick Jackson Turner wrote of the nine distinct American regions used by the Census Office to recognise the socio-economic differences that helped define the lives of American citizens.[3] What was clear to many commentators was that America was home to people with a multitude of ethnicities and economic lifestyles. It could be argued that there was never really one America, rather a federal collection of Americas. To an observer such as Frederick Marryat, America in 1839 was 'not yet . . . in the true sense of the word, a nation, [but a] mass of many people cemented together to a certain degree, by a general form of government'.[4] At this stage the 'cement' was still thin and far from solid.

A nation is created through the popular recognition of shared symbols and myths. During the period when the citizens of so many 'Americas' aspired to E Pluribus Unum, both recent history and folklore were utilised to forge a sense of unity. To supplement the by then traditional story of the Mayflower pilgrims and the War of Independence, were added the stories of frontier and Shakespeare. Richard Slotkin wrote of 'myth and historical memory', which, he argues, largely developed between the 1830s and 1840s, along with the 'development of true mass media with a national market'.[5] For Slotkin, 'to study national popular culture, we should see it not as a national folklore but as the myth medium of the victorious party in an extended historical struggle'.[6] In this case the 'victorious party' were the Anglo-Americans, and 'The makers of American myths and ideological formulae [were the] writers, journalists, preachers, and politicians'.[7]

While acknowledging the ethnic, economic and geographical diversity, it is still possible to recognise certain aspects or experience that characterise the early nineteenth century, a period dominated by Jacksonian politics. The term 'Jacksonian', while referring to a specific political movement, conveniently describes a period when characteristics, present within the new republic since the War of Independence, became more recognisable

and were celebrated as being 'American'. Acknowledging the problem of
attempting generalisation, Edward Pessen suggested that the era was characterised by an acceptance of uncompromising individualism and violence,
of personal vanity and anti-intellectualism.[8] In an attempt to summarise the
period, Frederick Jackson Turner wrote, 'Jacksonian Democracy implied a
fuller trust in the common people and in their right and capacity to rule.'[9]
He regarded the Jacksonian period as a distinct epoch in which 'An optimistic and creative nation was forming and dealing with democracy and
with things, in vast new spaces, in an original, practical, and determined way
and on a grand scale.'[10] As Lawrence Levine observed, 'Nineteenth-century
America, . . . was fertile ground for these attempts to fix certain aspects of
the shifting landscape of modernity into the unchanging relationship with
a symbolic past.'[11]

These are some of the characteristics of a period in which the confidence
of ordinary Americans rose. According to Turner,

> It was because Andrew Jackson personified these essential Western traits that . . .
> he became the idol and the mouthpiece of the popular will; [his] triumph . . .
> marked the end of the old era of trained statesmen for the Presidency. With him
> began the era of the popular hero.[12]

There was an identifiable Jacksonian energy that encouraged the population
to take personal ownership of all aspects of life in the republic.

The people that made up this 'nation of nations', while still in the process
of adopting the 'symbols and myths' that would unite them, were offered a
naturalised Shakespeare in political speeches, in orations, on the stage and
in newsprint. Rather than a ridiculed representative of a foreign literature,
'Shakespeare and his drama had become . . . an integral part of American
culture.'[13] In what Turner called the 'crucible of the frontier',[14] 'Americans,
prepared by a national cult of the individual, quickly embraced the romantic
characterization' that was so much a feature of Shakespeare's plays.[15]

SHAKESPEAREAN IMAGERY AND LANGUAGE

An early example of the way imagery more usually associated with
Shakespeare and Elizabethan theatre was to be linked with what would
later become American national consciousness can be detected in an early
poem about America. In 1606, Michael Drayton, 'Shakespeare's Warwickshire friend and fellow poet',[16] published a poem in England that associated
the heroic imagery and spirit of the English victory at Agincourt with the
adventurers who were to establish the first colony of Virginia.[17] This type

of suggestion of noble aims and a valiant heritage would be repeated as Americans visualised themselves in romantic terms far removed from the gritty reality of subduing the continent they had now won. Many years later, Ashley Thorndike commented, 'I like to fancy that the American temper has a close kinship with the Elizabethan joy in experience, the venturesomeness in deeds, the heedlessness as to dogmas.'[18]

Another romantic, William Adams Slade, would offer a justification to his American audience for their claim to Shakespeare, describing how, along with the Bible, copies of Shakespeare had accompanied the heroic pioneers across the American continent. For Slade, these American pioneers were like Elizabethan adventurers, 'sailing' across dangerous seas for the benefit of the commonweal:

Starting at the Atlantic seaboard, [Shakespeare] has gone on from coast to coast, the spectator of the country's growth, moving from frontier to frontier, sometimes in the company of, sometimes only a measurable distance behind, the westward-moving pioneers, those later, free-hearted adventurers, descendants in the spirit of Drake and Hawkins and Frobisher. As once the Golden Hind, so now the prairie schooner dared the yet unknown, and Elizabethan idioms, many of them forgotten in the land of their origin, sometimes gave a flavor to the speech heard along the trail.[19]

The term 'prairie schooner' used by Slade was part of American idiom during the nineteenth century. The large ox-drawn covered wagons are seen as 'ships', sailing across oceans to establish new colonies of freedom and material plenty. The image of an ocean of grass being crossed by sturdy schooners, crewed by heroic colonisers, functions within the romantic myth that surrounds the American West. The ability to romanticise the process of western expansion is a feature of the Jacksonian epoch and something that helped fix the heroic within the American consciousness.[20] American citizens, apparently so practical, readily embraced images that cloaked western expansionism with Elizabethan, if not actually Shakespearean, imagery, and one can speculate that this in turn helped make Shakespeare fit so easily within American values and tastes.

The brief reference by Slade to 'Elizabethan idioms, many of them forgotten' repeats the suggestion that certain Shakespearean phrases could be understood more readily in communities in nineteenth-century America than in Victorian England. As early as 1789, Noah Webster, creator of the first American dictionary, wrote of his belief that 'American yeomanry' spoke 'the most *pure English* known in the world'.[21] In his opinion, the inhabitants of New England understood a form of English that had now been lost in the mother country, following many years of foreign influence and fashionable corruptions.

Richard Grant White, editor of an American edition of Shakespeare (1865), remarked in his notes to the plays that he had discovered a number of Elizabethan words, then unknown in England, that were still part of colloquial speech in America. One example White offered was the term 'pheese' used in the opening scene of *The Taming of the Shrew*. The textual note suggested to the reader that whereas an Englishman would need this term explained, 'It is hardly necessary to remark [to an American] that "pheese" means "worry".'[22] White later published two books on the use of the English language in America, in which, like Webster, he argued that, contrary to the opinion of English critics and journalists, many educated Americans spoke an earlier, 'purer' form of English than the citizens of England:

The English of the period when Shakespeare wrote and the Bible was translated has been kept in use among people of education somewhat more in the new England than in the old. All over the country there are some words and phrases in common use, and in certain parts of New England and Virginia there are many, which have been dropped in British England, or are to be found only among the squires and farmers in the recesses of rural counties.[23]

The suggestion was that most Anglo-Americans had arrived in the colonies prior to the 1707 Act of Union with Scotland. From this date onwards, perhaps due to the greater influence of European courtiers and fashions, language usage in England underwent changes (White regarded such changes as errors), and consequently spoken English was, by the nineteenth century, subject to numerous 'Briticisms'. In White's opinion, many Americans had continued to speak and write English in a form that was closer to the English of Shakespeare than the language, now denuded of many Elizabethan terms and riddled with Briticisms, generally spoken in England.

White informed his American readership that 'we shall have the reason to suspect that there is at least the beginning of a new language, – the British –, and that the English tongue and English sense has fled to the Yankee across the sea'.[24] This wonderfully provocative statement managed to unite several aspects of American tradition that had developed during the nineteenth century both to serve the appropriation of Shakespeare and to boost American nationalism. For White, the Americans were able to understand the language of Shakespeare because this was their shared spoken language. Thus, and seemingly paradoxically, language, and the philosophical and cultural text that was Shakespeare, contained the American cultural heritage. By implication White appears to have suggested Shakespeare spoke the language of America.

AN AUDIENCE LIVING IN A FRONTIER ENVIRONMENT

Life in the American South and West could be harsh. At times nature itself appeared to be at war with the settlers and pioneers. Complete with tornadoes, blizzards, droughts and thunderstorms, nature was dramatic, and to succeed Americans on the frontier had to fight to survive. In addition to nature, the continued savage conflict with the numerous nations of American Indians brutalised both sides in the fierce dispute over land, further encouraging the general acceptance of violence that was one of the characteristics of Jacksonian society. What Richard Slotkin identified as part of *The Fatal Environment* ensured that for the American audience or reader violence was real and part of daily existence.[25] In an earlier book Slotkin went further when he suggested that, to some degree, American character was a result of a 'regeneration through violence'.[26] The acceptance of the existence of conflict represents part of the 'values and tastes' shared by Jacksonian and Shakespearean audiences.

Visiting New Orleans in 1817, Henry Fearon described an example of the 'Shakespearean' style of entertainment present in frontier society. He detailed the contents of an advertisement for a 'public amusement' to be held the next Sunday 'near the circus'. The 'amusement' was to be 'an extraordinary fight of furious animals'.[27] The four main 'fights' were variations on the bear-baiting that once competed for audiences with Shakespeare's Globe Theatre. The advertisement went on to suggest that if a bull that was part of the show survived an attack by dogs, 'several pieces of fireworks will be placed on his back, which will produce a very entertaining amusement'.[28] Fearon did not attend.

In Shakespeare's England the audience also understood the excitement of violence, and plays featuring bloodshed and retribution, such as Thomas Kyd's *Spanish Tragedy* or Shakespeare's *Titus Andronicus* or *Hamlet*, were highly popular entertainment. While some audiences in cities such as 'Puritan' Boston or 'Quaker' Philadelphia might be expected to have disapproved of representations of filial murder and revenge, in the many other frontier states the plays appeared to be contemporary in that respect at least, and to have been written with America in mind. Between Shakespeare and his American audience there was a shared acceptance that conflict was part of everyday existence. For American audiences and critics, what appears to have concerned them most about a play such as *Hamlet* was not whether the young prince should take violent revenge on his uncle Claudius, but why he found it so difficult to decide to act.

Presented in the theatre, the type of conflict that is a feature of many of Shakespeare's plays perhaps helped the audience come to terms with traumatic aspects of nineteenth-century American society. Many of those who watched conflict portrayed on the stage recognised themselves, and outside the theatre these same citizens frequently resorted to brutality to serve what they regarded as 'popular justice'. Joe Cowell, an English actor in America for over thirty years during the early nineteenth century, recounts an anecdote about fellow actor Junius Booth 'the elder', who, after taking against two itinerant preachers, played a joke on the pair. While the preachers were sleeping, Booth hid his wallet in their belongings and then reported the 'theft' to the captain of the riverboat. When the preachers were discovered to be in possession of Booth's wallet, the boat was stopped. Cowell reports that the two men made 'in vain their protestations of innocence . . . and they according to "Lynch law", were to receive a severe flagellation and then be left in the wilderness'.[29] When Booth saw the extreme reaction of the captain and other passengers to his 'joke' he confessed and the preachers escaped mob justice.

Henry Irving also observed the extent to which recourse to violence was a daily part of life for American audiences in the West. While in Colorado a touring company had 'condensed' a performance of a play into an hour and a half in order to catch a train to their next engagement. On the occasion of their next visit to the city, 'they were met *en route*, some fifty miles out, by the sheriff, who warned them to pass on by some other way as their coming was awaited by a large section of the able-bodied male population armed with shot guns'.[30]

Nineteenth-century American writers, whether in political articles, journalism or fiction, consistently represent society in the American South and West as characterised by conflict endured and practised by strong individuals. Mark Twain, in his fiction and 'reminiscences', revealed aspects of life in the South and West that reflected a society not dissimilar to that of Shakespearean drama. The blood feud between the Shepherdsons and Grangerfords in *The Adventures of Huckleberry Finn* reflects an aspect of the West that would have struck a chord with audiences watching the family feuds of *Romeo and Juliet*, and this in a book which features a supposed Shakespeare production by two confidence tricksters who themselves run the risk of retaliatory violence.[31]

In *Roughing It*, Twain described his own experiences in California and Nevada, and from his description of 'Utah [as] an absolute monarchy and Brigham Young [as] king' to the suggestion that the first twenty-six graves in the cemetery of Virginia City, Nevada, were of 'murdered men',[32] he presents the South and West in the mid-nineteenth century as a place where Shakespearean drama would have appeared to be not only 'American' but of immediate relevance. So close was the connection that a convicted murderer named Lovett, contemplating his own execution in January 1866, bequeathed his skull to actor Edwin Booth so that the actor might have a real 'prop' for his future performances of *Hamlet*.[33]

Shakespeare's plays often include the violence of the battlefield, the castle dungeon or the market place. These plays, now performed on the stage in Natchez, St Louis or Denver, were, in some way, appreciated and welcomed by an American audience because they dealt with many elements of their daily lives. Whilst many in the New York or Boston audience perhaps saw their personal interest in Shakespeare as validating their intellectual pretensions, frontier audiences enjoyed a form of theatrical melodrama that nonetheless captured some of the essence of Slotkin's *Fatal Environment*.

THEATRE FURTHER WEST

In Elizabethan London, at the height of Shakespeare's popularity, there were seven functioning theatres. As cities mushroomed across America, theatres also multiplied, and as the first towns were established west of the Alleghenies, enterprising actors soon followed. Theatre manager and actor Joe Cowell was to comment on the speed of theatre construction in the Ohio valley in 1829. As he observed, 'New towns must have new theatres, sometimes even before they have new churches, and Frankfort, Lexington, Louisville, and Cincinnati had been so adorned for several years.'[34] Actor Henry Irving was later to remark that 'The number of the theatres in America and the influence they exercise constitute important elements in the national life.'[35]

Further from the Middle West, the prospect of a free-spending audience in the gold-rush territories ensured that a constant stream of touring companies and star performers were induced to make the long and arduous journey from the east coast. There was big money to be made by such performers. Newspapers were to report that Edwin Forrest had been offered 'fifty thousand dollars to act fifty nights in California [and] six thousand dollars to act twenty nights in St. Louis'.[36] A report in the *Colored American* decrying the huge sums being amassed by actors and theatre owners stated that a dancer known as 'Madame Celeste' had, in ninety days of performances in New York, Philadelphia, Mobile and New Orleans, earned 'twenty-six thousand dollars'.[37] Actress Charlotte Cushman was so successful during her American tour of 1849–52 that she felt able to 'retire' from full-time acting to live in England and Rome. At her death she is said to have left a fortune of approximately $500,000.[38] With financial rewards such as these, theatre, the fictional characters from the plays and the actors who performed them all became part of everyday conversation for the fortune hunters and pioneers of America.

But the people living in the new cities were not the only Americans to be offered Shakespeare's plays. The prospectors, miners and assorted 'service' industries in the small boom towns received visits from travelling entertainers attracted by the potential earnings, and 'it has been estimated that by 1850 there were more than fifty stock companies' bringing a form of cultural conditioning to western audiences.[39]

In *How Shakespeare Won the West*, Helene Koon suggested that a 'Travelling company averaged $300 a night throughout the gold fields', and this figure was boosted by the gold dust and nuggets that were often thrown onto the stage as tributes by enthusiastic audiences.[40] Once the gold had been exploited and the territory settled down to a period of more sustained economic development, however, the travelling companies reduced in number. As Koon concluded, 'Shakespeare's popularity reached its height in the seven years between 1849 and 1856, when the gold madness flourished and hard earned nuggets were freely spent.'[41]

Bayard Taylor reported for the east-coast press on the development of western cities. Published in 1850 as a book entitled *Eldorado or Adventures in the Path of Empire*, his reports suggest both the type of audience and the apparent level of enthusiasm demonstrated for Shakespeare. Written in late 1849, Taylor described a theatre in the city of Sacramento in the early gold-rush period. The theatre was a 'Canvas building' with a sign identifying the 'Eagle Theatre . . . nailed to the top of the canvas frame'.[42] An audience of up to four hundred prospectors and miners paid three dollars each for a seat in a 'box' and two dollars for the 'pit' three times a week. The Eagle was the first commercial theatre established in California and it opened to an enthusiastic crowd of fortune hunters on 18 October 1849. While Sacramento was the site of the first theatre in California (there had been an earlier amateur performance of *Othello* at Sonoma in 1847), the Eagle Theatre, notable as it was, survived only until 4 January 1850, when it was washed away by the flooding Sacramento River. Encouraged by their commercial success, the company then moved to San Francisco to continue offering Shakespeare to the men and women of the new frontier.[43] Subsequently, at the grandly named Olympic Circus in San Francisco, just one month after the loss of the Eagle, the first of Shakespeare's plays to be performed was *Othello*.

The tent that had served as the first Sacramento theatre contrasts with the splendid edifice built for the population of Salt Lake City in Utah. Horace Greeley, in a report entitled 'An Editor Goes West, 1859', described the brick and stucco Saints Theatre which had cost Brigham Young $250,000 to build and could seat an audience of eighteen hundred. Brigham Young could often be seen amidst the thrice weekly audience with 'a dozen . . . wives side by side, and long seats quite filled with his children'.[44]

The decoration of this and many other theatres celebrated the new national symbols of America. Once again Shakespeare was associated with the enthusiasm for nationhood. The curtain of Ludlow and Smith's New Orleans theatre carried the image of 'Shakespeare borne in a halo of light on the pinions of the American eagle'.[45] It appears that in some theatres, William Shakespeare 'in the claws of the American eagle'[46] was regarded as a writer sharing the spirit of the American nation rather than an effete literary figure associated with America's main foreign rival.

A DEMOCRATIC AUDIENCE

For Philip C. Kolin, writing about Shakespeare in the South, the 'pluralistic' audience of nineteenth-century America mimicked the Bankside audience of seventeenth-century London, made up of 'day labourers, apprentices, law students, merchants, franklins, lords and ladies'.[47] Kolin notes that 'Southern audiences interested in Shakespeare included all strata of Mason-Dixon culture – slaves and free men and women, riverboat captains and their crews, the petit bourgeois, the landed aristocracy.'[48] To emphasise his point about the demographics of the audience for Shakespeare, Kolin referred to the *Daily Picayune*, 14 March 1844, which states, 'The play-going portion of our Negro population feel more interest in, and go in greater numbers to see, the plays of Shakespeare represented on the stage, than any other class of dramatic performance.'[49]

This inclusive audience, representing the spirit of Jacksonian America, was renowned for consisting of unrestrained pleasure seekers. Washington Irving, writing many years earlier in 1801 under the pseudonym Jonathan Oldstyle, remarked, 'I was much amused with the waggery and humour of the gallery, which, by the way, is kept in *excellent* order by the constables who are stationed there. The noise in this part of the house is somewhat similar to that which prevailed in Noah's ark.'[50]

Henry Fearon also visited many theatres during his travels. His comments are similar to those found in the reports written by later, more celebrated European visitors. In Pittsburgh, in 1818, Fearon saw a performance of *Hamlet* followed by a farce entitled 'Turn Out'. Fearon observed, 'The acting was equal to the audience, perhaps superior', and noted that the actor who played Horatio 'was dead drunk, and extremely dirty'.[51]

Tocqueville and Beaumont both commented on American theatre, and it is clear that they found the audiences more entertaining than some of the plays. In a note relating specifically to Philadelphia and New York, Beaumont described the sort of people who made up a theatre audience in the 1830s:

The public which goes to the theatre is generally thus composed: first, strangers who go because they do not know where else to pass their evenings; prostitutes, drawn by the presence of the strangers; young Americans of dissipated character; and finally a few shopkeeper's families . . . Persons more distinguished in fortune and position do not make theatre going a habit; only something out of the ordinary will attract them there – for example, the presence of a celebrated guest actor. On such occasions, many go to the theatre, not because they like it, but because it is fashionable.[52]

Beaumont claimed that the audience regarded theatre in a relaxed manner and stage drama as popular entertainment rather than 'high art'. He also complained that 'they chat, they argue, they fidget about, they make it an occasion to drink together; the interest of the play is entirely lost to view'.[53] While Beaumont may have disapproved of the audience reaction to stage drama, it was perhaps just this sort of healthy disrespect for what Levine described as 'highbrow' art that encouraged so wide an acceptance of Shakespeare.

Beaumont's reference to the presence of prostitutes in the audience introduces another aspect of the way theatre, and with it Shakespeare, became part of the vibrant life of many cities. While all plays, not just Shakespeare, 'benefited' from a mixed audience made up from a broad section of American society, the fact that Shakespeare was consumed by both 'service providers' and customers indicates another way the plays became known by so many Americans.

In a journal entry made in New Orleans on 1 January 1832, Tocqueville describes an audience and its class structure as delineated by the various 'tiers': 'Strange spectacle offered by the chamber. First stalls white, second

grey, coloured women, very pretty, white ones among them, but the remain-
der of African blood. Third stalls black.'[54] He also noted social events where
there were a large number of 'the very pretty coloured women' and mainly
'white' males, and drew the conclusion that the primary aim was to facilitate
sexual liaisons.

Charles Murray, writing about a visit to a theatre in the southern city
of Natchez, commented favourably on the appearance of the audience. He
observed that 'the Gallery was in the undisputed possession of some dozen
swarthy goddesses'.[55] Not only does this comment confirm earlier evidence
that citizens from all socio-economic groups attended the theatre, it also
suggests that the gallery or third tier was a place where unaccompanied
single women could be found in public. While Murray, like many writers
of the period, does not specify as much, it is highly likely that, as in many
theatres, the gallery in Natchez was occupied by working prostitutes.

In her essay 'That Guilty Third Tier: Prostitution in Nineteenth-Century
American Theaters', Claudia D. Johnson revealed the extent to which the
theatre, as well as providing entertainment to the audience of all ranks,
allowed men to make contact with prostitutes. While outwardly frowning
on what it considered as immoral activity, society quietly permitted 'the
oldest profession' to operate openly within theatres across America. It could
be argued that this aspect, prevalent within nineteenth-century culture,
aided the economic viability of theatres in so many newly founded western
cities. According to Johnson, 'By the 1830s and 1840s the relinquishing of
the third tier to prostitutes had become an established national tradition,
not only in New York, but in most cities, including Boston, Chicago,
Philadelphia, St. Louis, Cincinnati, Mobile, and New Orleans, among
others.'[56]

Johnson's essay also suggests that theatre designers might even have created a separate stairway to provide easy access to the third tier, allowing the
'entire inhabitants of houses of prostitution' to arrive en masse without disturbing the main body of the theatre. Joe Cowell makes a discrete mention
of the 'third tier' in a book on his life in the United States. Commenting
on his leased theatre in Baltimore (1827), he wrote, 'The gallery, which had
become an unprofitable nuisance, I dispensed with entirely, and made that
entrance serve for the third tier, effectually separating the visitors to that
section from the decorous part of the house.'[57]

The third tier was an aspect of American theatre not usually mentioned
by American writers of the east-coast cities intent on 'boosting' the public
perception of American culture in the expanding republic. But while
attending theatre productions of Shakespeare became a significant part of

American popular culture, 'The primary business of the gallery was not to watch the play but to make arrangements for the rest of the evening.'[58] Shakespeare had entered the lives of Americans by many different pathways, and even the most disinterested theatregoer might find a subliminal association between the dramatic action portrayed on the stage and the promise of more 'earthly' transactions later. Just as in the brothels and 'stews' of Elizabethan Southwark, when the democratic entertainment of theatre finished members of the American audience were able to continue their escapism through the medium of bacchanalian revelry.

AUDIENCE AND ACTORS

For audiences in America, Shakespeare was democratic entertainment, and they therefore expected those on stage to respect their wishes and hear their opinions. American equality extended to the audience and interaction between the stage and the audience was not always to the taste of visiting actors, but it did reflect the way Shakespeare had become part of folk culture rather than the property of those who regarded themselves as 'artists'. In the words of Jennifer Lee Carrell, 'Western audiences preserved and even heightened an exuberant tradition of theatregoing dating back to the Elizabethan audiences that Shakespeare knew.'[59]

In 1817, a Cincinnati newspaper reported the wild behaviour of a band of youths 'who were in the habit of besieging the theatre, pelting it with stones during the performance'.[60] Joe Cowell observed that men in the theatre 'generally, wore their hats; at all events, they consulted only their own opinion and comfort in the matter'.[61] Ralph Leslie Rusk, quoting several other examples, concluded that evidence from newspaper reports tended to support Fanny Trollope's often discounted opinion of Cincinnati and western society.

In Denver's Tabor Grand Opera House in 1886, during a performance of *Othello*, the actor Tommaso Salvini, in a note to the occupants of one of the boxes, complained about the 'laughter and popping of champagne corks'.[62] Horace Tabor, Denver's 'Silver King', loudly retorted, 'my theatre is a playhouse as much for the audience as for the actors', adding, 'if that Eytalian wants to pray let him go to church'.[63] The American audience, rather like the groundlings of Bankside, regarded the theatre as their territory rather than a place where an educated elite could dictate behaviour.

American audiences expected the actors to respond to their appreciation or criticism of the play or performance. If the audience enjoyed a particular soliloquy or speech, the actor could expect to have to repeat it several times until the audience allowed the play to continue. If nationalistic passions had been aroused in any way, the play might have to be temporarily suspended while the audience sang patriotic or popular songs of the day. In addition to the audience shouting, stamping and clapping their approval, Cowell observed that 'from ten to twenty dollars, and sometimes much more, would be thrown on the stage during . . . comic singing: a tribute of admiration not at all uncommon in those days in the South and West'.[64]

Within the detail of the public argument between Edwin Forrest and William Macready can be detected the difference between American and British audiences. During a visit to Britain in 1846, Forrest stated in a letter to *The Times* that he considered hissing to be one of two legitimate and justified methods by which an audience could express their opinion of an actor's performance.[65] He went on to add that in addition to hissing parts of a Macready performance that he considered an 'abuse', he also 'warmly applauded several points', noting with regret that no one else in the Edinburgh theatre joined him in this type of response. What is clear is that, for Forrest, hissing and applauding in the middle of a performance of a Shakespearean tragedy was to be expected. A response to Forrest's letter published in *The Times* two days later condemned this type of audience behaviour, suggesting that 'possibly it may be a Yankee fashion'.[66]

BURLESQUE SHOWS

Americans who had travelled westward were very willing to pay their hard-won dollars to see and hear Shakespeare performed as part of popular burlesque variety shows, and, along with rapidly built theatres, even riverboats were utilised to bring 'democratic' entertainment to the scattered population.

In *The Adventures of Huckleberry Finn*, Mark Twain portrayed the type of humorous individual that regarded Shakespeare as entertainment and sometimes as opportunity. The novel includes a comic episode in which two confidence tricksters, significantly employing aristocratic titles, attempt to swindle the public by supposedly staging a performance of *Hamlet*.[67] As Lawrence Levine notes, 'Twain's humor relies on his [readers'] familiarity with *Hamlet* and [their] ability to recognise the duke's improbable coupling of lines from a variety of Shakespeare's plays.'[68] Twain was confident that his readers would recognise both the form of the 'burlesque and

[the] parodies of Shakespeare',[69] so widespread had the acceptance of both become.

Now recognised by a substantial proportion of the American population, Shakespeare could be incorporated into any and every form of popular entertainment. John Brougham presented a musical at Burton's Theatre in New York in 1852, entitled 'Much Ado about a Merchant of Venice'. The lyrics of this early 'Broadway musical' included such wonderful lines as

> She has varmoosed far away,
> Far away from old Shylock,
> There's noone left to comfort me.
> All at my sorrows mock.[70]

A theatre poster preserved in the scrapbooks kept by Philadelphia attorney J. Parker Norris shows how several elements of so-called 'highbrow and lowbrow' entertainment could be combined to create an evening of popular culture. It advertises a show by the Cotton and Reeds New York Minstrels for 18 October 1875, in which 'songs and dances, enjoyable Ethiopian sketches and Burlesque Operas' are followed by an intriguing item called 'Shakespeare in the Kitchen'. A ticket for this evening of mixed entertainment cost just one dollar.[71]

As part of the widespread acceptance of Shakespeare there were minstrel burlesque versions of his plays: *Richard Ye Third, Hamlet the Dainty, an Ethiopian Burlesque, Hamlet Travesty* and comedy versions of *Antony and Cleopatra* and *The Tempest*.[72] Even when not part of the 'main attraction', Shakespeare was added to the entertainment. As part of a programme advertised for 18 January 1861, a poster for 'The Lone Star Minstrel and Dramatic Group' offered a Friday-night entertainment at the Melodeon, Mechanic Street, which, along with what was described as a 'roaring farce . . . *The Nigger Door-Keeper*', presented their audience with a 'rehearsal' of *Richard III*. Entrance just twenty-five cents.

In some cases, American producers rewrote or adapted the scripts of burlesques that had first been performed in London to reflect American colloquial humour. While the reason for the popularity of these burlesques is open to interpretation, for the humour to be successful the majority of an audience needed to have a basic knowledge of the Shakespearean original. One example of both parody and the Americanisation indicative of appropriation was *Ye Comedie of Errours*.[73] First performed by a minstrel company in 1858, the burlesque is set in New York, and concludes with the following lines:

> Luff me explain,
> It am de custom, at de Featres I mean –
> To end de tragemdy all well, dat's plain.
>
> . . .
>
> If in your mind, of doubt a shadow lurks,
> Just read it all in massa Shakespeare's works.

Hamlet received similar treatment, reflecting both the fashion for 'Ethiopian burlesque' and contemporary American imagery. In *Hamlet the Dainty* (consisting of just three scenes), Hamlet observes, 'Horatio, I've not seen such scenes since I was in Boston eating pork and beans.'[74]

Some commentators have regarded the fact that Shakespeare regularly appeared as part of musical burlesque and minstrel shows to be a sign of the decline of Shakespeare's artistic status in America. Lawrence Levine suggests, however, that it 'may be understood more meaningfully as [a sign of the audience's] having *integrated* him into American culture'.[75] Just as at Shakespeare's Bankside, theatre entertainment included all aspects of performance without the rigid barriers that would develop later. In Jacksonian America there was a democratisation of Shakespeare.

THE AUDIENCE AS READER

The diversity of the audience was matched by that of the readership. As literacy increased and the population was introduced to Shakespeare via the schoolroom, the stage, political debate and orations, it became normal for families and individuals to own a copy of the plays. Shakespeare was part of popular culture across America and this included the log cabin and the campfire. Migrants heading westwards to start a new life made space for two books of choice, the Bible and Shakespeare. In 1863, Jim Bridger, described as a 'mountain man' and 'Indian fighter', then nearly sixty, traded a 'yoke of cattle, then worth about $125, or almost a month of his wages', for a copy of Shakespeare from a passing westward-bound wagon, and this despite his not being able to read.[76] Bridger is the archetypal western man of the mythical proportions of Kit Carson and Jim Bowie. Amongst other things, he was an explorer who is said to have visited both the Great Salt Lake and the Yellowstone regions in 1824. He worked on the Oregon trail and founded Fort Bridger in 1843, was a Scout for the United States Army and is said to have had 'three Indian wives'. This man, living in Wyoming in 1863, far from the theatres and society of New York, plainly placed a high value on Shakespeare.

Jennifer Lee Carrell writes of the way mountain men, adventurers and prospectors used Shakespeare in their daily language. Scattered amidst the abandoned mines and ghost towns of the West can be found evidence that the works of a naturalised playwright occupied the minds of the prospectors after a hard day in the hills. Carrell has found record of mines in Colorado called 'Shakespeare', 'Ophelia', 'Cordelia', 'Desdemona' and 'Timon of Athens'.[77] There are also a town and a canyon in New Mexico, a mountaintop in Nevada and a reservoir in Texas all named 'Shakespeare'.[78]

While the citizens of each new town quickly felt the need to award themselves a theatre where a mixture of music, song and dance, lectures and so forth were offered as nightly entertainment, Shakespeare was more than just part of the community social life. His work was popular amongst the tough people of the frontier, and not, perhaps, because they had pretensions to elevated social status or appreciation of poetry or theatrical drama. Shakespeare was popular in the West for reasons other than the celebration of art. In the novel now credited with popularising the 'western' genre, Owen Wister's Wyoming cattle-droving hero, 'the Virginian', comments on the qualities of Shakespeare. He remarks during a card game, 'he makes men talk the way they do in life . . . It's a right down shame Shakespeare couldn't know about poker. He'd have had Falstaff playing all day at that Tearsheet outfit.'[79] The suggestion that 'cowboys' personally identified with Shakespeare is further emphasised when the Virginian parallels the story of *Othello* with an 'affair down in Arizona', and goes on to state that he prefers the nature of Mercutio to that of Romeo. For the Virginian, Mercutio is 'man' whereas Romeo allows his friend to be killed.[80]

An anecdote from Montana rancher Philip Ashton Rollins affirms that Shakespeare appealed to people who had little formal schooling. After listening to the 'dogs of war' speech from *Julius Caesar*, a cowhand reportedly expressed the view that 'Shakespeare could sure spill the real stuff. He's the only poet I ever seen was fed on raw meat.'[81] The 'manly' values and tastes of cowboys of this sort were satisfied by Shakespeare's plays partly because they contained characters that could fit comfortably within frontier society.

As suggested by Carrell, the campfire 'tale' aspect of Shakespeare was very compatible with oral tradition in nineteenth-century America. James Bridger, being illiterate, had to employ a German boy at forty dollars per month to read him the stories from his 'expensively' purchased book, but was soon able to 'give quotation after quotation'.[82] Despite increases in literacy, nineteenth-century America 'remained an oral world in which the spoken word was central'.[83] The soliloquies and dialogues of Shakespeare found a ready and enthusiastic audience in a nation that continued to expect fiery political debates and impassioned weekly church sermons. In a period in American nation building when public oration and storytelling were recognised and celebrated, Shakespeare supplied both. He was a storyteller of the campfire and the bunkroom, supplying images of people reacting to life with unrestrained passion. Shakespeare's characters fought and died; they were people who murdered and were in turn punished for their greed and other failings.

It would appear that the stories contained in Shakespeare's plays, though set in Italy, England or Denmark, when read aloud in the dust and dark of the western frontier seemed to be 'local'. As Carrell writes, 'Because Shakespeare . . . was shared by so many people, it became a kind of imaginary meeting place',[84] but while this place was indeed 'imaginary', it was a world in which Americans plainly seem to have felt at home, a place that welcomed people from the mine, the cattle ranch or the wagon trail.

Long before Mark Twain utilised Shakespeare as a comic device, the editor of *Russell's Magazine*, William Gilmore Simms, wrote a novel targeted at a readership that he knew would readily identify with a protagonist inspired by Shakespeare. *Border Beagles, a Tale of Mississippi* (1855), about a 'back-woods boy' turned actor and 'law enforcer', has epigraphs from Shakespeare for thirteen of its chapters and relied on the fact that the readership would recognise and understand the references to Shakespeare's plays and characters.[85] Simms included in this edition a preface or 'Advertisement', in which he made the following claim for his novel:

The history upon which it is founded, is beyond question, and I can confidently affirm that all the leading characters are drawn from life. Even my actor, absurd as such a character may seem, emanating from the wild woods of Mississippi, is no less real as a personage than any of the rest.[86]

This 'back-woods' actor is a character named Tom Horsey. The reader is introduced to him by his father, who complains that the theatre and Shakespeare have led Tom astray: 'This son of mine, got in with some of those player fellows at Mobile or Orleans, and they carried him to their blasted stage-houses, where he got possession of these Shakspere books, and he's never been worth a picayune since that day.'[87] The protagonist, Horsey, proceeds through his adventures humorously quoting passages from Shakespeare and commenting on the plays, contemporary American actors and theatres, while rounding up a gang of Mississippi outlaws. This man of action, we are told, would not take 'twenty dollars' for his pocket edition of Shakespeare.

In this early adventure novel, an American Shakespeare-reader is the comic all-action hero. He is a man of the time and Simms considered him a representative American.

DIME NOVELS

Part of the folk imagery celebrated by Americans during the Jacksonian period centred on the heroic story of settlers moving westwards to disseminate American civilisation. Popularising this imagery, mass-produced fiction in the form of story paper, dime novel and the cheap library was published in the 1840s to entertain and satisfy what was a growing market for reading material. The type of stories that most characterise this truly American literature were the 'tales of the frontier and of Indian fighting'.[88] The imagery and terminology first associated with the dime novels and later utilised in Hollywood adventure films carry many subtle references to a period and culture in which stage drama was enthusiastically consumed. Not surprisingly, references to Shakespeare can be found even in these novels, further demonstrating how completely Shakespeare was part of popular culture.

In a comic episode that predates Twain's *The Adventures of Huckleberry Finn*, dime novelist, actor and playwright Albert W. Aiken portrayed an entertainment performed in the city of Yreka, California, at the 'Theatre Royal . . . over Joe Smith's store'.[89] A programme including items such as a 'Trick Violin', a tableau and a poetry recital also featured the following:

> *Scene from Hamlet.*
> *Hamlet . . . . Mr. J. Lysander Tubbs.*
> *Ghost . . . . Mr. J. L. Tubbs.*
> *The Queen Mother . . . . Mr. Tubbs.*
>
> *To conclude with the great quarrel scene from*
> *Shakespeare's masterpiece,*
>
> *JULIUS CAESAR.*
> *Cassius . . . . Mr. Tubbs.*
> *Brutus . . . . Mr. Tubbs.*
> *Mark Antony . . . . Mr. Tubbs.*
> *The Ghost from Philippi . . . . . Mr. Tubbs.*
> CARDS OF ADMISSION . . . 4 BITS.

As in the case of *Huckleberry Finn*, the humour of this piece relied on a substantial number of dime-novel readers recognising both Shakespeare and the type of burlesque presentation that was common in frontier society.

Another dime novel, comprehensively entitled *Deadwood Dick's Doom; or, Calamity Jane's Last Adventure, a Tale of Death Notch*, introduced a character styled as 'William Henry Shakespeare, ther poet o' ther West, an' philosophical protection of the wimmen's rights'.[90] This character, also known as 'the bullwhacker poet', fights his way through the novel from barroom to poker game, while reciting poetry and throwing knives. The extent to which Shakespeare was both freely appropriated and celebrated can be seen in a passage where 'the bullwhacker poet' introduces a travelling performer to a saloon full of assorted desperadoes:

> as Shakespeare, Sr., sed:
> 'A maiden fair wi' voice like a dream-er,
> She sings an' she plays – s'e's a reg'lar screamer.'

And again,

As my late lamented namesake, Shakespeare, has been known on several occasions to remark:

> 'Ketch a bird on ther wing,
> And force it ter sing,
> An' all in god time,
> You'll hev music sublime.'

This combination of a dime-novel cult hero, western vernacular and corruption of Shakespearean imagery typifies the popular culture of the Jacksonian era.

Theatres, newspapers and magazines were all key parts of the machinery that allowed invented tradition and unifying symbols to be popularised across such a huge landmass. The main characters in this tradition were pioneer men and women who, in real life, found Shakespeare's stories and characters not too dissimilar to the romanticised constructs of contemporary popular fiction. As Levine has suggested, 'Americans were able to fit Shakespeare into their culture so easily because he *seemed* to fit – because so many of his values and tastes were, or at least appeared to be, close to their own.'[91] There was, of course no one 'typical' America reader. The diverse population that made up this new nation was scattered across the differing geographical regions. Reflecting this diversity, their response to the political and social environment was also varied. While Ralph Waldo Emerson might have lectured on Shakespeare to an audience in Boston, his interest in the plays was very different from that of a man such as James Bridger.

Emerson and the pioneer, as Americans, shared the appropriated symbols and characters of Shakespeare, while responding to different qualities. The New Englander and the frontier pioneer, both fiercely patriotic, could not have conversed together about many subjects, but they shared The US Constitution and Shakespeare. As national symbols, both helped to unify the many Americas of Walt Whitman's poetry. As Thorndike would claim, 'Shakespeare has been a symbol of unity, a moving force.'[92] Shakespeare became one of the symbols that allowed the Bostonian, the Californian and the New Mexican to recognise themselves as Americans. For Emerson, Shakespeare might have been an exemplar. For Edwin Forrest, the actor, he was a muse. For the ladies of the third tier, he was an opportunity, and for Bridger, he was a yeoman folk hero. However the diverse social groups chose to categorise Shakespeare, the fact is that they all felt drawn to this playwright, now in his naturalised form. William Shakespeare was a key figure during this period precisely because he was accepted by both the American intellectual elite and the masses that constituted Jacksonian democracy.

NOTES

1. Levine, *Highbrow/Lowbrow*, p. 36.
2. Walt Whitman, *Leaves of Grass and Selected Prose*, ed. Ellman Crasnow (London: Everyman, 1993). See 'Song of Myself' (1855), p. 41.
3. Frederick Jackson Turner, *The United States, 1830–1850* (New York: Henry Holt & Co., 1935), p. 4.
4. Frederick Marryat, *Diary in America with Remarks on Its Institutions* (New York: William H. Colyer, 1839), p. 3.
5. Richard Slotkin, *The Fatal Environment: The Myth of the Frontier in the Age of Industrialization 1800–1890* (Norman OK: University of Oklahoma Press, 1985), p. 32. See also chapter 5, 'Ideology and Fiction'.
6. Ibid., p. 30.
7. Ibid., p. 10.
8. Edward Pessen, *Jacksonian America: Society, Personality, and Politics* (Homewood IL: Dorsey Press, 1969). See particularly chapter 2, 'The Jacksonian Character'.
9. Turner, *The United States*, p. 578.
10. Ibid., p. 591.
11. Levine, *Highbrow/Lowbrow*, p. 229.

12. Frederick Jackson Turner, *The Frontier in American History* (New York: Henry Holt & Co., 1920), p. 254.
13. Levine, *Highbrow/Lowbrow*, p. 15.
14. Frederick Jackson Turner, 'The Significance of the Frontier in American History' (annual report of the *American Historical Association*, 1893), in Turner, *The Frontier in American History*, p. 244.
15. Richardson, 'In the Shadow of the Bard', in Fisher and Watt, eds., *When They Weren't Doing Shakespeare*, p. 126.
16. Adams, 'The Folger Shakespeare Memorial', p. 212.
17. Michael Drayton, *The Ballad of Agincourt and the Ode to the Virginian Voyage* (London, 1606).
18. Thorndike, *Shakespeare in America*, p. 22.
19. Slade, '*The Significance of the Folger Shakespeare Memorial*', p. 59. This 'paper' was part of a eulogy written for the funeral of Henry C. Folger. The term schooner originated in New England, describing a development in ship design.
20. See various poems by Walt Whitman, such as 'Pioneers! O Pioneers!', in *Leaves of Grass*, p. 202.
21. Noah Webster, *Dissertations on the English Language, with an Essay on a Reformed Mode of Spelling* (Boston MA, 1789), p. 288.
22. *The Works of William Shakespeare*, ed. White, p. 485.
23. Richard Grant White, *Words and Their Uses, Past and Present* (New York: Sheldon & Co., 1871), p. 184.
24. Ibid., p. 194. See chapters 5, 'Misused Words', and 6, 'Briticisms'.
25. Slotkin, *The Fatal Environment*, pp. 77–8.
26. Richard Slotkin, *Regeneration through Violence: The mythology of the American Frontier, 1600–1860* (Middletown CT: Wesleyan University Press, 1973).
27. Fearon, *Sketches of America*, p. 274.
28. Ibid.
29. Cowell, *Thirty Years Passed among the Players*, p. 73.
30. Henry Irving, 'The American Audience', *Fortnightly Review*, 43 (1 February 1885), p. 199.
31. Mark Twain, *The Adventures of Huckleberry Finn* (London: Penguin Classics, 1985), pp. 154–76.
32. Mark Twain, *Roughing It* (London: Penguin Classics, 1985), pp. 137 and 346.
33. The Booth Family Scrapbook, Folger Shakespeare Library, Washington DC, newspaper clipping dated 12 January 1866. An alternative version of this story states that Junius Booth Sr paid a lawyer to help Lovett, who was imprisoned in Louisville for horse theft. Later, Lovett bequeathed his skull to Booth. Edwin Booth used the skull in *Hamlet*, but from 1888 had it mounted on a wall bracket in his apartment in the New York gentleman's club the Players. See Laurence Hutton, *Edwin Booth* (New York: Harper & Bros., 1893), pp. 45–6.
34. Cowell, *Thirty Years Passed among the Players*, p. 87.
35. Irving, 'The American Audience', p. 197.

36. *National Era* (Washington DC), 24 May 1855.
37. Rev. Robert Turnbull, 'Expensiveness of the Theatres', *Colored American* (New York), 21 March 1840.
38. In addition to female roles, Cushman was to take the male roles of both Romeo and Hamlet.
39. Wilmeth and Bigsby, eds., *The Cambridge History of American Theatre*, pp. 17–19.
40. Koon, *How Shakespeare Won the West*, p. 13.
41. Ibid., p. 15.
42. Bayard Taylor, *Eldorado or Adventures in the Path of Empire*, 2 vols. (London: Richard Bentley, 1850), vol. II, p. 30.
43. Koon, *How Shakespeare Won the West*, p. 4.
44. Warren S. Tryon, ed., *A Mirror for Americans: Life and Manners in the United States, 1790–1870*, 3 vols. (Chicago: University of Chicago Press, 1952), vol. III, p. 745.
45. John Smith Kendall, *The Golden Age of the New Orleans Theater* (Baton Rouge LA: Louisiana State University Press, 1952), p. 210. See also Grimsted, *Melodrama Unveiled*, p. 112.
46. Grimsted, *Melodrama Unveiled*, p. 112.
47. Kolin, ed., *Shakespeare in the South*, p. 7.
48. Ibid.
49. Quoted here from Kolin, ed., *Shakespeare in the South*, p. 126, n. 7.
50. *Morning Chronicle* (New York), 1801. Quoted here from Montrose Jonas Moses and John Mason Brown, *The American Theatre as Seen by Its Critics 1752–1934* (New York: W. W. Norton & Co., 1934), p. 40.
51. Fearon, *Sketches of America*, pp. 209–10.
52. Beaumont, *Marie*, p. 231.
53. Ibid.
54. Quoted here from George Wilson Pierson, *Tocqueville and Beaumont in America* (New York: Oxford University Press, 1938), p. 628.
55. Charles Murray, *Travels in North America during the Years 1834, 1835 & 1836, Including a Summer Residence with the Pawnee Tribe of Indians in the Remote Prairies of the Missouri and a Visit to Cuba and the Azore Islands* (London: Richard Bentley, 1839), p. 180.
56. Claudia D. Johnson, 'That Guilty Third Tier: Prostitution in Nineteenth-Century American Theaters', in Daniel Walker Howe, ed., *Victorian America* ([Philadelphia]: University of Pennsylvania Press, 1976), p. 113.
57. Cowell, *Thirty Years Passed among the Players*, p. 82.
58. Johnson, 'That Guilty Third Tier', p. 114.
59. Carrell, 'How the Bard Won the West', p. 106.
60. *Liberty Hall* (Cincinnati), 20 January and 31 March 1817. Quoted here from Rusk, *The Literature of the Middle Western Frontier*, vol. I, p. 431. For a fuller contemporary critique of theatre audiences, see 'Popular Amusements in New York', *National Era* (Washington DC), 15 April 1847.
61. Cowell, *Thirty Years Passed among the Players*, p. 57.

62. Carrell, 'How the Bard Won the West', p. 106.
63. Ibid.
64. Cowell, *Thirty Years Passed among the Players*, p. 87.
65. *The Times*, 4 April 1846. Forrest wrote in response to a news story, 'Professional Jealousy', *The Times*, 12 March 1846.
66. *The Times*, 6 April 1846.
67. Twain, *The Adventures of Huckleberry Finn*, pp. 190–9.
68. Levine, *Highbrow/Lowbrow*, p. 13.
69. Ibid.
70. Grenville Vernon, *Yankee Doodle-Doo: A Collection of Songs of the Early American Stage* (New York: Payson & Clarke, 1927), p. 164.
71. See J. Parker Norris Scrapbooks, Folger Shakespeare Library, Washington DC.
72. Koon, *How Shakespeare Won the West*, p. 12.
73. John F. Poole, *Ye Comedie of Errours, a Glorious, Uproarous Burlesque. Not Indecorous nor Censorous, with Many a Chorus Warranted Not To Bore Us, Now for the First Time Set before Us* (New York: Samuel French [*c.* 1858]). Quoted here from Stanley Wells, *American Shakespeare Travesties (1852–1888)*, 5 vols. (London: Diploma Press, 1978), vol. v, pp. 75–6.
74. G. W. Griffin, *Hamlet the Dainty, an Ethiopian Burlesque on Shakespeare's Hamlet* (n.p., 1870). Quoted here from Wells, *American Shakespeare Travesties*, p. 123. For further comment on the use of Shakespeare within American burlesque, see Granqvist, *Imitation as Resistance*.
75. Levine, *Highbrow/Lowbrow*, p. 23.
76. Carrell, 'How the Bard Won the West', p. 99. See also J. Cecil Alter, *James Bridger, Trapper, Frontiersman, Scout and Guide; a Historical Narrative* (Salt Lake City UT: Shepard Book Co., 1925).
77. Ibid., pp. 100–1.
78. 'Shakespeare', New Mexico, located south of Silver City and just forty miles north of the Mexican border, is now a ghost town and tourist site.
79. Owen Wister, *The Virginian* (New York: Macmillan & Co., 1902), p. 155. The Virginian cowboy had been under the tutelage of his fiancée.
80. Ibid., p. 278.
81. Carrell, 'How the Bard Won the West', p. 102.
82. Alter, *James Bridger*, p. 403.
83. Levine, *Highbrow/Lowbrow*, p. 36.
84. Carrell, 'How the Bard Won the West', p. 104.
85. William Gilmore Simms, *Border Beagles, a Tale of Mississippi* (New York: W. J. Widdleton, 1855).
86. Ibid., p. 1.
87. Ibid., pp. 33–4.
88. Michael Denning, *Mechanic Accents, Dime Novels and Working-Class Culture in America* (New York: Verso, 1987), p. 13.
89. Albert W. Aiken, 'Richard Talbot of Cinnabar; or, The Brothers of the Red Hand', *Saturday Journal*, 530 (14 August 1880). See also Albert Johannsen, *The House of Beadle and Adams and Its Dime and Nickel Novels: The Story of*

a *Vanished Literature*, 3 vols. (Norman OK: University of Oklahoma Press, 1962).

90. Edward L. Wheeler, *Deadwood Dick's Doom; or, Calamity Jane's Last Adventure, a Tale of Death Notch* (New York: Deadwood Dick Library [Beadle and Adams], 1899).

91. Ibid.

92. Thorndike, *Shakespeare in America*, p. 10.

CHAPTER 5

Context for appropriation in nineteenth-century America

The master of our Thought, the Land's first Citizen.

Bayard Taylor

The promotion of a naturalised Shakespeare, which had started with the 'First American Edition' in 1795, continued with a second 'complete works' published in 1802 by Munroe & Francis of Boston.[1] This mail-order subscription edition of sixteen 'paper-covered parts'[2] cost the subscriber $-.35 per part, 'payment on delivery', amounting to a total price of just $5.60. As a result of these early, relatively low-cost American editions of Shakespeare there was a viable commercial market and a mass readership for the newly adopted Elizabethan playwright.

Before considering the probable reasons for the huge increase in the consumption of printed editions of Shakespeare's works, it is important to recognise that each edition represented an incidence of new marketing rather than new scholarship. Giles E. Dawson has shown that a large number of what appear to be new editions of Shakespeare are in fact reprints or re-presented versions of earlier scholarship. In evidence, Dawson has cited an 1823 edition of Shakespeare from publisher H. C. Carey & M'Carthy of Philadelphia that was reprinted at least thirty-six times by six different American publishers.[3] Each new publisher would create a personalised title page, despite the fact that the text that followed was an exact copy of earlier work. One reason for this simple 're-presentation' was to reduce distribution costs. To help overcome the problem of transporting heavy finished books across the great distances that divided major cities, it became common practice for printers to create copy stereotype plates and sell these easily transportable items to other publishers. The growing population with its scattered locations encouraged an increase in the number of publishers in the United States, and each in turn offered at least one edition of Shakespeare.

As demonstrated above, the decade beginning 1850 marked the point from which the rise in the number of booksellers and the availability of Shakespeare became a cultural phenomenon. While during this period many more businesses set out to capitalise on the commercial opportunity, the fact is that there was a significant increase in the demand for Shakespeare. Americans started to consume Shakespeare in huge quantities, and it is clear that by the middle of the nineteenth century much had happened in America to make Shakespeare appear important or at least useful. There was a political and social context for the appropriation of Shakespeare, beyond people's personal values and tastes, and this needs to be considered if we are to understand why Shakespeare was so readily consumed by so many Americans. It was this context that made it possible for a naturalised playwright to meet the needs of the still emerging nation of America.

THE CONTEXT OF AMERICAN EXPANSIONISM

The rapid increase in the availability and distribution of Shakespeare occurred simultaneously with the territorial expansion of America to occupy land from the Atlantic to the Pacific Ocean. The original thirteen east-coast colonies that declared themselves a sovereign nation in 1776 had used a combination of diplomatic pressure, military force and quantities of gold to expand their sphere of influence to a large part of the western hemisphere. This expansion of the United States occurred exactly at a time when the British and other European powers were expanding their respective empires in Africa and Asia.

The imperial aspirations of the future American republic can be detected from as early as 1783. Benjamin Franklin had, during the peace negotiations in Paris that ended the War of Independence, asked Britain to cede all Canada to the United States as a gesture of conciliation. Other important political figures regarded the whole northern continent as potentially one single republic. Thomas Jefferson considered both Cuba and Canada to be territories that should be added to the American 'empire'. In a letter to his successor James Madison, dated 27 April 1809, Jefferson stated that, in his view, European countries would be preoccupied with warring against each other, and that America

should then have only to include the North [Canada] in our confederacy, which would be of course in the First War, and we should have such an empire for liberty as she has never surveyed since the creation: & I am persuaded no constitution was ever before so well calculated as ours for extensive empire & self government.[4]

The contents of this letter demonstrate the importance attributed by American political figures to the military conquest of foreign states and peoples, integral to the process of establishing their 'empire of Liberty'. The expansion of the American state, a process that history has often presented as somehow benign and part of a natural democratic revolution, was in some ways similar to the imperial expansion of many European nations during the nineteenth century.

This American expansion included the purchase of Louisiana from Napoleon in 1803 (seemingly together with any inhabitant of the territory), the acquisition of Florida and Oregon through diplomatic treaty, and the military annexation of Mexican territory that became Texas, California, Nevada, Arizona and New Mexico.[5] The years between the first census of 1790 and 1850 saw the physical territory of the United States more than triple in size. As with the territory, American self-belief also grew.

In less than sixty years not only had the American republic swept across the continent but its people had also seen all foreign challengers concede to their supremacy. Americans watched as the numerous sovereign nations of American Indians were forced to retreat in front of Anglo-American territorial and cultural expansion. The Indian Removal Act of 1830 was to confirm the dominant political philosophy that Americans had the right to take land from any foreign nation in the name of democracy and national security. Americans also saw the once powerful nations of Spain and Russia surrender territory to America, and, importantly, citizens celebrated the defeat of both Britain and Mexico in the wars of 1812 and 1845–9 respectively.

For Americans, '[the] century had been characterised by an expansion of territory, population, material wealth and power that appeared almost miraculous'.[6] Taken together, the events combined to justify the widely held belief that Americans, or at least one dominant group of Americans, were 'exceptional' and racially supreme.[7] The expansion of American territory and power could be considered as the creation of an empire, centred on Washington DC, that paralleled the expanding empires of the European nations.

In 1845, a phrase was coined that, in just two words, both captured and disguised the growing belief in American supremacy. John L. O'Sullivan, then editor of the *New York Morning News* and personal friend of Nathaniel Hawthorne, used his newspaper to express his opinion on the 'problem' of Mexico and Oregon and his conviction that Americans had 'the right of [their] manifest destiny to over spread and to possess the whole continent'.[8] The phrase 'manifest destiny' was immediately adopted by American politicians and was repeatedly used to justify any and all actions that ensured that Anglo-Americans, and other northern Europeans assimilated into the national identity, dominated not just ownership of the land but also American culture.

The important issue of territorial expansion still occupied the minds of many citizens even as the nineteenth century drew to a close. Though Americans occupied the continent from the east coast to the west, there was still the land to the north that was not part of the United States. In 1890, James Harrison Wilson argued that

the refusal of England to give us a fair share of that conquest which decided that the North American continent should be forever dominated by the Anglo-Saxon race, cannot be permanently settled till that domination is exercised exclusively by our own government . . . [Americans] feel the North American continent was created a unit for their use and occupation, and that their manifest destiny is to possess it.[9]

This belief in a greater 'destiny' was also to feature in the writings and actions of Theodore Roosevelt. He was to write of 'the spread of the English-speaking peoples' and of his belief that there was a special cultural quality possessed by Anglo-Americans.[10]

In a century of almost unbounded expansion, some Americans, who had witnessed their apparently unstoppable cultural power and military success, searched for reasons to explain and justify their dominance. The reason for this cultural superiority was assumed to be racial supremacy, and Shakespeare was the product of the culture and the racial stock that had given rise to many of the early colonisers whose descendants now dominated America. While not directly contributing to this dominance, Shakespeare was embraced as a symbol of the assumed cultural superiority of English-speaking people.

THE CONTEXT OF IMMIGRATION

While many today regard cultural pluralism as healthy and beneficial to a democracy, in the nineteenth century few shared this belief.[11] Reflecting the growing concern of the federal government, the 1850 United States 'decennial census' featured for the first time a question requiring citizens to indicate their country of birth. A recent study of this census data by Campbell J. Gibson and Emily Lennon presents the 'Nativity of the Population for the 25 Largest Urban Places and for Selected Counties'.[12] When retabulated this data shows that 35 per cent of the recorded population of America were 'foreign born'; for the city of New York, however, the foreign-born percentage was 45 per cent, for Cincinnati, 47 per cent and for Chicago, 52 per cent. These figures suggest that in 1850, for 35 per cent of the American population, English was not necessarily the first language or the language used by the family at home. English was not their 'mother tongue' or cultural conditioner.

To further emphasise the significance of this data, it is important to consider not just the people recorded by the census but, perhaps more importantly, those not recorded. A large section of the population was excluded. The list is extensive: American Indians, African-Americans (neither 'freemen' nor slaves), the entire Chicano population of the ex-Mexican territories of California, Arizona, New Mexico, Nevada, Texas, and of course anyone who, for various reasons, wished to remain outside the law. When the large number of Americans excluded from the census are considered, it is easy to deduce, although not prove, that, for the majority of Americans, English was not the 'first' language or the language used within the home. English, albeit the language of the American establishment, was a minority language, and the continued cultural dominance of Anglo-Americans was severely under threat.

This situation had been brought about both by American territorial expansion and by a change in the pattern of immigration. While in the seventeenth century the English had made up the majority of emigrants to the new American colonies, the situation in the eighteenth century had been very different. By 1790 'people of English ancestry composed less than one-half of the population'.[13] The combination of changing European political and economic conditions meant that, increasingly, immigrants to America were from non-English backgrounds. The long-running and often bloody rivalry between America and Britain also discouraged further immigration from England. One respected academic later made the claim that anti-English sentiment did 'mischief in more ways than one. It drives British emigration from American shores to Australia at a time when the self-governing element in this country is in danger of being swamped by alien elements.'[14]

While a survey of articles published in a wide range of nineteenth-century journals demonstrates that many Anglo-Americans strongly believed that their destiny was to rule the American continent, others expressed increasing alarm. There was a widespread fear that Anglo-American destiny was threatened by the arrival of immigrants, people the 'nativists' considered might ultimately undermine their future dominance and prosperity.

Hostility to the perceived threat of foreign influence increased. As part of this hostility, on 17 November 1837 a congressman and judge, George Washington Woodward, proposed amendments to the Constitution of Pennsylvania, the effect of which would have been to bar foreigners from voting or taking part in American politics. His view was that 'they have no sympathy in common with us; they have no qualifications to render them fit recipients of these high political privileges'.[15] While the proposal was later withdrawn, this type of expression of hostility towards immigrants from non-Protestant, non-Anglo-Saxon countries became increasingly common.

The Louisiana Native American Association was formed as early as August 1835 to represent the interests of second-generation or older Americans. In a twenty-page pamphlet, it urged the repeal of naturalisation laws that allowed 'paupers and vagrants' to become American citizens, qualifying for the same rights as 'native'-born Americans.[16] At a time when the United States was pushing its borders westward and American citizens hoped to maximise their financial gains, new immigrants from the 'old world' claimed the same advantages and competed for wealth and position. Rather than share the great opportunities that expansion offered, many Americans sought to brand the immigrants as inferior 'freeloaders'.

In Louisiana, itself a state within the Union only from 1812, the call was to the base instincts of the population to defend themselves from contamination. The writer of the above-mentioned pamphlet promised, 'like those patriots, seeing portentous evils approaching our country from foreign influence, like them though far inferior, [we] will never cease to warn the people, till those evils are corrected or averted'.[17] There was an evangelical zeal to maintain 'purity' of culture, blood and privilege. The intention of the publication was to raise fear and hostility, and the arguments used would return again when the 'Red Scares' and the McCarthy 'witch-hunts' created anti-Communist hysteria. But in 1839 the claim was

That two thirds of the teachers in our schools, seminaries, and institutions for the education of our youth, and the instruction of the rising generation, consist of foreigners, who have themselves been brought up in distant lands, – imbued with feelings, prejudices and aspirations alien to our own . . . we tell our countrymen, that many of the professors in our Colleges and Universities are foreigners, and that the press, the great moral lever of Nations, has almost been absolutely monopolized by Foreigners.[18]

The fear was that people who did not share Anglo-American traditions would introduce 'alien' culture to America. To better defend the status quo, people who regarded themselves as native-born Anglo-Americans rallied behind symbols of national identity.

Another person involved in the nativist movement was Samuel Morse, the respected Massachusetts-born painter and inventor of the telegraph and code. In 1835, the title of the pamphlet *Imminent Dangers to the Free*

Institutions of the United States through Foreign Immigration succinctly conveyed his concerns to his fellow citizens.[19]

The populist response to this type of fear was the emergence of the political movement that became commonly known as the Know-Nothings. This nativist organisation campaigned strongly against further immigration from Catholic countries and anywhere considered to be non-Anglo-Saxon. The organisation's political tenets supported the promotion of 'one great homogeneous American race'. The idea of rapid assimilation of immigrants into an Anglo-American nationality was captured in their slogan 'Nationalize before We Naturalize'.[20] The clear understanding was that Americans were made not just born. The Know-Nothings opposed any immigration of people who were thought not able or prepared to learn to be American. As a political force, the party rose to prominence and importance in 1854, gaining the governorships of Massachusetts and Delaware.[21] It adopted the name 'the American Party', fought and lost the 1856 presidential election after a fight with the newly established Republican Party, and then disbanded around 1860 as the threat of the War of Secession loomed.

While the fears expressed by the members of the Know-Nothings and other American nativists might seem irrational and bigoted to a modern reader, the party was formed as a direct reaction to the challenges presented by further expansion of the Union. There had been an ultimately unsuccessful but co-ordinated attempt to create self-sustaining 'colonies' of Catholics across America, the intention being to ensure that the Catholic faith and culture were not undermined by the influence of the greater Protestant population. An Irish-American, D'Arcy McGee, and a newspaper called the *American Celt* were both prominent in the campaign to co-ordinate Catholic immigration and settlement. The *American Celt*, published in New York in the 1850s and edited by a Catholic bishop, promoted the idea that to preserve their culture Catholics should unite and settle land for a future Catholic state.[22] Mary Gilbert Kelly, in a study of Catholic societies established in the nineteenth century, repeatedly mentions the Know-Nothings, and it would appear that the idea of Catholic 'colonies' and nativists' fears were both born out of reactionary responses.

The fact that some groups of immigrants proposed organising themselves around ethnic or religious loyalties, buying land and creating associations that would ultimately lead to townships based wholly on sectarian criteria, indicates the potential problems that the American nation faced during the nineteenth century. Up to this point, many Americans had felt secure living and prospering within a political union where the English language and

Protestant religious belief, while not guaranteed by the Constitution, were considered key elements of American tradition. The increasing independence demonstrated by some new immigrants undoubtedly undermined this sense of security. In the minds of some Americans the original idealistic concept of E Pluribus Unum now appeared to be under threat. The response was to boost American nationalism in all its many forms. Nationalism can perhaps be regarded as a common response to a collective perception of threat, and Americans, from as early as the colonial period, seem to have been particularly susceptible to this type of collective paranoia.

AMERICAN ETHNOGENESIS AND THE CULT OF ANGLO-SAXONISM

During the main period of appropriation of Shakespeare one term came to signify the emergence of an American cultural tradition, and it resonated throughout the United States. That term was 'Anglo-Saxon'. American independence and the American continental 'empire' had been established by a people who increasingly regarded themselves as largely Anglo-Saxon in origin, and this racial and cultural signifier was to dominate the media in the nineteenth century.

As early as 1774, Thomas Jefferson had appropriated a 'Saxon' identity for 'British America' when he argued that the people had inherited the right to Saxon law free from Norman feudalism, and in the nineteenth century this claim to Anglo-Saxon ancestry became even more important.[23] The Anglo-Saxon mastery in America occurred during a period when the other 'Anglo-Saxons', those in Britain, were successfully establishing an empire that would dominate significant parts of the world outside the Americas. These two empires were established by rival nations that, it was argued, originally shared one common heritage, that of Anglo-Saxon traditions, and one common language. This language, a signifier of cultural conditioning, was the language of Shakespeare, and Shakespeare now became increasingly important to an American people who welcomed the existence of an 'Anglo-Saxon prophet' of Homeric if not biblical proportions. I use the term 'prophet' in the same manner as Charles Mills Gayley in his *Shakespeare and the Founders of Liberty in America*, in the sense not of 'someone who foresees or foretells the future' but of someone who provides a voice for the spiritual and cultural inheritance of Anglo-Saxon people born in America.[24]

Reginald Horsman described how writers in England and America throughout the first half of the nineteenth century developed their ideas of Anglo-Saxon supremacy.[25] One of the people he identified was Thomas

Carlyle, and Horsman suggests that his 'popularity both in England and the United States did much to disseminate the idea of a superior Anglo-Saxon race with a world mission to fulfil'.[26] It was as if, just when Americans needed to make sense of their territorial expansion and their oppression of weaker peoples within the American continent, a racial and cultural justification became available that was easy both to accept and to communicate. Horsman states: 'The new ideas fell on a fertile ground in the 1830s and 1840s. In a time of rapid growth and change, with its accompanying insecurities and dislocations, many Americans found comfort in the strength and status of a distinguished racial heritage.'[27] Horsman maintained that writers such as Carlyle, Thomas Arnold, Robert Knox and the poet and novelist Sir Walter Scott communicated 'ideas [that] permeated the American periodicals and in the second half of the century formed part of the accepted truth of American schoolbooks'.[28]

The popularity of Scott's novels, denounced by Mark Twain as a 'debilitating influence' on the South,[29] is consistent with the wide acceptance of the romantic myth associated with the concept of pre-English freedoms. Not being English himself, Scott was not seen as being tainted by negative associations. Most of those of his works that were published in the United States concerned the struggle of the Scottish people to preserve a separate identity from that of the conquering English. His 1814 novel *Waverley* depicted the Jacobite rebellion against the English, while his most successful novel, *Ivanhoe* (1819), romanticised the struggle between the heroic twelfth-century Anglo-Saxon population and the tyrannical aristocratic Normans. For many Americans, Scott's novels helped both to support the cult of Anglo-Saxonism and to boost their 'Fourth of July' prejudice against the English. Like Shakespeare himself, Scott was seen as a writer whose stories provided a heroic mythology stressing a heritage of ancient freedoms. The idea that Anglo-Saxons 'had selected themselves through immigration to escape the British (Norman) yoke and bring the torch of freedom to America was a quintessential myth of ethnogenesis'.[30]

While Anglo-Saxonism became associated with the popular concept of manifest destiny, not everyone was pleased by this promotion of mythology. In 1849, a learned American, Charles Anderson, was to comment on the popularity of this Anglo-Saxon myth in an address: 'I find our whole people, without regard to . . . distinctions, apparently abandoning themselves to a sentiment, which is a fallacy in philosophy, an untruth in history, and a gross impiety in religion.'[31] Anderson sought to counter the popular acceptance of the myth of Anglo-Saxonism that permeated American consciousness. He asked his audience if they had not observed how decided and how universal is the belief amongst the North Americans and Englishmen of this age, that there is, in what they call (for what reasons I know not,) the '*Anglo Saxon*' Race, some extraordinary power, or capability of accomplishing greater things, than in any other family of men.[32]

While Anderson declared that there had never been a single racial group or nation of Anglo-Saxons, he failed to confront the political needs that had led so many seemingly practical and logical people in America to embrace such a potentially pernicious cult. Without any means to counter the ideological cause that encouraged acceptance of the myth, Anderson's argument was overwhelmed by the rush to embrace a national identity based on precepts that benefited the members of the Anglo-American elite.

While today the term 'Anglo-Saxon' is perhaps mainly understood to suggest a racial grouping, in nineteenth-century America it also implied an ethnicity that was thought to have flourished in pre-Norman England. While a belief in racial purity can be detected in many nineteenth-century writings and political speeches, what marked the American cult of Anglo-Saxonism was the idea that a person could become a 'naturalised' Anglo-Saxon by the adoption of the cultural traditions thought to symbolise Anglo-Saxon tradition. There was the possibility of cultural conversion, and it was to help facilitate this process that Shakespeare was appropriated.

While Anglo-Saxonism did not originate in America, it became central to the process of American ethnogenesis. It assisted the process by which a new nation of people were able to celebrate a cultural inheritance, while at the same time reject the political entity called England. To allow Americans to promote widespread acceptance of Shakespeare while England itself was seen as the enemy, heritage and the political system of England had to be separated. The cult of Anglo-Saxonism made this necessary division possible. To proclaim Anglo-Saxon heritage in the nineteenth century suggested that there had been a return to an earlier cultural purity, free from the affectation and pollution that had enveloped Norman England.

The appropriation of Shakespeare as a form of cultural talisman was made easier by this subtle if complex differentiation between good – i.e. Anglo – and bad – i.e. English – cultural dominance. An Anglo-American was someone who celebrated symbols of Anglo-Saxon heritage while believing that England was largely a nation of serfs and tyrants and as such an anachronism.

Another reason for the popularity of Anglo-Saxonism was that as Americans became more prosperous they sought to understand their success in terms that offered a dignified history to rival that of the 'old world'.

There was a desire to create an origin myth for America that was equal to that of ancient Greece or Rome. To satisfy this desire for origins, Thomas Jefferson's early design for the Great Seal of the United States was to have 'On one side . . . two mythical Anglo-Saxon warriors, Hengst and Horsa; on the other, he wanted to portray the Chosen People following a pillar of fire.'[33]

Jefferson's interest in and association of America with Anglo-Saxon traditions extended to introducing the ancient Anglo-Saxon land measurement of 'hundreds' into the state of Virginia civil administration and adding the Anglo-Saxon language to the syllabus of the University of Virginia. While Jefferson was demonstrably hostile to eighteenth-century England, he believed there was an essential Anglo-Saxon inheritance that could be separated from the political and national construct of Britain. The Anglo-Saxon tradition, once separated from the heart of the enemy, could form the basis for an American cultural inheritance and a focus for American pride and exceptionalism. In Jefferson can be seen evidence of the institutionalised ambivalence towards the culture of England that would later become so much a part of American nationalism. The foundations of American Anglo-Saxonism, partly laid by Jefferson, created the impetus for the later separation of Shakespeare from the nation of his birth, and his appropriation as an American cultural icon. Whereas Hengst and Horsa failed to become recognised by the American nation, Shakespeare became a cultural icon and a symbolic guarantor of American cultural pedigree.

Evidence of the popularity of Anglo-Saxonism can be found in newspapers and magazines covering a wide range of contemporary issues. A substantial article in the *North American Review* in July 1851 entitled 'The Anglo-Saxon Race' highlighted two new books about the Anglo-Saxon language. The writer commented that both the publication and the titles of these volumes were 'significant signs of the times'.[34] The article went on to repeat a theme found in many contemporaneous writings. The suggestion was that since the Anglo-Saxon did not mix blood with other races the race remained 'strong and vigorous'. This was in marked contrast to the French and the Spanish, who were thought to intermarry with aboriginal peoples, the result of which was that their colonies declined.

Anglo-Saxon heritage and culture, which appeared to have overwhelmed other colonial traditions, was considered to be vital to the continued success of the American state. Rivalry between America and England even stretched to Anglo-Saxonism, the writer making the claim that 'New England is more Anglo-Saxon than Old England'.[35] This strongly supremacist article was published in a respected Boston-based magazine, perhaps reflecting not only how widespread the ideas had become but also the lack of opposition to the type of ideology it undoubtedly represented.

Even many of those closely involved in the abolition movement shared the belief in Anglo-Saxonism. Harriet Beecher Stowe's *Uncle Tom's Cabin*, though written as an abolitionist treatise, nevertheless reflected the almost universally held American belief in the superiority of the Anglo-Saxon race. In Stowe's words, 'To the Anglo-Saxon race has been entrusted the destinies of the world.'[36] As a writer Stowe did not champion equality of the races. What she promoted was Christian compassion for an oppressed people. Like many others in the New England abolitionist movement, she saw slavery as a stain on the soul of the Anglo-American, and in her 'Concluding Remarks' made it clear that she believed the ultimate future of freed slaves was to live in Liberia, not in the United States.[37]

THE ANGLO-SAXON MISSION

In 1850, a book written by Massachusetts-born Unitarian minister Abiel Abbot Livermore confirmed several contextual aspects of American political and social life at the mid-point of the nineteenth century. Livermore produced a critique of the Mexican War and in the process reflected the popular concepts of manifest destiny and Anglo-Saxonism. Livermore suggested that the war with Mexico had been fought partly to 'show our republican manhood [to the] crumbling, bankrupt, starving, war-taxed, and groaning kingdoms of Europe'.[38] Writing that 'The Anglo-Saxons have been apparently persuaded to think themselves the chosen people, the anointed race of the Lord, commissioned to drive out the heathen, and plant their religion and institutions in every Canaan they could subjugate', his contempt for what he appeared to regard as 'blasphemy' was barely concealed.[39] He harangued his countrymen and argued that in the war with Mexico Americans were acting as 'tyrants' and as if they had the 'divine' right of 'old world' kings.

For Livermore, however, the latest European emigration was largely responsible for this tyrannical behaviour. He maintained that 'Hundreds of thousands, with all their old-world ideas, unbaptized into the spirit of liberty, except it be as licence, have been transplanted into the vast regions of the Middle States, the West and South West', and from this foreign-born population 'no inconsiderable part of the American army' had been formed.[40] Livermore argued that these immigrants, untouched as yet by Anglo-Saxon culture, were responsible for much of the brutality that had materialised in the process of enacting manifest destiny. In his opinion,

Americans such as himself had been unable to influence the behaviour of this army now that 'The true American ideas have been supplanted by a system of Bedouin morality in the minds of not a few, cast beyond the control of a high-toned public conscience.'[41] While opposing the expansionist philosophy of America, Livermore nevertheless regarded Anglo-American culture as an agent of civilisation and thereby supported the rapid 'conversion' of immigrants to the 'higher' cultural values that he believed constituted Anglo-Saxon heritage.

In 1860, William Gilpin, the son of a Pennsylvania Quaker, an ex-major of the Mexican War and first governor of Colorado, published a book in which he set out the 'mission' of the United States, using 'geographical, social and political' data to argue that America was the Anglo-Saxon 'promised land'.[42] Though a soldier and an unapologetic supporter of the continued 'pursuit of property', Gilpin regarded himself as a type of 'lay' preacher. He maintained that 'The American realizes that "Progress is God". He clearly recognizes and accepts the *continental* mission of his country and his people.'[43] This mission was the establishment of 'the *republican empire* of the people of North America',[44] the true and legitimate successor to all the ancient empires that had been recorded by historians. The book concluded by repeating part of a presentation Gilpin had made before the United States Senate on 2 March 1846. His belief was that 'The *untransacted* destiny of the American people is to subdue the continent.'[45]

As an appendix to his book, Gilpin included a number of speeches he had delivered between 1847 and 1868. In addition to glorifying the role of the frontier, he repeated the now familiar rhetoric about the importance of unifying under a single dominant culture. He argued that the nations of Europe had failed because 'upon each river dwells a distinct people, differing from all the rest in race, language, habits, and interests . . . The history of these nations is a story of perpetual war and mutual extermination.'[46] The cult of Anglo-Saxonism and the importance of the English language were then associated with the need to solidify the American nation. Unlike Europe, America was to succeed by 'forming a single people, identical in manners, language, customs, and impulses: preserving the same civilization, the same religion: imbued with the same opinions, and having the same political liberties'.[47]

The ethnogenesis of the American nation was to be based on Anglo-Saxon cultural mythology. While for Gilpin racial supremacy was a significant element of Anglo-Saxonism, it is clear that ethnicity was also important. Immigrants could become Anglo-American by assimilation. There would be 'the instinctive fusion into one language and one new race, of Germans, English, French, and Spanish, whose individuality [was to be] obliterated in a single generation!'[48]

THE ACHIEVEMENT OF ANGLO-AMERICAN DESTINY

The combination of elements comprised by American nationalism encouraged a belief in the manifest destiny of the American republic. This destiny was for the United States to control the North American continent and ultimately dominate the culture of the world. There were Americans who prophesied that all other cultures would disappear, to be replaced by a unifying Anglo-American culture accomplished by use of the English language and by the cultural and political texts of the American nation.

From as early as 1789, American writers started to popularise the concepts that were to lead in part to the later appropriation of Shakespeare. Noah Webster, writing on the subject of the English language, suggested that as the United States would never be conquered by any nation 'we have therefore the fairest opportunity of establishing a national language, and of giving it uniformity and perspicuity, in North America, that ever presented itself to mankind'.[49] Webster was not suggesting that America should copy English pronunciation and form. He believed that America should have the freedom to develop its own 'dialect' of American 'English'. The important point for Webster was that this language would be uniform across America.

In 1787, Joel Barlow, a Connecticut-born graduate of Yale and one of the so-called 'Hartford wits', published a poem entitled *Vision of Columbus*, which he then revised and republished in 1807 as *The Columbiad*. With this epic poem, Barlow created a kind of 'American *Iliad*' that recounted the discovery of America, told the story of the heroic War of Independence against England and finally prophesied that the United States would rise to a position of worldwide cultural dominance. Within the poem Barlow predicted for his fellow citizens that there would be an 'Assimilation and final union of all languages', the language of America rising to dominate all others.[50] In the words of the poem,

> At this blest period, when the total race
> Shall speak one language and all truths embrace,
> Instruction clear a speedier course shall find,
> And open earlier on the infant mind.
> No foreign terms shall crowd with barbarous rules
> The dull unmeaning pageantry of schools;
> . . .
> One living language, one unborrow'd dress
> Her boldest flights with fullest force express.[51]

While this poem was unlikely to have been read by the democratic majority, *The Columbiad* does suggest that, for some influential Americans, 'foreign terms' were unacceptable and that there was a belief in a single unifying culture that would enable the nation to rise to fulfil a grand destiny.

Ideas of American destiny based on ethnocentric supremacy became a subject for popular discussion. The spirit energised Caleb Cushing, a New Englander, congressman, general in the Mexican War, scholar admired by Ralph Waldo Emerson, American diplomat and associate of several American presidents. For Cushing, the Americans were 'people consist[ing] chiefly of different branches of the Teutonic race, as Dutch, German, Swedish, Saxon and Norman, the combination of the latter predominating over all others'.[52] Cushing's prophecy was that the power of Anglo-American culture would come to dominate all others. The message supporting a single Anglo-American national identity was that 'the time is near at hand . . . when the United States will possess more than a hundred million inhabitants, nearly all speaking the same language, – having one general civilization, literature, and national character, – similar laws and religion'.[53] For many Americans such as Cushing, the future for peoples with a non-Anglo-American tradition and culture matched that of the American Indian, in that 'Their gradual extinction . . . is chiefly to be ascribed to the personal qualities of each race',[54] a view shared and later expressed by Theodore Roosevelt.[55]

Similar opinions on the need for Americanisation were held by Harriet Beecher Stowe's father. Beecher preached a message that Americans of the East, particularly of New England, had to ensure that the immigrants to the new territories in the West were rapidly assimilated into Anglo-American ideals. For him, there was a danger to American civilisation from immigrants who had not been exposed to Protestant republicanism. Beecher insisted to his readers that 'We must educate! We must educate!, or we perish by our own prosperity.'[56]

Another orator, Benjamin Hunt, stressed the importance of the English language in the process of nation building. For Hunt, 'the uniformity of language which is destined to prevail over so vast a country . . . is an important element in forming a national character'.[57] To protect Anglo-American democracy there was a need to promote the unifying American language. Several years later, repeating the same doctrine, an article in the *New York Herald* asserted that 'The population is the Anglo-Saxon race, absorbing the Celtic and all other nationalities except the African, and assimilating them to itself. There is one language, the English, that which the immortal Shakespeare wrote.'[58]

This type of association between language and the destiny of the American people was frequently made. In 1855, an article entitled 'Our

Language Destined To Be Universal' reiterated many of the interrelated themes that had become part of nationalist discourse.[59] After reviewing the fate of several of the world's fallen empires, the article suggested that the destiny for the American people was to be different and result in the 'regeneration of the world', this task achieved through 'universal Christianity . . . offered up in our language'.[60] What was referred to as the 'Anglo-American tongue' was the replacement for the lost 'pre-Babel, Adamite' language mentioned in the Bible.[61] This 'Anglo-American tongue' was not only to advance the fortunes of a unified American nation but also to fulfil a divine mission.

The American Home Missionary Society captured the nationalistic and cultural supremacist tone that is implicit in the idea that America had the destiny to become the centre of the Protestant world. One sermon text from 1851 suggested that

Europe is but a congregation of Nations of different languages, habits and religions. But power, as it passes into our hands, comes to one people, speaking the same language, the language of Milton, Shakspeare, and the English Bible, having one literature, and one common soul.[62]

Commending the progress towards establishing one American identity, the author Reverend David Hunter Riddle remarked, 'Amidst all other ominous aspects, it is cheering to see how soon the process of homogeneity and nationalization is perfected here.'[63] For Riddle, the motto on the Great Seal of the United States and the American dollar, E Pluribus Unum, had become a form of religious tenet.

Riddle preached the establishment of a new empire centred on American Protestant Christianity. Contrary to the main policy of the nativist organisations, however, Riddle supported increased immigration precisely to allow the United States to dominate a future civilisation. Riddle suggested that Americans should not fear Catholic immigrants but work to convert them to American Protestantism.

This combination of Anglo-American destiny and missionary zeal can be found in another Home Missionary Society pamphlet, written by a J. M. Sturtevant. Sturtevant was a member of a New England family, a friend of Abraham Lincoln, a doctor of divinity and a university professor at Jacksonville, Illinois. Sturtevant claimed that 'The American people shall yet convert the world to Christ, by their voluntary and spontaneous migrations.'[64] The migrations that Sturtevant believed would convert the world were from one group of American Christians. It was, he insisted, 'the Anglo American emigrant [who] holds North America in his grasp'.[65]

Sturtevant went on to predict that what he regarded as the inferior French and Spanish bloodlines, together with their Catholic beliefs, would gradually die out. The special American 'trinity' of Anglo-Saxon strength, Protestantism and the English language would conquer and fulfil their destiny as prophesied. It is interesting to consider that at this time Sturtevant was not thought to be a political extremist and that he, like many of the influential figures of the American Establishment, was from New England. This writer and scholar who was espousing the 'conversion' of foreign bloodlines by the superior 'Anglo-American emigrant' represented the powerful group of Americans who from the Declaration of Independence had shaped republican democracy in a form that best suited their ethnic cultural values.

The most influential series of publications from the Home Missionary Society was *Our Country*, the final version of which was written by Josiah Strong and published in 1886. Though born in Illinois, Strong was another member of a New England family. A recent edition of *Our Country* claims that it sold 'one hundred and seventy-five thousand copies . . . before 1916, and individual chapters were reprinted in newspapers and magazines, and published separately in pamphlet form'.[66] According to the editor, Jurgen Herbst, 'This book . . . mirrors the thoughts and aspirations of this dominant segment of American society towards the close of the nineteenth century, and is therefore a historical document of major importance.'[67] The American readership had been well prepared for Strong's 'sermon', as earlier versions of *Our Country*, written by other authors, complete with similar themes and conclusions, had appeared in 1841, 1842 and 1858. The project of the Home Missionary Society had been to convert all Americans, and this, the latest and most complete *Our Country*, continued the task. As Herbst observed,

The conversion of the unconverted Americans in the West was viewed not only as Christian duty, but also as patriotic challenge, for the writers of *Our Country* assumed that Protestant America was God's special instrument in His great work, and so to be a Protestant Christian and an American patriot was one and the same.[68]

The content of Strong's text confirmed his sensitivity to the issues of immigration, and he referred to the yet to be published 'Eleventh Census' and the estimate of the 'present foreign-born population'. Using data from the Tenth Census, Strong argued that 'So immense a foreign element must have a profound influence on [American] national life and character',[69] combating this influence being one of the main missions of the society he represented. Strong gave warning of a further moral contamination of the American population, maintaining that 'a considerable element of our American-born population [is] apparently under the impression that the Ten Commandments are not binding west of the Missouri'.[70] Rhetoric reminiscent of early nineteenth-century nativists was employed to suggest that these non-American-born citizens were likely to form political blocks that would distort American democracy, as this important text of 1886 attempted to argue that 'Immigration is the mother and nurse of American socialism.'[71]

With the threat now clearly outlined, Strong joined together the key issues of religion, language and cultural traditions. While immigrants were necessary for America to grow, the task for patriots was to 'convert' these immigrants to Anglo-American values as speedily as possible. As Strong pointed out, 'Many American citizens are not Americanized. It is as unfortunate as it is natural that foreigners in this country should cherish their own language and peculiar customs.'[72] The Americanization that had been needed to combat these 'peculiar customs', while not at this point stated, was clearly to be found within the English language and the influential cultural text supplied by the American publishers of Shakespeare.

Strong echoed the beliefs of the American Establishment by entitling chapter 14 'The Anglo-Saxon and the World's Future'. He credited the Anglo-Saxon race, now supremely centred in the United States, with the establishment of 'pure spiritual Christianity [and] civil liberty'.[73] Strong predicted that the future of the world was in the hands of Anglo-Americans and the cultural heritage that sustained them. He predicted that by 1990 the Anglo-American population would be 373 million, and that together with the other Anglo-Saxon dominated countries (i.e. Canada, Australia, South Africa and Britain) it would 'give its civilization to mankind'.[74] Strong proposed a world vision for an Anglo-American empire that would outclass all other races and cultures. He suggested to his American readership that 'Nothing can save the inferior race but a ready and pliant assimilation' and that 'no war of extermination is needful'.[75] To demonstrate his capacity for humanitarian concern, and perhaps his awareness of the plight of the American Indians, he added, 'Whether the extinction of inferior races before the advancing Anglo-Saxon seems to the reader sad or otherwise, it certainly appears probable.'[76]

As a powerful conclusion to this picture of American assimilation of weaker cultures, Strong suggested that the world could be Anglo-Saxonised via the English language. Quoting a German philologist named Jacob

Grimm, Strong predicted that the English language would 'rule in future times . . . all corners of the earth [and] that the language of Shakespeare would eventually become the language of mankind'.[77]

Behind this association of Anglo-Saxon symbolism with American supremacy lay a complex ideology designed to boost a sense of national identity. While there was undoubtedly a widely held belief in the myth of racial Anglo-Saxon purity, what Strong's text demonstrates is that beyond this belief there was also an idea that people could become Anglo-Saxons by assimilation. The diverse group of people who were now American citizens could be 'converted', provided the cultural values, literature and religion of the Anglo-Saxons were all vigorously promoted. Conditioning was all that was necessary. If an American believed in Anglo-Saxon values, celebrated the symbols and demonstrated observance, then he/she became Anglo-Saxon by conversion. It was an American citizen's patriotic duty to become Americanised. It was a required act of faith.

During the nineteenth century Anglo-Saxonism was increasingly utilised to homogenise American culture and create the sense of a shared inheritance. A powerful wave of supremacist belief and Anglo-Saxon romanticism swept through the nation that had been created vowing to reject European influence. While, Americans had taken every opportunity to decry English arrogance and a hierarchical society based on inherited aristocratic qualities, Anglo-Americans now felt entitled to boast of their inherited destiny. This is the context in which the rapid appropriation of Shakespeare must be seen.

American ethnogenesis was not the product of a melting pot accommodating all the different ethnic traditions arriving with the immigrants from Europe. Eric Kaufmann has suggested that American ethnicity was Anglo-American ethnicity. It was this group that developed the 'myth-symbol complex' from which we now recognise the identity we call American. For Kaufmann, 'The United States was not an exception to the rule that nations are formed by core ethnic groups which later attempt to shape the nation in their own image.'[78] The evidence, when considered together, suggests that the rise of nativist sentiment, Anglo-Saxon romanticism and the increase in the consumption of Shakespeare may have been interrelated.

Shakespeare's words heard on the stage, read in affordable printed collections or declaimed in the schoolroom became part of the cultural Anglo-Saxon folklore that carried within it a conditioning that would both unite and help to influence the expanding American population on its path to the fulfilment of manifest destiny.

NOTES

1. *The Dramatick Works of William Shakespeare, Printed Complete* (Boston MA: Munroe & Francis, 1802).
2. Westfall, *American Shakespearean Criticism*, p. 97.
3. Giles Edwin Dawson, *Four Centuries of Shakespeare Publication* (Lawrence KS: University of Kansas Libraries, 1964), p. 19.
4. Thomas Jefferson, manuscript letter 149, Manuscript Division, Library of Congress, Washington DC.
5. See Thomas G. Paterson, ed., *Major Problems in American Foreign Relations*, 2 vols. (Lexington KY: D. C. Heath, 1989), vol. 1, chapters 4 and 8.
6. Slotkin, *The Fatal Environment*, p. 3.
7. Ibid. See particularly chapter 11, 'The Ideology of Race Conflict, 1848–1858'.
8. Paterson, ed., *Major Problems in American Foreign Relations*, p. 271.
9. Gen. James Harrison Wilson, 'Do Americans Hate England?', *North American Review*, 150/403 (June 1890), pp. 771–5.
10. Theodore Roosevelt, *The Winning of the West*, ed. Christopher Lasch (Greenwich CT: Fawcett Publications, 1964). First published 1899.
11. Tyler Anbinder, *Nativism and Slavery: The Know Nothings and the Politics of the 1850s* (New York: Oxford University Press, 1992), pp. 3–5. Anbinder writes that the growth of American 'nativism' coincided exactly with high levels of immigration. See also Slotkin, *The Fatal Environment*, on the subjects of immigration and metropolis.
12. Gibson and Lennon, 'Historical Census Statistics on the Foreign-Born Population of the United States: 1850–1990'.
13. Jon Gjerde, ed., *Major Problems in American Immigration and Ethnic History* (Boston MA: Houghton, Mifflin Co., 1998), p. 1.
14. Goldwin Smith, 'The Hatred of England', *North American Review*, 150/402 (May 1890), p. 548.
15. George Washington Woodward, *Woodward on Foreigners* (Philadelphia: H. B. Ashmead, 1863), p. 5. This is a pamphlet against the immigration of non-Anglo-Saxons.
16. Louisiana Native American Association, *Address of the Louisiana Native American Association, to the Citizens of Louisiana and the Inhabitants of the United States* (New Orleans: D. Felt & Co., 1839), p. 6.
17. Ibid.
18. Ibid., p. 7.
19. Samuel Morse, *Imminent Dangers to the Free Institutions of the United States through Foreign Immigration, and the Present State of the Naturalization Laws* (New York: E. B. Clayton, 1835).
20. Anbinder, *Nativism and Slavery*, p. 121.

21. As an example of the often unconscious link between politics and Shakespeare, in Harrisburg, Pennsylvania, the local Native American Party held an election meeting at the Shakespeare Saloon on 12 July 1851.

22. 'An Irish Colony – Why Not?', *American Celt* (New York), 3 February and 3 March 1855. See Mary Gilbert Kelly, *Catholic Immigration Colonization Projects in the United States, 1815–1860* (New York: United States Catholic Historical Society, 1939). The bishop was John Timon and the last issue of the newspaper 6 June 1857.

23. Jefferson, 'A Summary View of the Rights of British America', p. 118.

24. Gayley, *Shakespeare and the Founders of Liberty*, p. 127.

25. Reginald Horsman, *Race and Manifest Destiny: The Origins of American Anglo-Saxonism* (Cambridge MA: Harvard University Press, 1981), pp. 62–71.

26. Ibid., p. 65.

27. Ibid., p. 5.

28. Ibid., p. 157. Between 1813 and 1823, more than five million copies of Scott's *Waverley* novels had been 'pirated' and sold in America. See Mott, *Golden Multitudes*, pp. 68–9.

29. Mark Twain, *Life on the Mississippi* (New York: Oxford University Press, 1996), p. 416: 'The South has not yet recovered from the debilitating influence of his books.'

30. Eric Kaufmann, 'American Exceptionalism Reconsidered: Anglo-Saxon Ethnogenesis in the "Universal" Nation, 1776–1850', *Journal of American Studies*, 33 (1999), p. 456.

31. Charles Anderson, *An Address on Anglo Saxon Destiny: Delivered before the Philomathesian Society, of Kenyon College, Ohio, August 8th, 1849: and Repeated before the New England Society of Cincinnati; December 20th, 1849* (Cincinnati: John D. Thorpe, 1850), p. 4.

32. Ibid.

33. Allen J. Frantzen, *Desire for Origins* (New Brunswick NJ: Rutgers University Press, 1990), p. 204. See chapter 7, 'Nationalism, Internationalism, and Teaching Anglo-Saxon Studies in the United States', pp. 206–17.

34. 'The Anglo-Saxon Race', *North American Review*, 152/73 (July 1851), pp. 34–71.

35. Ibid., p. 39.

36. Harriet Beecher Stowe, *Uncle Tom's Cabin or Life among the Lowly* (New York: Penguin, 1981), p. 610. First published 1852.

37. Ibid., chapter 45, 'Concluding Remarks'.

38. Abiel Abbot Livermore, *The War with Mexico Reviewed* (Boston MA: W. Crosby & H. P. Nichols, 1850), p. 8.

39. Ibid.

40. Ibid., p. 10.

41. Ibid., p. 11.

42. William Gilpin, *Mission of the North American People, Geographical, Social, and Political* (Philadelphia: J. B. Lippincott, 1873). First published 1860 as *The Central Gold Region: the Grain, Pastoral, and Gold Regions of North America*.

43. Ibid., p. 99.
44. Ibid., p. 106.
45. Ibid., p. 124.
46. Ibid., p. 142. Gilpin appears to consider the frontier in a very similar manner to Frederick Jackson Turner in his famous 1893 thesis 'The Significance of the Frontier in American History'.
47. Gilpin, *Mission of the North American People*, p. 143.
48. Ibid.
49. Webster, *Dissertations on the English Language*, p. 36.
50. Joel Barlow, *The Columbiad, a Poem* (Philadelphia: C. & A. Conrad & Co., 1807), argument to Book IX, p. 352.
51. Ibid., Book X, lines 450–60, pp. 373–4.
52. Caleb Cushing, *An Oration on the Material Growth and Territorial Progress of the United States, Delivered at Springfield, Mass., on the Fourth of July, 1839* (Springfield MA: Merrian, Wood & Co., 1839), p. 22.
53. Ibid.
54. Ibid., p. 24.
55. See Roosevelt, *The Winning of the West*.
56. Lyman Beecher, *A Plea for the West*, 2nd edn (Cincinnati: Truman & Smith, 1835), pp. 31–2.
57. Benjamin Faneul Hunt, *An Oration Delivered by Their Appointment before the Washington Society, in Charleston, South-Carolina, on the 4th of July, 1839* (Charleston: S. S. Miller, 1839), p. 35.
58. 'Would the Abolition of Slavery Save or Would It Destroy the Union?', *New York Herald*, 30 September 1861, a pro-Union but pro-slavery article.
59. 'Our Language Destined To Be Universal', *United States Democratic Review*, 35/4 (April 1855), pp. 306–14.
60. Ibid., p. 313.
61. Ibid., p. 310.
62. Rev. David Hunter Riddle, *A Sermon on Behalf of the American Home Missionary Society, Preached in the Cities of New York and Brooklyn, May 1851* (New York: American Home Missionary Society, 1851), p. 14.
63. Ibid.
64. Rev. Julian Monson Sturtevant, *American Emigration* (New York: American Home Missionary Society, 1857), p. 9.
65. Ibid., p. 11.
66. Josiah Strong, *Our Country*, ed. Jurgen Herbst (Cambridge MA: Belknap Press, 1963), introduction, p. ix. First published 1886.
67. Ibid.
68. Ibid., p. xi.
69. Ibid.
70. Ibid., p. 53.
71. Ibid., p. 55.
72. Ibid.

73. Ibid., pp. 201–2.
74. Ibid., p. 205.
75. Ibid., pp. 214–15.
76. Ibid.
77. Ibid., p. 217.
78. Kaufmann, 'American Exceptionalism Reconsidered', p. 456.

CHAPTER 6

The American heroic and ownership of Shakespeare

Shakspeare, – that awful name!
A household word with us, – him too we claim.

George Calvert

American national myth and tradition, from its genesis during the War of Independence, identified anyone fighting against 'tyranny' as a hero and patriot. At the same time that the mythology of the heroic pilgrim settlers and frontier pioneers developed, the popularity of the yeoman playwright, together with his numerous robust and individualist protagonists, increased. The imagery of the death of tyrants and regicide in plays such as *Julius Caesar, Richard III, Hamlet* and *Macbeth* found a receptive audience in republican America, perhaps affirming the idea that acts of heroic rebellion were necessary to secure freedom. From presidents to 'political activists', men chose to invoke Shakespearean imagery to engender the spirit of American patriotism.

LEADERS AND HEROES

The early American heroes who had helped to found colonies prior to the heady days of the nineteenth-century republic were not immune from posthumous association with Shakespeare. Retrospectively, commentators attempted to forge links between the colonial writers and the playwright. For some Americans, intellectual credibility was reaffirmed by any apparent appreciation of Shakespeare, and many were therefore prepared to go to great lengths to show that several (if not most) important Americans felt a common bond with this naturalised playwright. To suggest a relationship scholars searched through personal library catalogues and correspondence noting anything that could indicate knowledge of Shakespeare.

Some American writers have suggested that New England Puritans such as John Harvard and Cotton Mather owned copies of Shakespeare's plays.[1]

There is, however, no evidence that any seventeenth-century New Englander read or referred to Shakespeare's plays. Despite this, the desire to make a link has remained. While admitting the absence of evidence, Esther Dunn still 'attempt[ed] the impossible',[2] speculating at length that the symbolically important pilgrims could have spent many a dark winter evening reading plays. For Dunn and other Americans, the 'picture of Cotton Mather poring over the pages of Shakespeare's First Folio [was] too good to lose'.[3]

The oft-repeated supposition that Cotton Mather owned a Shakespeare First Folio has recently been exposed as myth. William H. Scheide has provided new evidence that connects the nineteenth-century descendants of Mather to a First Folio proven to have been owned by a Judge William Parker of Boston in 1791. Samuel Parker, the son of the judge, inherited this copy and in 1802 married Hannah Mather Crocker, a great-granddaughter of Cotton Mather. It is likely that it was from this Mather family connection that the tradition of early 'Puritan' ownership of a First Folio developed.[4]

While any association between Puritan New England and Shakespeare amounts to little more than romantic speculation, the possibility of early awareness of Shakespeare by some Virginian colonists is more likely. In *Shakespeare and the Founders of Liberty in America*, Charles Mills Gayley maintained that there is substantial evidence that William Shakespeare was personally acquainted with members of the Virginia Council that began its work in the City of London in 1606. Gayley presented an interesting thesis that 'of the eighty-five members of the council during the ten years preceding Shakespeare's death . . . at least seven were men with whom Shakespeare had personal intercourse'.[5] The suggestion was that the playwright shared their vision for the creation of an experimental democratic society and that many of Shakespeare's plays contain ideas that were similar to those of the Virginia 'patriots'. However, this thesis relied on the assumption that any association or friendship between Shakespeare and investors in the Virginia Council signified his agreement with their aims and ideals.

While once again evidence of a direct link between Shakespeare and the early colonists is at best circumstantial, Gayley did demonstrate that some of the basic plot and certain parts of the text of *The Tempest* can be traced to a confidential unpublished letter written by William Strachey, available only to senior members of the London Virginia Council in September 1610. The possibility that Shakespeare, through his association with the earl of Southampton, the earl of Pembroke, Christopher Brooke and others, discussed and debated the affairs of the new Virginia Colony allowed Gayley to claim Shakespeare as an honorary American founding father.

While attempts to link the heroic colonists of America with Shakespeare reveal how comprehensive the appropriation of Shakespeare became, genuine examples of appreciation of Shakespeare by later American political figures can easily be found. John Adams once wrote in his journal of 'Shakspeare, that great master of every affection of the heart and every sentiment of the mind'.[6] George Washington had Shakespeare in his personal library and was a regular visitor to the John Street Theatre in New York, where, it would be easy to speculate, he could have watched *Richard III*. Thomas Jefferson, while not noted for his fondness for the British, owned at least two copies of Shakespeare (the first bought between 1786 and 1787 while he was resident in Paris), had four separate commentaries on various plays,[7] and was to present a rare set of quartos to the University of Virginia.

As the American populace enthusiastically embraced the cult of Anglo-Saxonism and the concept of manifest destiny, the name of Shakespeare was often linked to a heroic American heritage. As writer after writer championed Shakespeare and his plays, collectively the plays became associated with the assumed supremacy of the Anglo-American people. As Richard Grant White was to assert in 1865, 'only his race could have produced him'.[8] American heroism and Shakespeare were allied subliminally every time a newspaper or writer described Shakespeare as 'the greatest philosophic poet of the Anglo-Saxon race'.[9]

THE AMERICAN HEROIC

In 1850 Ralph Waldo Emerson remarked, 'It is natural to believe in great men. If the companions of our childhood should turn out to be heroes, and their condition regal, it would not surprise us.'[10] The propensity to celebrate achievement and glamorise named personalities as role models had already become a characteristic of the American nation. Shakespeare became one such celebrated personality.

America was regarded by its citizens as the 'home of the brave' and a nation made up of exceptional people. Unconsciously, Americans considered themselves collectively heroic, and increasingly extravagant displays of patriotism marked the national character. Alexis de Tocqueville suggested that Americans subconsciously felt their 'equality and precariousness of . . . social condition' to be at risk and therefore had to boost their own self-esteem and confidence by celebrating every possible sign of success.[11] To help create the matrix of interlocking symbols that helped reinforced the idea that was America, American success and American heroes were to be eulogised and promoted at every opportunity.

Frontier celebrities such as Jim Bowie, 'Wild Bill' Hickok, General George Custer and Kit Carson became cultural icons, and they were joined by Shakespeare to serve as powerful symbols for Anglo-America as it struggled to forge and promote a sense of nation to an increasingly diverse population. Richard Slotkin has written of American 'attempts to create literary myths or "living legends" out of the materials of current history'.[12] Characters such as Cooper's fictional Natty Bumppo or the real-life Daniel Boone and David Crockett were considered to epitomise American heroism and their names were recognised in the schoolroom and saloon. The existence of the frontier hero was seen as proof that America was populated by people of exceptional quality and that if these innate national traits were encouraged America would truly be the 'land of the free'. The heroes that nineteenth-century America chose to celebrate and promote were predominantly drawn from the single ethnic group thought to represent Anglo-Saxon heritage. Slotkin maintained that for nineteenth-century America, 'The worldwide triumph of the English over the continental powers argues the racial superiority of the Anglo-Saxon in general: and the victory of the American branch over the English argues the brief for Yankee superiority in particular.'[13] Shakespeare increasingly became appropriated to this chauvinistic cause as Americans learned to identify themselves with symbols they collectively regarded as heroic.

As the nineteenth century progressed, American editions of Shakespeare were read across the country. Tocqueville remarked that 'There is hardly a pioneer's hut that does not contain a few odd volumes of Shakespeare.'[14] The Frenchman added that the first time he read *Henry V* was in an American log cabin. In a country where the frontier mentality was celebrated, the heroic quality of many characters in Shakespeare's plays was perhaps appreciated by a people who increasingly regarded themselves as exceptional.

Confirming Tocqueville's comment about the popularity of Shakespeare on the western frontier, Karl Knortz, a German émigré who arrived in America in 1863, commented,

There is certainly no land on the whole earth in which Shakespeare and the Bible are held in such high esteem as in America, so much criticised for its love of money; should one enter a blockhouse situated in the far west . . . the Bible and in most cases a cheap edition of the works of the poet Shakespeare are nearly always found.[15]

The heroic tales of Greeks, Romans and the Renaissance dramatised within the plays both fed and fuelled the American tendency to romanticise the exploits of bold leaders and soldiers.

The heroic quality of the American nation was at once celebrated and linked to Shakespeare in everyday practical items such as *The Shakspeare Calendar or Wit and Wisdom for Every Day in the Year*.[16] This calendar had originally featured in the *Southern Weekly Gazette* during 1849, but it proved to be so popular that its author, William Carey Richards, extended the idea and produced a convenient pocket-sized volume for 1850. For each day there was both an anniversary and a quotation taken from Shakespeare. Along with anniversaries from world history, all the major American events and battles were recorded. Two examples from this calendar show how Shakespeare was appropriated to reinforce the impression of the American heroic:

June 6, Patrick Henry died, 1799.
'a foe to tyrants and my country's friend'
Julius Caesar, Act V, Scene 4.

June 17, Battle of Bunker Hill, 1775.
'one to ten! Lean, raw-boned rascals! Who would e'er suppose they had such courage and audacity?'
Henry VI, Part 1, Act 1, Scene 2.

In his elevated position as America's best-known writer, Shakespeare provided the politically charged 'sound bites' that, in the nineteenth century, captured the sentiment of a populace that appreciated American jingoism.

HEROIC CELEBRATIONS IN PAINT AND STONE

As Americans continued their process of nation building, the image of Shakespeare was associated with American visual arts. In 1860 the Cosmopolitan Art Association, choosing an engraving for their annual mass distribution to American members, settled on a painting by Scottish-born artist John Faed called *Shakespeare and His Friends*.[17] The following year another Shakespeare subject was selected, this time the rotund rogue Falstaff.[18] In his book on American popular culture, Carl Bode commented that 'it was hardly American art', but this ignores the fact that by 1860 Shakespeare was recognised by many Americans as part of their culture. In *Shakespeare in American Painting*, Richard Studing catalogued as many as 987 separate American paintings and pieces of visual art that were inspired by Shakespeare or his dramatic characters, the first example of this being recorded as early as 1760 with the work of Benjamin West.[19]

In November 1864, in recognition of Shakespeare's new status as an adopted American exemplar, the three American Booth brothers, Edwin,

Junius and John Wilkes, performed *Julius Caesar* at the Winter Gardens Theatre in New York, to help raise funds for a statue in honour of the playwright. As Brutus, Cassius and Mark Antony, these three American actors presented the Shakespeare play that, for many Americans, closely promoted democratic republican ideals over the threat of monarchy.[20] It was, however, to be another eight years before a statue by John Quincy Adams Ward was finally unveiled in New York's Central Park. It has been estimated that more than 6,000 people attended the dedication ceremony on 22 May 1872, where they listened to an orchestra of over a hundred performers create the atmosphere of grandeur suitable for a speech by William Cullen Bryant, a future editor of Shakespeare's works, who praised Shakespeare as 'our great dramatist'.[21] The cultural link between Shakespeare and the America nation was emphasised by Bryant, who honoured Shakespeare and compared his glory to that of the natural wonders of the sequoia trees of California and New York State's Niagara Falls.

SCENES FROM A TRAGEDY

As the South and its supporters started to understand the consequence of losing so costly a war, a Shakespearean actor took a grave step that was to connect dramatic imagery with American nationhood. Just five months after the benefit performance held to raise funds for the statue of Shakespeare in Central Park, the names of the Booth family and President Abraham Lincoln were to be permanently linked.

Twenty-six-year-old John Wilkes Booth was known by friends to be a Confederate 'patriot' having often been involved in heated debates with his two brothers, both of whom supported continuance of the Union. Booth, fresh from his role as Mark Antony in *Julius Caesar*, took to the American stage again in a significant parody of his previous performance. On the evening of Good Friday, 14 April 1865, at the Ford Theatre in Washington DC, while watching *Our American Cousin* by Tom Taylor, President Abraham Lincoln was assassinated by Booth. After shooting Lincoln and stabbing Major Henry R. Rathbone, Booth jumped from the presidential box onto the stage, where he then turned to face his audience. Walt Whitman, writing as a New York journalist, described the Shakespearean quality of the event for his readers:

Booth, the murderer, dress'd in plain black broadcloth, bare-headed, with full, glossy, raven hair, his eyes like some mad animal's flashing with light and resolution, yet with a certain strange calmness, holds aloft in one hand a large knife – walks along not much back from the footlights – turns fully towards the audience his face of statuesque beauty, lit by those basilisk eyes, flashing with desperation, perhaps insanity – launches out in a firm and steady voice the words *Sic Semper Tyrannis* – and then walks with neither slow nor very rapid pace diagonally across to the back of the stage, and disappears.[22]

The similarity between this description and a staging of Shakespeare's dramatisation of the assassination of Caesar was obvious to many Americans. In Shakespeare's play, a group of conspirators murders Caesar soon after he has been publicly hailed for his triumph in a civil war. The reenactment of this scene, performed by a well-known and admired Shakespearean actor, was designed to shock a nation familiar with the imagery of a play popular for its political significance.

Scavan Bercovitch described Booth as acting like a 'latter-day Roman patriot',[23] and it is clear that, while not responsible for Booth's action, Shakespeare's play influenced his chosen means to accomplish it and his misplaced idea of the heroic. Even the Latin phrase pronounced by Booth, 'sic semper tyrannis', was perhaps intended to parallel Shakespeare's dramatic use of the Latin 'Et tu, Brute?' during the murder of Caesar.[24]

Sic Semper Tyrannis is the state motto of Virginia, the official translation being 'Thus Always to Tyrants'. While the motto is not directly credited to America's third president Thomas Jefferson, it does reflect his stated belief that 'The tree of liberty must be refreshed from time to time with the blood of patriots and tyrants.'[25] This phrase also appears to have been influenced by the power of Shakespeare to dramatise and add substance to the classical stories of the republic of Rome and the 'heroic' action of its citizens.

The tragic assassination of President Lincoln, together with the theatrical imagery of an imposing assassin waving a symbolic blade, has become a key event in American national history. The assassination of Lincoln in revenge for the defeat of the Confederacy secured his iconic status and added sanctity to the monuments that later bore his name.

PILGRIMAGES TO THE TOMB OF AMERICA'S PLAYWRIGHT

In 1820, the comprehensive nature of the American appropriation of Shakespeare was reflected in Washington Irving's *Sketch Book*. Irving described his visit to Stratford-upon-Avon as a 'poetical pilgrimage',[26] and later many thousands of his fellow citizens were to follow his example. The fact that so many made this journey is significant. Before Stratford was linked to the rail network in 1860, visiting the town from London represented a considerable, very uncomfortable journey. And unlike many of the more usual tourist destinations of Europe, such as Paris, Rome or Venice, Stratford was not noted for its grandeur, works of art or unique cultural quality. In the Stratford of 1820 there was just a shabby butcher's shop with a room designated by the owner as the place where Shakespeare was born, together with a small, although attractive, parish church with a tomb bearing a curse but no name. Despite all this, Americans still came.

The visitors' books from the Birthplace and Holy Trinity Church reveal that Irving made this pilgrimage three times. The first, on 25 July 1815, provided the inspiration for the 'Sketch' that was destined to become the quasi-official guidebook for American pilgrims arriving in Stratford. He visited again on 10 September 1821, and then once more on 20 December 1831. This final visit was made in the company of Martin Van Buren, soon to be the eighth president of the USA.

Many other notable Americans were also to make this pilgrimage. It has already been stated that, long before Irving, future presidents John Adams and Thomas Jefferson had taken the time to visit. Henry Clay, influential congressman and senator from Kentucky, was to sign the book on 5 July 1815. Calvin E. Stowe, clergyman and future husband of Harriet Beecher Stowe, signed on 2 August 1836. Charles Sumner, senator, influential statesman and political orator, signed 6 January 1839.

Many Americans directly involved in the public debate over a national literature also made the journey. In 1846 Margaret Fuller visited, and like many of her fellow citizens she 'handled . . . the poker used to such good purpose by Geoffrey Crayon'.[27] Harriet Beecher Stowe followed in her husband's footsteps to visit the 'shrine of pilgrims'[28] in 1853, and, like Irving, she published her impressions in a collection of letters written during her European travels. While Stowe had a lot to convey about Shakespeare and his influence on Milton, she was none too impressed with Stratford or with the White Lion hotel, where she was unfortunately accommodated in a room designated 'Richard III'.

Nathaniel Hawthorne made what he described in his journal as 'our pilgrimage' on 27 June 1855. But even if it was a pilgrimage, Hawthorne regarded the visit as a nationalistic duty rather than an act of free will. After visiting Holy Trinity Church, Hawthorne wrote that he 'had now done one of the things that an American proposes to himself as necessarily and chiefly to be done, on coming to England'.[29] It was clear that he regarded the Birthplace as 'a worse house than anybody could dream it to be',[30] and a meagre reason to stop in the Warwickshire town. Herman Melville, who visited Hawthorne in Liverpool and was probably aware of his opinion of the Birthplace, nevertheless paid his respects on 3 May 1857, with a similar lack of enthusiasm.[31]

There were many more visitors. Perhaps equally significant are the visits made by the thousands of lesser-known Americans who still undertook the arduous journey from the cities of Liverpool and London to rural Stratford. The surviving records of both Holy Trinity Church and the Birthplace contain some of the names of those who wished to demonstrate their idolisation of Shakespeare. A few felt the need to write tributes, perhaps for other Americans to read. In January 1805, a T. Clifford, of Philadelphia, wrote a couplet connecting his/her country with the Warwickshire tomb:

> Shakespeare thy name across the Atlantic clime,
> Shall be rever'd until even endless time.[32]

A George Jones went further and added a poem he claimed to have composed while in the chancel of Holy Trinity. His visit came 'after an absence . . . of 17 years in the United States'.[33] He had returned to what he described as 'his native land', left when he was seven. Now twenty-four, having spent all his formative years in America, Jones wrote that 'he but recorded the noble feeling which America entertains for the genius of Albion's immortal poet!':

> A pilgrim from a foreign to his nature land,
> Kneels in devotion Shakspeare as thy works command,
> Calls forth homage where'er thy names unfurl'd,
> And the proud England's isle may boast thy lore
> Yet lives thy spirit upon Columbia's shore.
> In states unborn and accents yet unknown,
> Again shalt thy prophetic lance be thrown.

Jones was soon to return to Stratford and introduce an American tradition to the Warwickshire calendar. Before an audience on 23 April 1836, Jones gave an oration in which he described himself as a 'Pilgrim from the New-World'.[34]

The increasing popularity of Stratford as a destination for Americans was recognised by the English press. A writer in *The Times* commented on the 'unremitting . . . pilgrimage to Shakespeare's birthplace . . . the head pilgrims being the travellers from the United States, with whom it is almost a religion to worship at the shrine of the "Anglo-Saxon" poet'.[35] The numbers were so great that when actor Edwin Booth visited, his daughter reported his disappointment at finding himself surrounded by 'patriotic worshipers . . . who in the home of Shakspere petitioned for the autograph of Booth'.[36]

Margaret Fuller, writing of her visit to the house in 1846, noted that Shakespeare's birthplace had been 'an object of devotion only for forty years',[37] omitting to point out that these forty years coincided with the period in which Americans had so publicly demonstrated their interest. Recently Peter Rawlings has gone so far as to suggest that America was responsible for the 'invention of Stratford-upon-Avon'.[38] American ambassador Edward John Phelps helped affirm this relationship in a speech to a Stratford audience on 17 October 1887. Phelps referred to the town as 'A place to which Americans, by the pilgrimage of successive generations, have established a title as tenants in common with Englishmen by right of possession'.[39]

On this occasion Phelps was supported by Henry Irving, who stated for the same audience of dignitaries, 'The simplest records of Stratford show that this is the Mecca of American pilgrims.'[40] Later Henry James was to utilise this cultural phenomenon of American 'pilgrimage' as the setting for his short story 'The Birthplace' (1903).[41]

THE AMERICAN FORREST

A study of the lives of some prominent nineteenth-century American figures demonstrates the complex relationship between appreciation of Shakespeare and prevalent anti-English sentiment. This ambivalence can be seen in Edwin Forrest, actor, hero of American east-coast working men and partial cause of the Astor Place riot. Forrest was so representative of certain aspects of Jacksonian America that his biographer claimed, 'A review of his sixty-six tempestuous years, . . . means a review of sixty-six years in a nation's life.'[42]

Forrest was a contributor to Andrew Jackson's new Democratic Party, and this, combined with his oratory skills, resulted in his aspiring to political office in New York City. His stage career made him a wealthy man, and he was held in sufficient renown to have a steamship named in his honour.[43] Like so many of his compatriots he was a passionate nationalist and anti-monarchist. According to Charles Shattuck, 'His patriotism, fervid from the beginning, [was to develop] into a relentless hatred of all things English.'[44]

His career on the American stage became entwined with his political beliefs and it is perhaps not surprising that his first theatrical involvement, when just fifteen years old, was as 'entrepreneur', organising a performance of that most political of plays, *Richard III*. For Forrest, Shakespeare was a cultural colossus. He has been reported as saying, 'I hold that next to God, Shakespeare comprehended the mind of man.'[45] Like so many of his fellow

Americans he was to make his pilgrimage to Stratford, in his case on 1 July 1837, where he signed the visitors' book at Holy Trinity Church with a bold flourish taking up a full six lines.

Observing the now annual institution, on 4 July 1838 Forrest delivered a public oration in celebration of sixty-two years of American independence.[46] His words of condemnation of England and praise for those who would overthrow monarchy can be seen as a prologue to the political statements he would frequently make as an actor on stage. He described England as sitting with 'swollen pride of aristocratic grandeur [while it watched] guards in blood-red livery restore peace and order at the bayonet's point'.[47] He predicted a coming revolution in England led by 'riotous and incendiary sons of agriculture [and] the pale operatives of the manufactries'.[48] All this he contrasted with 'American Greatness' and foresaw that the nation would one day comprise 'hundred millions of co-sovereigns'.[49]

His actions and speeches suggest that he believed that the American people were 'natural aristocrats' unburdened by any of the formal class distinctions or affected manners that, for him, typified England. He used his position as an actor to promote these beliefs. In a letter to Forrest about the role of Coriolanus, William Leggett, a leading voice for the Democratic Party, suggested that despite the character not being 'so much of a democrat as you and I are [there] is no reason why we should not use him if he can do us service'.[50] According to Charles Shattuck, Forrest did just this and used 'Shakespeare to fight causes and to do down supposed enemies of himself and the state'.[51]

In order to provide himself with material that better suited his acting style and his political beliefs, Forrest funded several playwriting competitions. Three of the prize plays 'rode the coattails of American enthusiasm for "old Hickory" and for the Democratic attack on aristocratic privilege', so much so that Bruce McConachie described the plays as 'Jacksonian melodramas'.[52]

As if to encapsulate his political beliefs, Forrest, once described as an 'actor of an heroic mould',[53] adopted the theatrical role of Jack Cade and bought the rights to perform a prize-winning play of the same name especially to give life to the myth of a yeoman hero of a long-past English rebellion. The playwright, Robert T. Conrad, was to acknowledge the advice and help he received from Forrest in extending the part of Cade from an earlier version of the play.[54] The first performance of the 'new *Jack Cade*', with Forrest in the lead role, took place at the Park Theatre in New York on 24 May 1841. The play was an adaptation of the basic story of a Kent yeoman's rebellion against the English King, as told in Shakespeare's *Henry VI, Part 2*. However, where in Shakespeare's play Cade is portrayed as a foolish uncouth outlaw, Forrest presents him as an orator, glorifies his actions and creates a character of heroic proportions. Both the American audience and Forrest must have enjoyed this 'all-action hero' drama, which from Act 1 had Cade shouting, 'Alas! For England! Her merry yeomen, and her sturdy serfs, that made red Agincourt immortal, now are trod like worms into the earth. Freedom ne'er came too soon for wrongs like ours.'[55] One can well imagine the applause from the audience at the play's conclusion, with Forrest as Cade chanting unhistorically, 'Free! Free! The bondsman is avenged, my country Free!' This play and Forrest's role in it appear to encapsulate Jacksonian politics and populist American hostility to the British monarchist Establishment.

At the end of his life, Forrest retired to his substantial home with its expensive well-stocked library complete with a copy of the rare Shakespeare First Folio, and, with a single act, combined the various aspects that had dominated his life. With his last will and testament, dated 5 April 1866, he established a residential home for elderly or disabled actors, the 'Edwin Forrest Home'.[56] Article 9 of its 'constitution' described its mission as being to 'promote the love of liberty, our country, and her institution: [and] to hold in honour the name of the great dramatic Bard'.[57] In the same document Forrest also specified that two annual ceremonies were to be performed with all residents in attendance. On 4 July the Declaration of Independence was to be read, 'without expurgation', to be 'followed by an oration, under the folds of our national flag'.[58] In addition to this annual celebration of the American Revolution, fought to secure independence, on every 23 April a eulogy was to be delivered celebrating the life and works of Shakespeare.

The two American institutions that Forrest and many Americans had learnt to consider as complementary were the works of Shakespeare and the Declaration of Independence. Throughout his life and even while preparing for his death, Forrest embraced both as documents unequivocally representing the best of the American tradition.

WHO OWNED SHAKESPEARE?

The rivalry that marked the relationship between Americans and their former colonial masters in England manifested itself in a battle for language and for what came to be regarded as the symbol of that language, Shakespeare. As Gustave de Beaumont was to observe, 'The rivalry existing between the Americans and the English is not only industrial and commercial. These two peoples have a common language, and each claims to speak it better than the other.'[59] Early American writer and playwright Peter Markoe wrote an ode that captured the sentiment that was a key part of the later nineteenth-century appropriation:

> Monopolizing Britain! Boast no more
> His genius to your narrow bounds confin'd;
> Shakespeare's bold spirit seeks our western shore,
> A gen'ral blessing for the world design'd,
> And, emulous to form the rising age,
> The noblest Bard demands the noblest Stage.[60]

Americans regarded their country as a 'noble stage' and Shakespeare, with his 'bold spirit', as liberated from 'monopolizing Britain' to share their destiny in the 'new world'.

If England was the ever-present enemy for the American nation, then the ownership of items of common heritage became contentious. The paradox of considering England as a threat to American ideals and the reality of sharing a common language could not always be ignored. George Calvert highlighted the problem of language in a poem:

> We have a double heritage. Through speech,
> We share the 'Sceptred Island's' mental glory.[61]

This 'double heritage' including the 'mental glory' that would spawn American republican heroes also extended to embrace the 'second Adam' in the form of the American Shakespeare:

> And he, – a second Adam on the earth,
> Repeopling it, the one unparallel'd,
> Th' absolute Lord of pathos and of mirth,
> As if creation's growth he had beheld,
> And had espied the secrets of its birth,
> And drunk the subtle spirit as it well'd
> In being's fonts, – Shakspeare, – that awful name!
> A household word with us, – him too we claim.[62]

Shakespeare was indeed a household word, and a word that was to represent the complex ideological theory that allowed Americans to claim ownership of those traits that were considered to be worthy of the republic while at the same time rejecting any shared heritage of 'tyranny' or imperial tendencies associated with England.

As has already been shown, other statements professing national ownership of Shakespeare appeared in various American editions of the works. As they read Shakespeare Americans reasserted their claim to ownership of the playwright and the text. In an edition published in 1850, the editor James Halliwell wrote of 'Shakspere – a name which belongs as much to Saxon America as to Saxon England'.[63]

A formal invitation from the state of California to Edwin Forrest offers another example of the way heritage was stressed and American ownership pronounced. Appealing to Forrest's ego, the invitation of April 1857 suggested that 'as Shakspere is remembered and his works revered, your name, too, will be remembered with pride by all who glory in the triumphs of our Saxon literature'.[64] 'Triumph' and Saxon heritage were to be constantly associated with the name of Shakespeare, and as Gayley later wrote, 'American heritage is of the revolutionary fathers, of the colonial fathers . . . the contemporaries and friends of the poet and prophet of the race.'[65]

In 1876, as the American people celebrated their national centennial, an article published in the *New York Herald* again highlighted this one particular aspect of the appropriation of Shakespeare that had been noticeable throughout the preceding one hundred years. Joseph Watson's article 'Shakespeare in America' included an account of the arrival of English actor George Frederick Cooke in New York.[66] Cooke disembarked in 1810, just prior to the second war fought by America against Britain. Unsurprisingly, his first appearance on the New York stage was as *Richard III*, before what Watson described as 'the greatest house ever known in America'. Watson went on to relate an anecdote concerning a conversation between Cooke and an unnamed American, assumed to have taken place sometime between 1810 and Cooke's death on 26 September 1812. According to Watson, Cooke remarked, 'I observe that you Americans always say "our great poet", "our immortal and unrivalled dramatist", but you are not the countrymen of Shakespeare. What part has an American in the Bard of Avon?', to which the American replied, 'Precisely the same part that an Englishman of the present day can claim in him. As a descendant from Britons, I claim the same share in the heroes, poets and philosophers of former days as any Briton of this day can.'[67] This exchange, fictional as it may be, reflected the opinion of many nineteenth-century Americans, and certainly it repeats the belief expressed in 1828 by James Fenimore Cooper that an 'American has just as good a right to claim . . . Shakespeare . . . for his countrym[a]n as an Englishman'.[68]

The fact is, of course, that by the mid-nineteenth century the majority of American citizens were not the descendants of 'Britons', but the American nation nevertheless claimed Shakespeare as their own. Shakespeare was considered to be part of American heritage irrespective of how the American citizen in question traced his or her own ancestry.

Watson's article carried the suggestion that, at the close of its second century, America, 'an English speaking people under a republican form of government will find it the foremost nation of the world, not only in literature, but also in the arts and sciences'.[69] Watson credits both Shakespeare and the American theatre with helping the USA to achieve this position. In concluding, he suggested why Shakespeare had been so important to America:

[Shakespeare] laid bare the intrigues of crowns and faithfully illustrated the shameless deeds of royalty. The Republic of the United States, on the other hand, created a singularly free people, who could read these plays while untrammelled and uninfluenced by monarchial surroundings.[70]

During the nineteenth century Shakespeare joined the other new American exemplars precisely because he was considered to reflect the heroic values and populist temperament of the new republic. Without any better symbol for American cultural unity, Shakespeare was appropriated to fulfil an important role that would, in the twentieth century, be served by many far more home-grown heroic celebrities.

NOTES

1. Dunn, *Shakespeare in America*. See also Marder, *His Exits and His Entrances*, p. 296, and Adams, 'The Folger Shakespeare Memorial', p. 213.
2. Dunn, *Shakespeare in America*, p. 19.
3. Ibid., p. 25. See also Edwin Eliott Willoughby, 'The Reading of Shakespeare in Colonial America', *Bibliographical Society of America*, 30/2 (1936), pp. 45–56.
4. William H. Scheide, 'The Earliest First Folio in America?', *Shakespeare Quarterly*, 27 (1976), pp. 332–3.
5. Gayley, *Shakespeare and the Founders of Liberty*, p. 37. Gayley's book, written perhaps to capture the attention of American patriots in 1917, culminated in an emotional appeal to a reluctant United States to launch into the First World War to protect democracy and all those 'who speak the tongue that Shakespeare spake'.
6. Adams, *Works*, vol. II, p. 293, entry for 9 February 1772.
7. See E. Millicent Sowerby, *Catalogue of the Library of Thomas Jefferson* (Washington DC: Library of Congress, 1952).
8. *The Works of William Shakespeare*, ed. White, p. cxcv.
9. *Town Crier: New York Dramatic News*, 1 February 1878, from a review of Edwin Booth's portrayal of Shylock.
10. Ralph Waldo Emerson, *Representative Men* (Philadelphia: David McKay, 1892), p. 1. First published 1850.

11. Tocqueville, *Democracy in America*, vol. II, p. 237.
12. Slotkin, *The Fatal Environment*, p. 242.
13. Ibid., p. 228.
14. Tocqueville, *Democracy in America*, vol. II, p. 58.
15. Karl Knortz, *Shakespeare in Amerika* (Berlin: Theodor Hofmann, 1882). Quoted here in translation from Westfall, *American Shakespeare Criticism*, p. 60.
16. William Carey Richards, *The Shakspeare Calendar; or, Wit and Wisdom for Every Day in the Year* (New York: George P. Putnam, 1850).
17. Bode, *The Anatomy of American Popular Culture*, p. 84.
18. Ibid., p. 85.
19. Richard Studing, *Shakespeare in American Painting: A Catalogue from the Late Eighteenth Century to the Present* (Rutherford NJ: Fairleigh Dickinson University Press, 1993).
20. See Marder, *His Exits and His Entrances*, pp. 312–25.
21. William Cullen Bryant, *Orations and Addresses* (New York: G. P. Putnam's Sons, 1878), p. 375.
22. Whitman, *Prose Works 1892*, vol. II, *Collect and Other Prose*, p. 505.
23. Scavan Bercovitch, ed., *The Cambridge History of American Literature*, 7 vols. (Cambridge: Cambridge University Press, 1997), vol. I, p. 590. See also Wilmeth and Bigsby, eds., *The Cambridge History of American Theatre*, p. 6.
24. *Julius Caesar*, Act 3, Scene 1.
25. Thomas Jefferson, *The Papers of Thomas Jefferson*, ed. Julian P. Boyd et al., vol. XII (Princeton: Princeton University Press, 1955), p. 356, letter of 13 November 1787 referring to Shay's Rebellion. The phrase 'Sic Semper Tyrannis' reappeared in American history linked to Thomas Jefferson on Patriots' Day 1995 in Oklahoma City. On the day of the explosion the now convicted and executed bomber Timothy McVeigh wore a T-shirt with the image of Lincoln and the phrase uttered by John Booth on the front and the quotation from Jefferson, 'The tree of liberty must be refreshed . . . ', on the back. See Lou Michel and Dan Herbeck, *American Terrorist: Timothy McVeigh and the Oklahoma City Bombing* (New York: Regan Books, 2001), p. 226.
26. Washington Irving, *The Sketch Book of Geoffrey Crayon, Gent.* (New York: Penguin Classics, 1988), p. 209. First published 1820.
27. S. Margaret Fuller, *At Home and Abroad* (Boston MA: Roberts Bros., 1874), p. 166.
28. Harriet Beecher Stowe, *Sunny Memories of Foreign Lands* (London: Piper, Stephenson & Spence, 1854), letter 10, p. 76. Stowe was to describe Queen Elizabeth I as a 'most repulsive and disagreeable woman' (p. 87).
29. Nathaniel Hawthorne, *The English Notebooks*, ed. Randall Stewart (New York: Modern Language Association of America, 1941), p. 134.
30. Ibid., p. 131.
31. Herman Melville, *Journal of a Visit to Europe and the Levant, October 11, 1856–May 6, 1857*, ed. Howard C. Horsford (Princeton: Princeton University Press, 1955).

32. Shakespeare Birthplace Trust, Office of Records, Records ERI/24, vol. I.
33. 15 August 1834. See Shakespeare Birthplace Trust, Office of Records, Records ERI/24, vol. III, p. 58.
34. George Jones, *The First Annual Jubilee Oration upon the Life, Character and Genius of Shakspeare, Delivered at Stratford-upon-Avon, April 23rd, 1836, before the Royal Shakspearian Club* (London: Edward Churton, 1836), p. 52. Jones also delivered a suitably patriotic Fourth of July oration in Richmond, Virginia: *Oration on the National Independence, Richmond, Va., July 4, 1840 before the Franklin Society at the City-Hall, Written and Pronounced by George Jones, Tragedian* (Richmond VA: Franklin Society, 1840).
35. 'The Birthplace of Shakespeare', *The Times*, 26 October 1868, p. 5.
36. Edwina Booth Grossman, *Edwin Booth, Recollections by His Daughter, Edwina Booth Grossmann, and Letters to Her and to His Friends* (New York: Century Co., 1984), p. 19.
37. Fuller, *At Home and Abroad*, p. 166.
38. Peter Rawlings, ed., *Americans on Shakespeare 1776–1914* (Aldershot: Ashgate, 1999), p. 14.
39. 'Shakespeare and America', *The Times*, 18 October 1887, p. 6.
40. Ibid.
41. Henry James, 'The Birthplace', in James, *The Better Sort* (New York: C. Scribner's Sons, 1903).
42. Montrose Jonas Moses, *The Fabulous Forrest: The Record of an American Actor* (Boston MA: Little, Brown & Co., 1929), p. 344.
43. Unfortunately the ship was to sink with loss of life. Forrest gave one thousand dollars to the widows of three pilots who were drowned. See *Frederick Douglass's Paper* (Rochester NY), 4 May 1855.
44. Charles H. Shattuck, *Shakespeare on the American Stage* (Washington DC: Folger Shakespeare Library, 1976), p. xii.
45. Bode, *The Anatomy of American Popular Culture*, p. 17.
46. Edwin Forrest, *Oration Delivered at the Democratic Republican Celebration of the Sixty-Second Anniversary of the Independence of the United States in the City of New-York, Fourth July, 1838* (New York: J. W. Bell, 1838).
47. Ibid., p. 15.
48. Ibid.
49. Ibid., p. 24.
50. Quoted from Moses, *The Fabulous Forrest*, p. 184.
51. Shattuck, *Shakespeare on the American Stage*, p. xii.
52. Bruce A. McConachie, 'The Theatre of Edwin Forrest and Jacksonian Hero Worship', in Fisher and Watt, eds., *When They Weren't Doing Shakespeare*, p. 4.
53. *Literary World*, 10 (April 1847), p. 234.
54. Robert Conrad, *Jack Cade* (New York, 1841).
55. Ibid., Act I, Scene 4.
56. Gabriel Harrison, *Edwin Forrest: the Actor and the Man, Critical and Reminiscent* (Brooklyn, 1889), pp. 197–200.

57. The Forrest home was to be destroyed by fire in January 1873. It was re-established, however, and continued until finally disbanded in 1987. Forrest's First Folio, although damaged, survived the fire. As of November 1994 the Folio was displayed in a glass box at the Free Library of Philadelphia. See Anthony James West, *The Shakespeare First Folio: The History of the Book* (Oxford: Oxford University Press, 2001).

58. Harrison, *Edwin Forrest*, pp. 201–10. For more on Forrest, see James Rees, *The Life of Edwin Forrest with Reminiscences and Personal Recollections* (Philadelphia: T. B. Peterson & Bros., 1874).

59. Beaumont, *Marie*, p. 219.

60. Peter Markoe, 'The Tragic Genius of Shakespeare; an Ode', in Markoe, *Miscellaneous Poems* (Philadelphia, 1787), pp. 23–7.

61. George Henry Calvert, *Cabrio: A Poem* (Baltimore: N. Hickman, 1840), Canto II, XXXVI, p. 34.

62. Ibid., Canto II, XXXVIII, p. 34.

63. *The Complete Works of Shakspere: Revised from the Original Editions, with Historical Introductions, and Notes Explanatory & Critical; a Life of the Poet, and an Introductory Essay on His Phraseology & Metre. By J. O. Halliwell, Esq. F.R.S. F.S.A.* (New York: Tallis, Willoughby & Co., 1850), vol. I, p. ii. The edition was pirated by a publisher in England, as a consequence of which the editor suspended work on later volumes.

64. Moses, *The Fabulous Forrest*, p. 303.

65. Gayley, *Shakespeare and the Founders of Liberty*, p. 224.

66. Watson, 'Shakespeare in America', *New York Herald*, 26 February 1877, p. 6. This was in fact the second instalment of an article first published on 12 February 1877, p. 4, and was to become the pamphlet *Shakespeare in America: His Influence on American Taste and Education, a Review by Joseph Watson* (Baltimore: John T. Ford, 1877).

67. For similar views expressed by Willian Cullen Bryant, see a speech made in 1870 in Rawlings, ed., *Americans on Shakespeare*, pp. 278–81.

68. Cooper, 'Notions of the Americans', p. 9.

69. Watson, 'Shakespeare in America'.

70. Ibid. There is a marked similarity in the language utilised by Watson to express these views and that of a later piece by Walt Whitman, 'What Lurks behind Shakspeare's Historical Plays', first published in the *Critic*, 27 September 1884.

CHAPTER 7

Shakespeare as a fulcrum for American literature

> You must believe in Shakespeare's un-approachability or quit the country.
>
> Herman Melville

The American political and cultural construct that was at first primarily an 'idea' intended to improve the material prosperity of its citizens later looked beyond the dollar to the written word to express and promote its national self-confidence. If America were to challenge the intellectual 'snobbery' of England, then American citizens would have to match or exceed European artistic and literary creativity. To achieve this end, the plays of Shakespeare, now available in numerous American editions, were freely used to instruct and inspire American 'scholars' to better embody in print the essence of the American spirit.

THE INFLUENCE OF SHAKESPEARE ON THE GENESIS OF AMERICAN LITERATURE

Washington Irving is often described as America's first successful professional author and father of the literary sketch or short story. Irving wrote his *Sketch Book* while living in England in 1820, but, as indicated in his preface, it was primarily intended for an American readership. Despite or, more correctly, because of this fact, Shakespeare was a key element in its reflections on language, authors, literature and culture. 'The Mutability of Literature' is a sketch that highlights Irving's use of Shakespeare. Irving's narrator, after reflecting that old books and authors must make way for the new, is asked by an imaginary voice from Elizabethan England whatever became of a 'half educated varlet . . . I think his name was Shakspeare. I presume he sunk into oblivion.'[1] Following this introduction, Irving commented on the contemporary position of Shakespeare in American culture and the extent to which literary critics invoked his writings:

Shakspeare, whom we behold, defying the encroachments of time, retaining in modern use the language and literature of his day, and giving duration to many an indifferent author, merely having flourished in his vicinity . . . even he, I grieve to say, is gradually assuming the tint of age, and his whole form is overrun by a profusion of commentators, who, like clambering vines and creepers, almost bury the noble plant that upholds them.[2]

While Irving criticised the reverence afforded both to 'old' books and their authors and, perhaps ironically, to any American writer who appropriated Shakespeare for his or her own aggrandisement, he praised poets and 'bards', who, he claimed, were able 'to transmit the pure light of poetical intelligence from age to age'.[3]

With this book, which included the tales of 'Rip Van Winkle' and 'The Legend of Sleepy Hollow', both now regarded as quintessentially American literature, it has been suggested that Irving held 'firm to the idea of Shakespeare's universal appeal',[4] and indeed Shakespeare is featured in no fewer than thirteen 'sketches'.

A contemporary of Irving, and the man sometimes regarded as America's first novelist, James Fenimore Cooper, observed in 1828 that Shakespeare was 'the Great author of America'.[5] For him, Shakespeare had already become a cultural symbol. Cooper, like Irving, established a link between American romantic myth and Shakespeare by using '1,089 quotations from Shakespeare' as epigraphs for his popular tales of the American frontier between 1820 and his death in 1851.[6]

This process of literary appropriation, here expressed by two key American authors, moved apace, and Shakespeare became the name frequently invoked by journalists and critics when assessing the quality of American debutant writers.

THE CONUNDRUM FOR AMERICAN WRITERS

Many opinion-formers, politicians and writers entered the debate about the nature of American literature, an issue described by Walt Whitman as a 'tremendous and fearful subject'.[7] The question for many was whether America would produce an identifiable national literature to rival that of the 'old world'? Their anxiety was aggravated by the frequent derogatory comments about American authors that appeared within the media in England.

Perhaps the earliest and most influential figure in this debate was William E. Channing, a doctor of divinity and a founder of the Unitarian Church.

In 1823 he wrote an essay entitled 'Remarks on National Literature' that was to influence Ralph Waldo Emerson and others who later demanded distinct American literature.[8]

For Channing, the issue was of more than just literary interest. Like those who were to follow him, he maintained that 'The topic seems . . . a great one, and to have intimate connections with morals and religion, as well as with all [American] public interests.'[9] He argued that a national literature was 'the expression of a nation's mind in writing',[10] and that 'The great distinction of a country . . . is that it produces superior men.'[11]

For Channing, the concept of a national literature was linked to the development of worthy and moral citizens. The mere institutions of republican democracy, or the material symbols of financial success, were not sufficient to fulfil the destiny that awaited the American nation. The suggestion was that, through dedication and application, America could produce 'a nobler order of intellect and character', and that this would not come from the 'climate or soil' but from applying American liberty to thought and hence to achieving 'Perfection of Mind'.[12] Channing confronted his countrymen by confirming what they already knew, namely that, as yet, America had nothing that could be called a national literature. Predating Emerson's famous 'American Scholar' address (1837), Channing argued that America must move out of the shadow of Europe. He asked his readers the provocative question 'Shall America be only an echo of what is thought and written under the Aristocracies beyond the ocean?' 'A foreign literature,' he insisted, 'will always, in a measure, be foreign.'[13]

Having decried the continuation of European influence, however, Channing went on to identify William Shakespeare as a worthwhile example of someone who developed his inherited genius by learning to communicate philosophical thoughts via literature. Importantly, Channing chose not to taint Shakespeare with the categorisation 'foreign'. He was, rather, a man who had produced literature, and 'literature is the nurse of genius'.[14]

The comparison between American writers and Shakespeare served both to inspire and to frustrate authors who saw a need to reflect American nationalism while still being measured against an Elizabethan playwright. The apparent conflict between a desire to establish a literature as a distinct statement of American identity and the increasing recognition of Shakespeare as part of American heritage can be seen to co-exist within the writings of an important American of the mid-nineteenth century, transcendentalist Ralph Waldo Emerson. More than anyone else, if perhaps inadvertently, Emerson, through his magazine contributions, philosophical essays and extensive programme of public lectures, created a link between the cause of American nationalism and acceptance of Shakespeare as part of American national heritage.

Emerson suggested that Shakespeare was an example of intellectual and creative achievement that modern 'Man', particularly American 'Man', should learn from but, importantly, strive to surpass. For Emerson, and others of the American social elite, if a citizen was to achieve great things, it was necessary to study the work and lives of 'great men' and, having understood their essence, move 'forward', advancing knowledge and American civilisation. While for some Shakespeare was merely a source of pleasure, for Emerson his importance was as a cultural milestone, marking a point to be reached and then transcended.[15]

In his lecture 'The American Scholar' he both recognised the value of Shakespeare and criticised those who idolised him without aspiring to surpass his creative achievements.[16] Emerson informed his audience that 'The English dramatic poets have Shakespearised now for two hundred years.'[17] The implication was that, in Emerson's view, English poets had not yet moved forward, and Emerson insisted that 'Man Thinking must not be subdued by his instruments.'[18] For Emerson, Shakespeare, though important, was just one of these instruments. He nonetheless promoted Shakespeare as a source of inspiration, even while announcing that Americans had 'listened too long to the courtly muses of Europe'.[19] He called to the 'American Scholar' to move on and write an identifiably American literature.

Emerson made his first visit to England in 1832 at the age of twenty-nine. There he met Samuel Coleridge and Thomas Carlyle, both influential figures in philosophy and literature. Following another visit to England in 1848, Emerson confided to his diary his belief that America was 'the right home and seat of the English race; and this great England will dwindle again to an island which has done well but has reached its utmost expansion'.[20] The implication was that America had rescued the best attributes of the 'English race', Shakespeare included.

In *Representative Men* (1850) Emerson described the attributes of six Europeans worthy of close study, placing Shakespeare alongside Plato, Swedenborg, Montaigne, Napoleon and Goethe. Importantly for Americans, out of this list of European 'heroes' only Shakespeare's work was widely available to English-speaking citizens. Emerson suggested that 'Other men are lenses through which we read our own minds',[21] and again he supported the American propensity to celebrate and 'believe in great men'.[22]

For Emerson, the importance of Shakespeare did not simply lie in the quality of his plays. He informed his readers that he thought 'highly . . . of his dramatic merit, but still [thought] it secondary'.[23] Shakespeare was recommended to Americans because he was the 'Poet and Philosopher' who shared an Anglo-Saxon heritage and could inspire Americans to greater achievement.

In addition to writing Emerson undertook lecture tours, with Shakespeare and 'the English' as frequent topics for his oratory skills.[24] Between 1848 and 1856 he delivered more than forty lectures on English topics in America, and these were published in a revised form as *English Traits* (1856).[25] In this book Emerson publicly declared America to be the 'right home and seat of the English race' and suggested that it was therefore important for Americans to learn more about their heritage. For Emerson, the best of Anglo-Saxon characteristics had now reached 'the vast physical influences of [the American] continent'.[26] This book proved a commercial success both in the United States and in England, helped no doubt by almost fifty literary reviews in popular journals.[27]

Other prominent east-coast intellectuals joined the process of promoting Shakespeare. The lecture platform was popular both with citizens who desired self-improvement and with the speakers themselves. Along with notables such as Richard Henry Dana and historian George Ticknor, Henry Norman Hudson lectured on the subject of Shakespeare. Beginning in 1844, Hudson, an Episcopalian minister and later a professor of Shakespeare at Boston University, delivered lectures on Shakespeare 'from Cincinnati to Mobile to Boston'.[28] Promoting Shakespeare had now become a commercial enterprise, and 'by 1848 his lectures were popular enough to be published in two volumes'.[29]

The task of creating a distinctive national literature for America continued both to inspire and to haunt the minds of authors, who invariably found themselves compared with Shakespeare. It was not sufficient to write popular and critically acclaimed literature. Channing and Emerson had challenged American authors to write literature that represented and united the nation. As Whitman wrote in 1891, the object had been to write literature for 'forty-four Nations curiously and irresistibly blent and aggregated in ONE NATION, with one imperial language'.[30] The task was one of 'Patriotism, Nationality, Ensemble'.[31] It was a task attempted in the public gaze and the gaze most resented was that of the English.

William Dean Howells, as editor of *Harper's New Monthly Magazine*, responded to the continued self-conscious debate about national literature and the provocative journalism on the subject appearing in the London press. For Howells, the problem was self-created and perhaps insoluble. He told his readership that 'for all aesthetic purposes the American people are not a nation, but a condition. They are the old, well-known Anglo-Saxon race, affected and modified by the influence of the other strains, but not essentially changed by these.'[32] Howells suggested that the process by which the Anglo-Americans had created a culture and tradition for America precluded the invention of literature that was 'original' or unique.

While the literati continued to fret about their independence, in Howells's view the vast majority of successful American writers before 1866 'were not only of New England race, but of New England birth'.[33] Writing about 'Literary Boston', Howells identified a significant aspect of the problem associated with the quest for a national literature. According to this respected editor, for at least the first half of the century 'The literary theories [they] accepted were New England theories . . . Boston criticism.'[34] Those responsible for much of the literary output of America had been conditioned by the culture and tradition of New England. Howells went on, 'New England [has been a] nation in itself . . . and it will probably be centuries yet before the life of the whole country, the American life as distinguished from the New England life, shall have anything so like a national literature.'[35] The very people most insistent in demanding a national literature were from the region most noted for its homogeneity of Anglo-American culture. For Howells, unity and a truly national literature were as yet a chimera.

Yet while the genesis of a national literature was anything but painless, in several ways Shakespeare had already been naturalised as a writer for the American nation, even if the title had not as yet been officially conferred.

EDUCATION AND THE PROCESS OF APPROPRIATION

Public education increased during the nineteenth century, and the resultant high level of literacy of American citizens helped create a readership for Shakespeare. Free schooling had been available in Massachusetts from as early as 1827 and the same state made school attendance compulsory in 1852. Along with the number of public schools, the length of time children spent in education increased from 'four months and two days in 1800 . . . to twenty-two months and ten days in 1850'.[36] The region of New England, so important to the cult of Anglo-Saxonism, was to supply a high proportion of the writers of school books and classroom teachers. As Ruth Elson observed, 'In this period New England can justly be termed the schoolmaster of the nation.'[37]

Anglo-Saxonism and Shakespeare had both been appropriated to the cause of American nationalism and this was reflected in the content of the school books that were used to teach children of all ethnic backgrounds to read and write, consider history and understand American politics. It is important to note that, as the millions of Americans for whom English was not the 'mother tongue' learnt to speak 'American', they were introduced to Shakespeare as part of American rather than English culture.

The American education system had by now already recognised the value of using Shakespeare's text to encourage improved levels of expression from their students. From the frontier homesteads in the West to city schools in the East, young Americans were required to read selected passages of Shakespeare for declamation in front of their peers. From the publication in 1810 of John Walker's *Elements of Elocution*, 'the first text devoted specifically to Shakespeare',[38] to the well-known 'McGuffey Readers', school children were systematically introduced to Shakespeare. Plays were appropriated to the important task of instructing children from diverse national and linguistic backgrounds to read and speak the unifying American English.

The early 'readers' had been noted for their jingoism, largely choosing American texts, such as the Declaration of Independence and the Constitution, for the instruction of reading. By 1850, however, passages from Shakespeare were widely used to illustrate moral values and for elocution practice. At this point, Shakespeare was not studied as literature, either foreign or domestic, and this fact helped to ensure that the plays continued to be accepted by Americans as American popular culture.

The mass-produced McGuffey Readers were published in Ohio by William Holmes McGuffey,[39] and by the *Sixth Eclectic Reader* 'more than fifty pages' were devoted to Shakespeare.[40] Between 1836 and the beginning of the twentieth century, these McGuffey Readers sold as many as 120 million copies, joining other 'readers' from Goldsbury & Russell or Pickett, all of which used Shakespeare.[41]

From 1865 Shakespeare was gradually introduced into history of literature courses in high schools, and in 1869 Harvard specified a knowledge of Shakespeare as one of its college entrance criteria. Other American colleges soon followed Harvard's lead. The language of Americanisation was English and Shakespeare was the preferred cultural text. In 1897 Roosevelt was to write that he believed 'that English, and no other language, is that in which all the school exercises should be conducted',[42] and while it may not have been formally stated Shakespeare was now synonymous with the American nation and language.

Across the United States, familiarity with Shakespeare's text, brought about by exposure to it in the school classroom, helped to secure a position for Shakespeare within national culture, coming as it did at a time when

America was both choosing and celebrating symbols that were to represent American identity.

THE DESIRE FOR SELF-IMPROVEMENT

In her autobiography, Elizabeth Oakes Smith, poet and writer of dime novels, wrote of the period after her marriage in Portland in 1823. She often read Shakespeare aloud to her husband and others, but she commented that 'they little knew how I went to school to Shakespeare and absorbed his teaching into my Pilgrim blood . . . how women needed just such a creation as Richard Third to set them thinking'.[43] For Smith, Shakespeare provided education and personal inspiration.

In the preface to the 1859 edition of *Shakespeare's Works*, the editor Mary Cowden Clarke captured the feeling of Smith and many other Americans when she linked Shakespeare with themes of self-development, liberty and Anglo-Saxonism.[44] In the first line she informed the reader that 'Shakespeare's works are a library in themselves.' Clarke then went on to suggest that 'A poor lad, possessing no other book might, on this single one, make himself a gentleman and a scholar. A poor girl, studying no other volume, might become a lady in heart and soul.'[45] This preface was carefully constructed to appeal to the hopes and aspirations of the millions of 'new' Americans.

In a country where the Christian Bible had hitherto often been considered the only book needed to guide an American, Shakespeare was now offered as a supplement or even as a replacement. As Americans travelled westwards across the lands acquired as the result of 'manifest destiny', there was little room for books. Clarke argued that the works of Shakespeare should be an exception in that they were a 'library in themselves'.

Clarke's preface went on to link the vocabulary of Shakespeare (Clarke being the author of *The Complete Concordance to Shakespeare*)[46] with 'oratorical powers' that aided the cause of liberty, while she suggested that 'Shakespeare may be taken as a standard for language . . . manly [and] genuine Saxon English.'[47]

Though not American, Clarke was specifically chosen to write the preface for this edition by its New York publisher.[48] The preface was skilfully written to appeal to a wide American public, and her adoption of the now established style of publishing Shakespeare without 'distracting notes'[49] clearly identifies this edition with the mood of mid-nineteenth-century America. The publisher set out to capitalise on the acceptance of Shakespeare as a text to be read by all Americans, and perhaps especially by frontier families. This marketing of Shakespeare as an aid for families was undoubtedly helped by the fact that Clarke was a female editor. Indeed she was the first woman to break into the hitherto male-dominated world of Shakespearean scholarship.[50]

The concept of Shakespeare as a possible panacea for personal problems is present in a semi-autobiographical novel by New Englander Elizabeth Stoddard. In a story of a woman growing up in Massachusetts between 1830 and 1850, Stoddard's ailing heroine is advised by the fictional doctor to 'keep [her] feet warm . . . And read Shakespeare.'[51] Another respected novelist, Louisa May Alcott, reflected American interest in Shakespeare's educational properties. In *Little Women*, the heroine and aspiring author is given a copy of Shakespeare by her mentor, the volume described as one of his most treasured possessions. As he makes his gift, his words echo the sentiment of the preface by Mary Cowden Clarke. Alcott has her character offer Shakespeare as a 'library' all in a single book:

You say often you wish a library: here I gif you one; for between these two lids (he meant covers) is many books in one. Read him well, and he will help you much; for the study of character in this book will help you to read it in the world, and paint it with your pen.[52]

While American women writers worked to overcome the difficulties of succeeding in a 'masculine' society, Shakespeare can be seen to have influenced their progress, while at the same time his works were promoted to a wider readership.

American newspaper stories also confirm that many citizens looked to Shakespeare as a means to self-development. An item from Cincinnati highlighted the activities of 'F. J. Furnivall with others', who, like many, had started a society to study Shakespeare. The piece suggested that 'youths' who devoted a year or two to Latin and Greek were wasting their time. In the writer's view, they should rethink their priorities, as 'there is no-one, it matters not what is his calling or what his social position who could not derive pleasure and instruction from Shakespeare'.[53]

As Shakespeare and the societies set up to celebrate the drama he created became part of social activity, the American press across the country reprinted 'syndicated' stories and in so doing influenced many millions of Americans. In 1850, a story of how a society in New York celebrated Shakespeare's date of birth was regarded as news in New Orleans, but such was the interest in Shakespeare, or anything associated with Shakespeare, that newspaper editors happily recycled such items.[54] When a Cincinnati newspaper itself celebrated the anniversary of the playwright's birth, the editor confirmed for the readers what was obvious to many, that 'In almost every American community there is some organisation in the name of Shakespeare, a club or a society, the effect of which is at least to foster a taste for the poet.'[55]

The early life of writer and editor William Dean Howells provides an example of a young man living in a society motivated by the desire for self-improvement who turned towards Shakespeare. Howells was born in 1837 in the small town of Martin's Ferry, Ohio. His printer father's background was Welsh and his mother's German. At the age of sixteen, when living in Dayton, Ohio, Howells, already exposed to Shakespeare's plays on the stage, was inspired to read them by workers in his father's print shop. He was to write 'Printers in the old-time offices were always spouting Shakespeare more or less, and I suppose I could not have kept away from him much longer in the nature of things.'[56] For leisure, Howells would take a copy of Shakespeare into the countryside and, together with a friend, would read aloud, a process that would develop a number of the skills thought to be helpful to the advancement of a small-town boy. Though he later felt embarrassed by his adoration of the playwright, he was to confess that his 'worship of Shakespeare went to heights and lengths that it had reached with no earlier idol, and there was a supreme moment, once, when I found myself saying that the creation of Shakespeare was as great as the creation of a planet'.[57]

Howells's family background was not English. He was not wealthy or subject to the influences of a large eastern cosmopolitan city. Yet even in a small town in Ohio in 1853 Shakespeare was an 'idol' to whom he was happy to devote many leisure hours. Howells later wrote the presidential campaign biography for Abraham Lincoln and became a successful novelist and influential American literary critic.

Henry Thoreau, who had been a student at Concord Academy and was later to attend Harvard College, followed the now standard educational practice of performing declamatory exercises from Shakespeare.[58] He was another American who considered Shakespeare a tool for strengthening the mind of democratic America. In *Walden*, in a chapter entitled 'Reading', Thoreau promoted the 'classics' and ridiculed contemporary American fiction by describing it as 'gingerbread, baked daily'.[59] It was his contention that democracy was to be achieved through self-education: 'Instead of noblemen, let us have noble villages of men.'[60] 'Books,' he insisted, 'are the treasured wealth of the world and the fit inheritance of generations and nations. Books, the oldest and the best, stand naturally and rightfully on the shelves of every cottage.'[61] And not only every cottage:

When Vaticans shall be filled with Vedas and Zendavestas and Bibles, with Homers and Dantes and Shakespeares, and all the centuries to come shall have successively deposited their trophies in the forum of the world. By such a pile we may hope to scale heaven at last.[62]

While such lofty philosophical aims were not necessarily shared by the millions of Americans seeking self-improvement, it is clear that if they lacked native-born 'equivalents to Descartes, Pascal, or for that matter, Montaigne, Rabelais, Racine, Montesquieu and Rousseau',[63] at least Shakespeare had been positioned as their cultural philosopher. Anthony Trollope, son of Fanny Trollope, recounting his visit to America in 1863, observed, 'An American will perhaps consider himself to be as little like an Englishman as he is like a Frenchman. But he reads Shakespeare through the medium of his own vernacular, and has to undergo the penance of a foreign tongue before he can understand Molière.'[64] The point, while perhaps obvious, does emphasise why, at this point in American ethnogenesis, Shakespeare so quickly became the preferred text for citizens from all social backgrounds and ancestry.

SOUTH OF THE MASON-DIXON LINE

The issues that finally brought about the War of Secession (1861–5) went far beyond the abolition of slavery. When, during the first half of the century, writers and commentators in New England had espoused the creation of a national literature celebrating a common heritage, their counterparts in the South, such as the Charleston Group, had similar dreams. While the northern writers conceived the nation 'largely in their own image', however, the southern writers, born with a different cultural perspective, visualised the 'nation' in distinctly southern terms. In his poem 'Ethnogenesis' of 1861, the writer Henry Timrod, described by Alfred Lord Tennyson as 'the Laureate of the Confederacy',[65] expressed the hope that 'at last, we are a nation among nations'.[66] Despite the North–South cultural differences that would so tragically become polarised as a result of war, the national literature that both groups of writers hoped to create was constructed from a single language and a single 'old world' cultural source. This source was the now Anglo-Saxonised Shakespeare.

Just as national identity had been introduced into American editions of Shakespeare, so a concern with nation in the South also led in Shakespeare's direction. In his 'Address Delivered at the Opening of the New Theatre at Richmond',[67] a poem first read to the public in February 1863 as the death toll of the war mounted, Timrod symbolised 'history as a stage on which are enacted the various phases of southern culture, each represented by characters drawn from Shakespeare's plays'.[68] This contribution to the national literature of America was created using the characters and imagery that were well known to citizens of both North and South. Elements of *The Tempest*, *King Lear*, *Othello* and *Hamlet* were all incorporated in this poem that set out to tell the tale of a tragic, flawed, yet still 'romantic' world. To Timrod, the South was a distinct subculture, separate yet part of the developing political 'condition' that was America.

Christina Murphy has argued that before 1865 southern writers often compared their collective situation to that of Hamlet, in that, like him, the South had 'been chosen in a corrupt world for the role of bringing justice and creating an enduring peace in a new rule'.[69] Timrod makes this very comparison and Murphy paraphrases his poetry: 'Like the South, Hamlet is slow to rise to the call – "He pauses on the very brink of fact / To toy as with the shadow of an act" – but, once challenged, he fights bravely and is willing to sacrifice his life for the attainment of noble ideals.'[70]

At a time when Walt Whitman was declaring himself a bard for the American nation, Timrod, from his home in Charleston, wrote the essay 'Literature in the South' (1859), in which he 'saw clearly how indifferent southern culture was to the development of a significant national [American] literature'.[71] He was aware of the cultural gap between the southern experience and the American ideal of northern writers such as Whitman. In some ways Timrod tried to bridge that gap, and Shakespearean imagery was a codex that appeared to embody a shared set of cultural values for both North and South.

A CHURCHYARD IN FREDERICKSBURG

While many southerners were fighting for what they regarded as their democratic rights, others opposed to slavery chose to exile themselves in Europe. One such southerner was Moncure D. Conway, and he helped to provide an interesting episode in America's appropriation of Shakespeare.

In 1864, not surprisingly, there was no official American presence at the tercentenary celebrations of Shakespeare's birth in Stratford-upon-Avon. American journals did, however, carry reports of the memorial events. Conway, now a 'southerner in exile', wrote a ten-page report on the festivities for *Harper's New Monthly Magazine*. Pre-empting Charles Gayley's general thesis, Conway suggested that a friend of Shakespeare had been one of those who had joined the seventeenth-century Virginia colony. Conway, a Unitarian minister, friend of Emerson, born in Stafford County, Virginia, in 1832, and perhaps, as such, a credible local witness, claimed he personally remembered seeing

an old grave stone in the colonial parish church-yard at Fredericksburg, Virginia, on which it was written that beneath was the dust of one who had been 'a pall-bearer at the funeral of William Shakspeare', that being the one thing memorable in a life which ended in the early part of the 17th Century.[72]

Six years later, a poem entitled 'In the Old Churchyard at Fredericksburg', by F. W. Loring, helped to popularise this story of the Virginian grave of a 'friend' of Shakespeare.[73] Any link that could be forged between Shakespeare and American soil, now so heavy with the dead of the many battles fought around Fredericksburg, was timely, and Loring's poem appealed to romantic as well as nationalistic Americans:

> For in the churchyard at Fredericksburg
> Juliet seemed to love,
> Hamlet mused, and old Lear fell,
> Beatrice laughed, and Ariel
> Gleamed through skies above,
> As here, beneath this stone,
> Lay in his narrow hall,
> He who before had borne the pall
> At the funeral of Shakespeare.

Unfortunately, this Fredericksburg grave proved to be a pure fiction.

In 1886 Conway confessed his error and argued that the American grave of Shakespeare's 'pall-bearer' was a complete myth.[74] His six-page article for *Harper's*, published twenty-two years after he himself had first promoted the myth, documented how newspapers in America had happily repeated and 'improved' on a story that appears to have originated from a misunderstood transcription of a diary entry made by an unidentified American soldier at the 'Battle of the Wilderness' in 1864. Conway, stimulated by both the story and memories of happier times during his childhood around Fredericksburg, believed he had himself seen the gravestone together with its inscription. With his romantic interest in Shakespeare, and his desire to associate his nation with the playwright, he became involved in popularising a myth that lasted at least twenty-two years.

SHAKESPEARE BY OTHER MEANS

Along with Mary Cowden Clarke, many other women helped to encourage popular interest in Shakespeare. One such woman was Fanny Kemble, who became famous for her public readings of Shakespeare. She arrived in New York in September 1832 with her actor father, Charles Kemble, to undertake a theatrical tour that was to last until June 1834. The Kembles toured American theatres performing a variety of plays but chiefly those of Shakespeare. Despite being an actress, however, Fanny Kemble is best remembered for capitalising on the surviving Puritan concern about public morals and the negative influence of theatre entertainment.

True to their Puritan traditions, from as early as 1750 the city authorities in Boston had banned all theatrical performances, and it was not until 10 August 1792 that Shakespeare was openly performed in the Boston New Exhibition Room. In an effort to avoid the accusation of encouraging moral depravity, both *Hamlet* and *Romeo and Juliet* were advertised in the city not as plays but as 'moral lectures'.[75] The same fears haunted the authorities in Philadelphia and the same tactics were used to subvert their restrictions. On 25 July 1867, while the theatre in the city was still closed, *Hamlet* was performed under the disguised title of 'Filial Piety'.[76] In addition to Boston and Philadelphia, objections to theatre performances were later also voiced in the New York press. The Reverend Robert Turnbull attacked the American stage, suggesting that all the theatres should be destroyed. Turnbull wrote that he hoped to see (Shakespeare notably excluded) all the 'comedies, tragedies and farces in the world, heaped and blazing together in one grand funeral pile'.[77]

This type of concern over theatre and public morals was a subject of conversation at a dinner party attended by Fanny Kemble in Boston in 1833. In her journal she recounts a conversation with the Reverend William E. Channing, the man who first called for a national literature. Channing offered the opinion that Shakespeare could very well be broken up into passages for declamation in 'private assemblies', thereby avoiding the need for 'theatrical exhibitions'.[78]

Kemble seems to have taken Channing's suggestion seriously, as newspapers were soon reporting her success in giving 'Shakespeare readings in Boston and New York to crowded houses'.[79] In Washington a journalist reported that Mrs Kemble had given 'her readings of Shakespeare to as large a deeply interested audience as could be gathered in the Eastern cities'.[80] Raoul Granqvist referred to Kemble as 'the high priestess of the inspired Bard', touring America for twenty years from 1849 to 1869, 'reading from Shakespeare's plays for audiences who were opposed to theatre'.[81] Significantly, Fanny Kemble's readings, delivered over those twenty years, would reach many Americans who were not prepared to attend the public playhouse. Though theatre was disapproved of, Shakespeare was then so integral to popular American culture that, even for the puritan-minded, means had to be found to allow everyone to share in his imagery.

AFRICAN-AMERICANS AND AMERICA'S SHAKESPEARE

Some Americans who, on account of their origins, could not lay claim to a tradition of the English language or Shakespeare nevertheless responded to burgeoning cultural conditioning. William Wells Brown, an escaped slave, became one of the first African-American novelists.[82] His novel *Clotel*, although written while Brown was in London, was published in America in 1860, and Shakespeare was to provide epigraphs for two of his chapters. Another African-American, abolitionist and orator Frederick Douglass, used Shakespeare for the main epigraph of his only work of fiction, *The Heroic Slave. A Thrilling Narrative of the Adventures of Madison Washington, in Pursuit of Liberty*.[83] In his other role as newspaper editor, Douglass supplied his readership with stories of the struggle for emancipation, frequently interspersed with the name and subject of Shakespeare. Other newspapers that promoted the abolitionist cause were to utilise Shakespeare in a similar manner.[84]

However, it was the American theatre that first seemed to offer African-Americans the opportunity for greater expression of their aspiration towards equality. An episode that can be seen to combine several aspects of nineteenth-century society occurred in 1821, when William Henry Brown, a West-Indian-born American ex-seaman, founded the African Grove Theatre in lower Manhattan. After initially attracting an audience of African-Americans to shows of music and vaudeville entertainment, Brown formed a company of African-American actors. This theatre company launched the careers of actors such as James Hewlett and Ira Aldridge.[85] Both men readily accepted Shakespearean roles portraying free soldier-aristocrats. Significantly, the first of Shakespeare's plays to be performed by the African-American company was *Richard III*, which had been the first to be performed in New York seventy-one years earlier on 5 March 1750. It was no accident that the play chosen was one that portrays the Machiavellian villainy of a member of the English aristocracy. However, the newspapers of 1821 give an indication of the theatre establishment's reaction to the fact that Shakespeare was now being performed by African-American actors. The story of New York's newest theatre and a review of the performance of *Richard III* were written for the *National Advocate* by Mordecai Noah:

These imitative inmates of the kitchen and pantries . . . were determined to have some kind of amusement [and] they resolved to set up a play and the upper apartments of the neglected African Grove were pitched upon for the purpose. *Richard III*, after mature deliberation, was agreed upon, and a little dapper, woolly-headed waiter at the City Hotel personated the royal Plantagenet.[86]

The hostility and sarcasm of the reviewer was clear, and after further 'criticism' of the performance of actor James Hewlett, one-time waiter and ex-servant to the English actor George Frederick Cooke, Noah concluded his piece by informing his readers that at the end of the play 'Richard and Catesby were unfortunately taken up by the Watch' (i.e. they were arrested).[87]

Following this reversal of fortune, on 1 October 1821 the theatre company moved to a new address very close to the Park Theatre in Park Row, later to be known as Chatham Street. This new location brought Brown's African company into direct competition with the management of the Park Theatre, which had just reopened following a fire and which had a friend and supporting playwright in the personage of the editor of the *National Advocate*, one Mordecai Noah.

The hostility of both the New York press and the police was to continue, and a subsequent story provided added ingredients that some New Yorkers would perhaps have regarded as provocative. Although slavery had been abolished in the city as early as 1799, the practice of racial segregation was still enforced in New York theatres. As Henry Fearon had observed in 1818, 'A part of the gallery is allotted for Negroes, they not being admitted into any other part of the house.'[88] The company of William Brown was to invert this segregation. As the *National Advocate* reported, 'The gentlemen of color announce another play at their Pantheon, corner of Bleecker and Mercer Streets on Monday evening . . . they have graciously made a partition at the back of their house for accommodation of the whites.'[89]

The fact that African-American actors were now to present Shakespeare, adjacent to the prestigious Park Theatre, to a mixed-race audience with the 'white' New Yorkers segregated in the rear inflamed an already tense situation. Some New Yorkers were less than happy that what they regarded as 'freed slaves' were succeeding in the theatre business. When Gustave de Beaumont speculated about the cause of a later New York race riot (1834), he concluded that 'as long as the freed Negroes show themselves submissive and respectful to the whites, as long as they hold themselves to a position of inferiority, they are assured of support and protection',[90] and it can be surmised that establishing a theatre was considered an act that was far from submissive. For New Yorkers, this was perhaps one step too far towards E Pluribus Unum.

A newspaper report in the *New York American* on 10 January 1822 provides an account of the response by the city authorities. Under the headline 'Hung Be the Heavens with Black-Shakespeare', the piece describes how, after a closure order from the New York police had been defied, a pathetic if amusing scene took place:

> It appears that the sable managers, not satisfied with a small share of the profit and a great portion of fame, determined to rival the Great Park Theatre . . . and accordingly hired the hotel next door to the theatre. It was at length considered necessary to interpose the arm of authority, and on Monday evening a dozen watchmen made part of the audience. The play was Richard. The watchmen interrupted the royal Plantagenet in one of his soliloquies with 'Hello you – there – come along with me'. Richard replied with a real tragic grin 'Fellow begone – I'm not at leisure' . . . So forthwith Richard, Lady Ann, the dead King Henry, Queen Elizabeth and the Two young Princes were escorted . . . to the watch house.[91]

The image of 'English royalty' being led away under guard and imprisoned in a New York jail was, no doubt, quite to the taste of the readers, and the report concluded with the suggestion that the actors were finally released after they had promised 'never to act Shakespeare again'.[92] It is interesting to note that the works of other playwrights were not so proscribed, only those of Shakespeare. Thus, the first attempt by a group of African-Americans to share in what had become the cultural tradition of America was suppressed by members of the New York Establishment.

To better understand why the city authorities took such oppressive action, it is necessary to consider the restrictive laws of the period. At this time, some southern states regarded teaching a slave to read as a criminal act. In South Carolina, for example, even in 1835, the law imposed a fine of one hundred dollars on a master who taught his or her slaves to read.[93] In 1831, when reporting the rebellion led by Nat Turner, newspapers commented negatively on the fact that he had been taught to read, suggesting that this may have been responsible for his rebellious independent thought. Many in the South considered reading a dangerous pastime in African-Americans, and perhaps similar fears surfaced in New Yorkers when they discovered the African Grove Company not only reading but performing Shakespeare, complete with portrayals of the overthrow of tyrants.

With the suppression of the African Grove Theatre, the political elite underlined their conviction that Shakespeare could, in certain hands, promote the idea of liberty and democratic rebellion. For some

Anglo-Americans, the spectre of African-Americans learning from Shakespeare was something to be suppressed, not welcomed.

While responsibility for the final closure of what was now known as Brown's Theatre remains a matter for speculation, the involvement of New York officials in the process is clear. A key opponent of Brown's Theatre was Mordecai Noah. In addition to his role as journalist, he was also a sheriff, politician and writer of patriotic plays. Noah represents the type of complex character found in the post-Revolution period. Like so many of his contemporaries he was an American nationalist, and his biographer suggests that he had a 'reputation as waver of the flag and as patriot-in-chief to the management of the Park'.[94] Several years earlier, in 1809, Noah had reissued a book by New-York-born Charlotte Ramsey Lennox, first published in London in 1793.[95] This book suggested possible sources for the stories contained in Shakespeare's plays, and Noah added to Lennox's text his own criticism of the moral and religious content he regarded as typical of decadent England.[96] By this act Noah demonstrated his cultural interest in Shakespeare and betrayed the political overtones that would dominate his own theatrical offerings.

In the middle of the period when Brown's Theatre was facing opposition, Noah premiered a new play at the Park Theatre. On 'Evacuation Day', 25 November 1821, amidst festivities celebrating the removal of British forces from New York, *Marion, or The Hero of Lake George* was presented to an enthusiastic audience. Into this patriotic play about an American victory over the English troops during the War of Independence Noah interwove a motif from *Romeo and Juliet*,[97] thereby combining portrayal of anti-English sentiment with appropriation of Shakespeare.

But Noah's actions against Brown's Theatre and America's loss of acting talent was to be to England's advantage. Following the theatre's closure, actor Ira Aldridge left the United States for a successful stage career in England and Europe. In 1826, he made his London debut as Othello, billed as the 'African Roscius' after the great Roman comic actor, and he later toured Europe playing several Shakespearean roles, including King Lear and Macbeth. He became a British citizen in 1863.

THE CHEROKEE NATION

Shakespeare also played a small part in the cultural interaction between Anglo-Americans and American Indians. As early as 2 November 1752, *Othello* was performed in front of the 'Emperor and Empress' of the Cherokee nation.[98] Fifteen years later, in 1767, two newspaper reports tell the story of how three chiefs of the Cherokee nation, Atakullakulla, Ouconnostota and the Raven King of Toogoloo, together with six other 'chiefs and Warriors', were received by General Gage.[99] These Cherokee chiefs were entertained during their Saturday night in New York at the recently opened John Street Theatre with a performance of *Richard III*.[100] The newspaper reported that the Cherokees 'regarded the play with seriousness and attention' and that their 'Countenances and Behaviour were rather expressive of Surprize and Curiosity, than any other Passions. Some of them were much surprized and diverted at the Tricks of HARLEQUIN.' According to William Dunlap, this harlequin was part of a separate entertainment, a farce called 'The Oracle and Harlequin's Vagaries' staged by the American Company, and the visiting Cherokee dignitaries, unable to communicate their thoughts in any other way, attempted to reciprocate by offering their hosts a 'war dance'.[101]

While no evidence can be found that the Cherokees, the most 'assimilated' nation of American Indians, ever regularly became part of the audience for Shakespeare, an episode from their forced expulsion from Georgia once more demonstrates how Shakespeare became a form of American cultural lingua franca. A front-page report in the bilingual newspaper the *Cherokee Phoenix and Indian Advocate* carried details of a debate that took place in the US Senate concerning treaties signed between the Cherokees and the United States government. Senator John Forsyth, speaking on behalf of the state of Georgia, maintained that an agreement between itself and the federal government allowed Georgia to claim all land within state borders. 'I will have my bond, I will have my pound of flesh', he exclaimed.[102] Senator Peleg Sprague of Maine, cousin to Charles Sprague, took up this reference to *The Merchant of Venice* and argued against the injustice of Shylock's claim, hence supporting the continued presence of the Cherokee nation on their traditional lands. With this exchange, two parties, on opposite sides in a uniquely American dispute, communicated their ideals by use of the now widely recognised language of Shakespeare. The fact that this debate concerned the future of the Cherokee nation, and was reported in detail in the only newspaper published by and for American Indians, is an indication of the extent of Shakespeare's appropriation.

VOICES OF MALCONTENTS

While Americans on the frontier were learning to declaim Shakespeare in school or were enjoying rowdy burlesque performances on makeshift stages, some American writers imbued with the nationalist spirit struggled to accept Shakespeare as part of American heritage. As Peter Rawlings observed, 'For some, Shakespeare's location in the feudal past and the aristocratic values his plays were seen as advocating represented a threat to the republic.'[103] Rawlings named Orestes Brownson, George Wilkes and Jones Very, suggesting they considered Shakespeare a 'supreme problem for burgeoning American writers in search of cultural distinctiveness'.[104]

Herman Melville was another malcontent who, while personally deeply appreciative of Shakespeare, expressed concern about the extent of the populist appropriation and what he described as 'blind, unbridled admiration'.[105] That Melville had conformed to the nineteenth-century American 'norm' is demonstrated by his purchase of a copy of Shakespeare prior to completing *Moby-Dick*, and it seems likely that this purchase inspired what appears to have been a major change in the course taken by both the *Pequod* and the whale as Melville completed the manuscript.[106] In his personal copy of Shakespeare it is still possible to read the numerous marginalia he made, including notes about characters to be developed in *Moby-Dick*.[107]

Melville was later to draw even more directly on Shakespeare when he sketched a series of contemporaneous scenes for his novel *The Confidence-Man*. In it he included twenty references to Shakespeare, covering eleven separate plays. One character, perhaps reflecting Melville's personal concern, complained that 'Shakespeare has got to be a kind of deity. Prudent minds, having certain latent thoughts concerning him, will reserve them in a condition of lasting probation.'[108]

Despite his own literary appreciation of Shakespeare, Melville commented directly on the apparent paradox of American recognition of a 'foreign' playwright in the essay 'Hawthorne and His Mosses' (1850). In this essay Melville praised Nathaniel Hawthorne's literary skills and suggested that American readers should consider Hawthorne and Shakespeare as comparable. While he also argued against American authors continuing to write in the shadow of English writers, his praise for Hawthorne repeated the very practice to which he objected: 'I do not say that Nathaniel of Salem is greater than William of Avon, or as great. But the difference between the two men is by no means immeasurable.'[109] The suggestion was that both Hawthorne and Shakespeare were 'masters of the great Art of Telling the Truth';[110] it was just that Hawthorne was telling a truth as America experienced it.

For Melville, the combination of the appropriation of Shakespeare and the cause of American nationalism had become a frustrating problem, now that 'The absolute and unconditional adoration of Shakespeare has grown to be part of our Anglo-Saxon superstitions.'[111] He pointed out for his contemporaries 'that in his own lifetime, Shakespeare was not Shakespeare but only master William Shakespeare of the shrewd, thriving business firm of Condell, Shakespeare & Co.'.[112] With this Melville acknowledged the fact that from the publication of the 'First American Edition' in 1795 the process of appropriation had first created and then elevated a symbolic Shakespeare to a height greater than thought reasonable in his own time or in the country of his birth. Melville's quite rational appeal to his fellow citizens went largely unheard.

Melville criticised the then social reality that, as an American, 'You must believe in Shakespeare's un-approachability or quit the country.'[113] Melville, perhaps bitter and frustrated at the lack of public recognition his own work had received, chose to praise Hawthorne while attacking the idolisation of an English playwright. Self-interest and nationalism combined to provoke his appeal to his countrymen that 'no American writer should write like an Englishman, or a Frenchman; let him write like a man, for then he will be sure to write like an American'.[114] Melville echoed the anti-English journalism of the Fourth of July orations when he added, 'believe it or not England, after all, is, in many things, an alien to us'.[115] While comments such as these were critical of Shakespeare's popularity in America, however, it appears Melville's main target was the rowdy and unqualified acclaim by an unschooled populace rather than the plays themselves.

A short article published in Evert A. Duyckinck's *Literary World* provides an additional illustration of the issue that was to preoccupy some malcontents. The writer (possibly Melville or Duyckinck) again highlighted the extent to which, by the mid-nineteenth century, Americans consumed Shakespeare. Directly addressing America, the article declared, 'We have the plays of Shakspeare every night in scores of theatres in city and country, packet ships, halls, hotels, steamboats, sailing, steaming, constantly opening and taking their drinks and dinners in the name of Shakspeare.'[116] It went on to say, however, 'Shakspeare is not popular in America . . . he is but imperfectly understood, and is rather a tradition than a reality.'[117] These seemingly contradictory statements were to be explained as the article proceeded by criticising the lack of intellectual development of American citizens, who, it suggested, merely 'bolted' Shakespeare down like 'children', hungry diners consuming the 'greatest amount of animal food in the shortest time',[118] quite unlike a culturally mature people who might be expected to appreciate the finer subtleties of the drama. The message to American citizens was 'We are in a formative state, and have not yet reached the appreciation of such niceties. We must live and learn . . . We cannot as yet quite digest Shakspeare – he is rather too much for us.'[119] While the article was critical of the level of unbridled celebration of Shakespeare, once more censure was directed towards the behaviour of the populace.

Melville was not alone in his public pronouncements on the problems of appropriating Shakespeare for America while, at the same time, attempting to create a distinct national identity. Walt Whitman, while claiming that 'as a boy or young man I had seen (reading them carefully the day beforehand) quite all Shakspere's acting dramas',[120] also disputed Shakespeare's position in American culture. As the editor of the *Brooklyn Daily Eagle*, Whitman praised what he described as 'the indomitable energy of the Anglo-Saxon character', but in his role as the self-proclaimed 'national' poet he criticised the increasing popularity of Shakespeare as an Anglo-American icon.[121] In 1855 Whitman asked the question 'What play of Shakspeare, represented in America, is not an insult to America, to the marrow in its bones?'[122] In *Democratic Vistas* he argued that foreign poems, 'Shakspere included, are poisonous to the idea of the pride and dignity of the common people, the life blood of democracy'.[123] Whitman, like Melville, shared the spirit of nationalism that had now permeated nineteenth-century America and, like Melville, he sought the acceptance of his own work in a country that consumed increasing quantities from the pen of a 'foreign' playwright. While he appreciated the aesthetic quality of Shakespeare's plays, he felt that they presented the American audience with glorified examples of a society in which 'Feudalism is unrival'd'.[124]

According to Whitman, Shakespeare failed to meet the republican challenge. In the 1855 preface to *Leaves of Grass* he stated that 'The attitude of great poets is to cheer up the slaves and horrify despots.'[125] This assertion was omitted from later editions, perhaps to avoid a hostile response from any pro-slavery countrymen, but the implication was that 'great' poets had a responsibility to promote the American concept of republicanism. For Whitman, the work of Shakespeare and other British writers constituted the antithesis of what America believed it represented. Whitman was to write that 'Walter Scott and Tennyson, like Shakspere, exhale that principle of caste which we Americans have come on earth to destroy.'[126]

While Whitman was a very notable voice in arguing against the suitability of Shakespeare for nineteenth-century America, the strength of his expressed opposition diminished as the century progressed. Alwin Thaler observed that 'within ten years [of] *Democratic Vistas* Whitman had substantially qualified the assertion that the great poems are poisonous to the lifeblood of democracy'.[127] The 'qualification' supplied by Whitman was that in portraying the 'worse excesses' of European feudal society 'Shakspere . . . performs a service incalculably precious to . . . America.'[128]

But as we have seen, while not all America's aspiring writers were content that their fellow citizens so freely honoured and consumed Shakespeare, even when writing in protest their actions helped to confirm his pre-eminence within nineteenth-century popular culture. As the main evidence presented in this book suggests, the voice of these malcontents among the literati, whatever their number, proved to be weak and unable to curb the vigorous appetites of the democratic populace.

In this chapter I have argued that, unlike some writers such as Melville and Whitman, many Americans unreservedly regarded Shakespeare as an important icon and part of their collective cultural heritage. The producers of American popular culture and the population that consumed it, whether female or male, Anglo-American or African-American, generally accepted Shakespeare as part of their shared national literature. For many Americans, the Declaration of Independence, the US Constitution and Shakespeare were familiar documents around which ideas of a national identity revolved.

NOTES

1. Irving, *The Sketch Book of Geoffrey Crayon*, p. 106.
2. Ibid.
3. Ibid., p. 107.
4. Ibid., introduction by editor William L. Hedges, p. vii.
5. Cooper, 'Notions of the Americans' p. 20.
6. Marder, *His Exits and His Entrances*, p. 297.
7. Walt Whitman, 'Have We a National Literature?', *North American Review*, 152/412 (March 1891), p. 332.
8. William E. Channing, 'Remarks on National Literature', in *The Works of William Channing* (Boston MA: American Unitarian Association, 1866), pp. 243–77.
9. Ibid., p. 243.
10. Ibid.
11. Ibid., p. 245.
12. Ibid., pp. 245–51.
13. Ibid., p. 262.
14. Ibid., p. 266.
15. For an in-depth study of Emerson, transcendentalism and Shakespeare, see Matthiessen, *American Renaissance*.
16. Ralph Waldo Emerson, 'The American Scholar', in Emerson, *Nature Addresses and Lectures* (Cambridge MA: Houghton, Mifflin & Co., 1883). Delivered to an audience in Cambridge, Massachusetts, on 31 August 1837.
17. Ibid., p. 92.

18. Ibid.
19. Ibid., p. 113.
20. Merton M. Sealts, *Emerson on the Scholar* (Columbia: University of Missouri Press, 1992), p. 221.
21. Emerson, *Representative Men*, p. 8.
22. Ibid., p. 5.
23. Ibid., p. 215.
24. Sealts, *Emerson on the Scholar*, p. 223.
25. Ralph Waldo Emerson, *English Traits*, ed. Howard Mumford Jones (Cambridge MA: Belknap Press, 1966).
26. Sealts, *Emerson on the Scholar*, p. 221.
27. Ibid., p. 224.
28. Marder, *His Exits and His Entrances*, p. 298.
29. Ibid.
30. Whitman, 'Have We a National Literature?', p. 333.
31. Ibid., p. 335.
32. William Dean Howells, 'Editor's Study', *Harper's New Monthly Magazine*, 83/498 (November 1891), p. 963.
33. William Dean Howells, 'Literary Boston Thirty Years Ago', *Harper's New Monthly Magazine*, 91/546 (November 1895), p. 866.
34. Ibid., p. 867.
35. Ibid.
36. Ruth Miller Elson, *Guardians of Tradition* (Lincoln NE: University of Nebraska Press, 1964), p. 6 (US Bureau of Education data).
37. Ibid.
38. Marder, *His Exits and His Entrances*, p. 281. See also the chapter 'Un-willingly to School'.
39. Elson, *Guardians of Tradition*, p. 7.
40. Marder, *His Exits and His Entrances*, p. 282.
41. Henry W. Simon, *The Reading of Shakespeare in American Schools and Colleges* (New York: Simon & Schuster, 1932), p. 26.
42. Theodore Roosevelt, *American Ideals and Other Essays, Social and Political* (New York: G. P. Putnam's Sons, 1897), p. 26. See the chapter 'True Americanism'.
43. Elizabeth Oakes Smith, *The Autobiography of Elizabeth Oakes Smith*, ed. Mary Alice Wyman (Lewiston ME: Lewiston Journal Co., 1924), p. 56. Smith wrote a succesful dime novel, *Bald Eagle; or, The Last of the Ramapaughs, a Romance of Revolutionary Times* (New York: Beadle & Co., 1867).
44. *Shakespeare's Works*, ed. Mary Cowden Clarke (New York: D. Appleton & Co., 1859), pp. v–vi.
45. Ibid., p. v.
46. Mary Cowden Clarke, *The Complete Concordance to Shakespeare* (London: Bickers, 1886). First published 1845.
47. *Shakespeare's Works*, ed. Clarke, p. v.
48. Westfall, *American Shakespearean Criticism*, p. 150.

49. Ibid., pp. 79–80.
50. Ibid., p. 150.
51. Elizabeth Stoddard, *The Morgesons* (New York: Penguin, 1984), p. 87. First published 1862. Quotations from both *The Merchant of Venice* and *Antony and Cleopatra* also appeared.
52. Louisa May Alcott, *Little Women* (New York: Penguin, 1989), p. 343. First published 1868. Alcott's heroine Jo later notes in her journal, 'I could . . . talk now about "my library"; as if I had a hundred books.' There are also references to both *Macbeth* and *The Merchant of Venice*.
53. 'Shakespearean Study', *Daily Enquirer* (Cincinnati), 6 February 1876.
54. See 'St George's Day in New York', *Daily Picayune* (New Orleans), 9 May 1850.
55. 'Shakespeare', *Commercial Cincinnati*, 23 April 1877.
56. William Dean Howells, *My Literary Passions* (New York: Harper & Bros., 1895), p. 71.
57. Ibid., p. 73.
58. Walter Harding, *The Days of Henry Thoreau* (Newport: Alfred A. Knopf, 1966), pp. 18–38.
59. Henry Thoreau, *The Portable Thoreau*, ed. Carl Bode (New York: Penguin, 1947), p. 358. First published 1854.
60. Ibid., p. 362.
61. Ibid.
62. Ibid., p. 356.
63. Allan Bloom, *The Closing of the American Mind* (New York: Simon & Schuster, 1987), p. 53. Bloom suggests that America as a nation lacked its own philosophical writers and that Shakespeare filled this gap.
64. Anthony Trollope, *North America*, ed. Donald Smalley and Bradford Allen Booth (New York: De Capo Press, 1951), p. 493. First published 1862.
65. Christina Murphy, 'The Artistic Design of Societal Commitment: Shakespeare and the Poetry of Henry Timrod', in Philip C. Kolin, ed., *Shakespeare and Southern Writers: A Study in Influence* (Jackson MS: University Press of Mississippi, 1985), p. 45, n. 1.
66. Henry Timrod, *The Poems of Henry Timrod* (New York: E. J. Hale & Son, 1873), p. 100.
67. Ibid., p. 121. See also *Southern Literary Messenger*, 37/2 (February 1863), pp. 123–4.
68. Murphy, 'The Artistic Design of Societal Commitment', p. 40.
69. Ibid., p. 42.
70. Ibid.
71. Ibid., p. 29.
72. Moncure D. Conway, 'The Shakspeare Tercentenary', *Harper's New Monthly Magazine*, 29/171 (August 1864), p. 342.
73. Frederic Wadsworth Loring, 'In the Old Churchyard at Fredericksburg', *Atlantic Monthly*, 26/155 (September 1870), pp. 273–4.
74. Moncure D. Conway, 'Hunting the Mythical Pall-Bearer', *Harper's New Monthly Magazine*, 72/428 (January 1886), pp. 211–17.

75. Jane Belle Sherzer, *American Editions of Shakespeare: 1753–1866* (Baltimore: Modern Language Association of America, 1907), p. 639.
76. Mary C. Diebals, *Peter Markoe (1752?–1792): A Philadelphia Writer* (Washington DC: Catholic University American Press, 1944), p. 33.
77. Rev. Robert Turnbull, 'Expensiveness of Theatres', *Colored American* (New York), 21 March 1840.
78. Kemble, *Journal of a Young Actress*, p. 169.
79. *Banner of Light* (Boston), 3 March 1858, p. 4.
80. *National Era* (Washington DC), 13 December 1849.
81. Granqvist, *Imitation as Resistance*, p. 186.
82. William Wells Brown, *Clotel; or The President's Daughter: a Narrative of Slave Life in the United States. With a Sketch of the Author's Life* (London: Partridge & Oakey, 1853).
83. Boston, 1853. The epigraph is taken from *Henry VI, Part 2*, Act 4, Scene 1.
84. For further examples of Shakespeare in the African-American press, see *Frederick Douglass's Paper* (Rochester NY), 4 September 1851, and subsequent issues of 8 January 1852 and 10 June 1853. See also *Freedom's Journal* (New York), 21 March 1829, and *Colored American* (New York), 3 August 1839.
85. Herbert Marshall and Mildred Stock, *Ira Aldridge, the Negro Tragedian* (London: Rockliff, 1958).
86. Mordecai Noah, *National Advocate* (New York), 21 September 1821. See Marshall and Stock, *Ira Aldridge*, p. 33.
87. Ibid., p. 34.
88. Fearon, *Sketches of America*, p. 87.
89. *National Advocate* (New York), 27 October 1821. See also Marshall and Stock, *Ira Aldridge*, p. 34. The social significance of this attempt to provide seating segregation in favour of African-Americans amused Fanny Trollope when writing of her visit to New York in 1831. Perhaps utilising a still popular anecdote, she was to comment on a theatre where 'but negroes perform' and 'whites' were restricted to the gallery. See Trollope, *The Domestic Manners of the Americans*, p. 271.
90. Beaumont, *Marie*, p. 242.
91. 'Hung Be the Heavens with Black-Shakespeare', *New York American*, 10 January 1822. See also Marshall and Stock, pp. 35–6.
92. Ibid.
93. Beaumont, *Marie*, pp. 191–2.
94. Isaac Goldberg, *Major Noah: American-Jewish Pioneer* (New York: Alfred A. Knopf, 1937), p. 181.
95. Mordecai Noah, *Shakespeare Illustrated, or, The Novels and Histories on Which the Plays of Shakespeare are Founded, Vol. I. Collected and Translated from the Originals, by Mrs. Lennox; with Critical Remarks and Biographical Sketches of the Writers, by M. M. Noah* (Philadelphia: Bradford & Inskeep, 1809). First published 1753.
96. Westfall, *American Shakespearean Criticism*, pp. 72–3.
97. Goldberg, *Major Noah*, p. 176.

98. Westfall, *American Shakespearean Criticism*, p. 48. Glenn Hughes gives the date as 9 November 1752. See Glenn Hughes, *A History of the American Theatre, 1700–1950* (New York: Samuel French, 1951), p. 17.

99. *Pennsylvania Gazette*, 24 December 1767. Reports filed in New York, dated 14 and 17 December 1767.

100. 12 December 1767. It is assumed that this production was the same as had been presented at the 'new Theatre, in Southwark' (Cedar Street, Philadelphia) with Mr Hallam in the role of Richard, and Mr Douglas as Buckingham. See *Pennsylvania Gazette*, 4 December 1766.

101. William Dunlap, *History of the American Theatre* (New York, 1832), p. 55.

102. *Cherokee Phoenix and Indian Advocate* (New Echota), 3/2 (3 July 1830).

103. Rawlings, ed., *Americans on Shakespeare*, p. 3.

104. Ibid., p. 5.

105. Herman Melville, 'Hawthorne and His Mosses', in Melville, *The Complete Shorter Fiction* (London: Everyman, 1997), p. 239. First published in two parts in Evert A. Duyckinck's *Literary World*, 7 (17 and 24 August 1850).

106. Herman Melville, *Moby-Dick; or, The Whale* (London: Penguin, 1986). First published 1851. For more on Shakespeare's influence on Melville, see William Ellery Sedgewick, *Herman Melville: The Tragedy of Mind* (Cambridge MA: Harvard University Press, 1945).

107. *The Dramatic Works of William Shakspeare; with a Life of the Poet, Original and Selected*, 7 vols. (Boston MA: Hilliard, Gray & Co., 1836). Melville was to later comment upon its 'glorious great type, every letter whereof is a soldier'. See Charles Olson, *Call Me Ishmael* (London: Jonathan Cape, 1967), p. 41.

108. Herman Melville, *The Confidence-Man* (Oxford: Oxford University Press, 1989), p. 229. First published 1856. See also the fictional debate about the moral value of Shakespeare and the advice offered by Polonius, pp. 226–33.

109. Melville, 'Hawthorne and His Mosses', p. 241.

110. Ibid., p. 239.

111. Ibid., p. 240.

112. Ibid.

113. Ibid.

114. Ibid., p. 243.

115. Ibid., p. 242.

116. 'Shakspeare in America', *Literary World*, 7 (July–December 1850), p. 348. Originally published in the edition of 2 November 1850, subtitled 'Review of Thomas De Quincey's *Biographical Essays*'.

117. Ibid.

118. Ibid.

119. Ibid., p. 349.

120. Walt Whitman, *The Collected Writings of Walt Whitman*, ed. G. W. Allen and S. Bradley (New York: New York University Press, 1964), p. 21.

121. *Brooklyn Daily Eagle*, 13 October 1846. Quoted here from Horsman, *Race and Manifest Destiny*, p. 235. Whitman was responding to American military action against Mexico in 1846.

122. Walt Whitman, 'An English and American Poet', *American Phrenological Journal*, 22/4 (October 1855), pp. 90–1.
123. Whitman, *Leaves of Grass*, p. 525.
124. Ibid., p. 476.
125. Ibid., p. 495.
126. Whitman, *Collected Writings*, p. 476.
127. Thaler, *Shakespeare and Democracy*, p. 19.
128. Whitman, *Collected Writings*, p. 476.

CHAPTER 8

The American Scholar and the authorship controversy

The names of the plays that Shakespeare wrote are household words in the mouths of mighty nations.

Theodore Roosevelt

As Shakespeare became widely accepted as a heroic exemplar, a new academic phenomenon arose that appeared to challenge the still emerging bardolatry. Published first in America, questions were raised as to Shakespeare's authorship of the plays. This was not simply a challenge to the accepted identity of the playwright, however. The most prominent name behind the authorship controversy sought to link the playwright irrevocably with the revolutionary ideology behind the foundation of the American nation.

The first public challenge to William Shakespeare's authorship was made in an obscure book by Joseph C. Hart, a New York lawyer and journalist and later a consul for the United States.[1] In 1848 Hart published *The Romance of Yachting*, a book presented to readers as an account of a sailing trip across the Atlantic to Spain. Despite the title, it contained a discourse on 'several favorite and prevailing historical assumptions, which the author . . . made object of [his] dissent'.[2] Among these 'dissents', Hart proposed to rename the city of New York removing what he argued was the 'badge of colonial slavery',[3] and he attacked the tradition of the iconic New England Puritans, preferring to champion the role of the 'Knickerbocker race'[4] of Dutch New Amsterdam. Both these 'dissents' suggest the continuing prevalence of an anti-English sentiment that perhaps also lay behind Hart's challenge over Shakespeare.

With more than thirty-five pages of text he presented a considered and well-argued attack on the idea that all thirty-seven plays had a single author and that this author was William Shakespeare of Stratford-upon-Avon. According to Hart, it was 'a fraud upon the world to thrust his surreptitious fame upon us'. Significantly, he suggested that in future years 'the enquiry will be, *who were the able literary men who wrote the dramas imputed to him?*[5] This question, now made public, appears to be the starting point for much subsequent scholarship. Hart did not himself make any attempt to identify the 'able literary men', however. For him the issue was one of English conceit and a fraud originated primarily by Nicolas Rowe in 1709. Hart concluded his expression of dissent by asking his readers, 'How much good Christian ink has been spent in writing up a worthless subject, I mean Shakspeare in person'.[6]

Though Hart attempted to destroy Shakespeare's personal reputation, he nevertheless seemed to admire the plays. Elsewhere in the book he quoted from *Othello*, while writing on the history of the Moors, and, for his readers' amusement, from Falstaff's celebration of the qualities of Spanish sherry from *Henry IV, Part 2*.

It is difficult to estimate how wide a circulation this book achieved, but it did represent the first published critique of the idea of Shakespeare the solus playwright. What is clear, however, is that some American literati were aware of Hart even if they did not share his views. One such person was Herman Melville, who refused to write a review of the book for his friend Evert Duyckinck.[7]

While Hart may have initiated the process, it is an American woman who is best known for publicising the question of Shakespeare's authorship. In January 1856, Ohio-born Delia Bacon became the first person to raise the issue in an American journal. This time, however, in addition to challenging Shakespeare's authorship, Bacon offered a new and radical approach to the process of appropriating Shakespeare to American tradition. For this new development, the plays were to be distanced not just from the rural folk background and monarchist traditions of England but also from the Warwickshire yeoman family. The difference between Delia Bacon's approach and that of Joseph Hart was that she sought to link the plays with a group of men who she believed to be prophets of republican America. Her leading article in *Putnam's Monthly, A Magazine of Literature, Science, and Art* was to have repercussions that startled many in nineteenth-century society, and it continues to interest some academics today.

For many commentators and writers 'post-Bacon', the focal issue has been the task of unmasking a secret author for the plays. From 1856 to date more than four thousand books and articles have been published on this subject. For the present study, however, the possible existence of an anonymous playwright is not an issue. What is important is the possible motive behind Bacon's search for a secret writer and the link between this motive and the nineteenth-century drive to create an American national tradition that included Shakespeare.

Bacon's assertion that Shakespeare was not responsible for the plays credited to him was recognised by the editor of the respected magazine as controversial, if not mildly heretical. While recognising a journalistic 'scoop', he felt the need to distance his magazine from any criticism that might be provoked by the article. A footnote to 'William Shakespeare and His Plays: An Inquiry Concerning Them' stated that

> In commencing the publication of these bold, original and most ingenious and interesting speculations upon the real authorship of Shakespeare's plays, it is proper for the Editor of *Putnam's Monthly*, in disclaiming all responsibility for their startling view of the questions, to say that they are the result of long and con-scientious investigation on the past of the learned and eloquent scholar, their author; and that the Editor has reason to hope that they will be continued through some future numbers of the Magazine.[8]

The editor of *Putnam's* thus indicated his support for the credentials of Bacon while distancing the magazine from the consequences of her thesis.

With this first article, Bacon set out to create, or in her view discover, the real author or authors of the plays. Her new view of Shakespeare rejected the idea of a mere rural poetic genius in favour of a reformist political writer and democratic republican philosopher. The 'new' Shakespeare was to be liberated from any moral taint or 'player's mercenary motive'[9] associated with the theatre of Elizabethan Southwark in order to fulfil a greater destiny as a proto-American and as a type of founding father.

Connecting Shakespeare with contemporary nineteenth-century schol-arship on the Greek poet Homer, Bacon pointedly chose to employ emo-tive and nationalistic language, referring to Shakespeare as '*our* poet – our Homer'.[10] With this reference, Bacon appeared to claim Shakespeare on behalf of the American people, fully conscious of the heady political atmo-sphere of mid-nineteenth-century America. For Bacon and her audience, Americans were the inheritors of the mantle of a western civilisation that had begun with the Greeks and been passed via the Romans to the English and that had now found its true home with Anglo-Americans. The new Shakespeare that Bacon sought to liberate from what she regarded as Tudor oppression was now part of American tradition, and she argued that it was his 'works . . . that have given our English life and language their imper-ishable claim in the earth'.[11] While Homer may have provided the 'song of the nation'[12] for the Greeks, Bacon now sought to credit Shakespeare with having performed a similar service for America.

For Bacon, the Homeric 'Shakespeare', while being a repository of the tales of Anglo-centric history and civilisation, was too much a passive person of mystery to be worthy of veneration in republican America. While Shakespeare was considered culturally Anglo-Saxon and therefore a member of the 'race' then considered by some Americans to be predestined to advance mankind, Bacon argued that his background and lowly business interests prevented him from creating pre-eminent philosophical texts. The *Putnam's* article makes it quite clear that for Bacon Shakespeare of Stratford-upon-Avon was merely a vulgar actor. Indeed, she compared him to her American contemporary Barnum, 'the prince showman . . . in that stately oriental retreat of his, in Connecticut'.[13] Shakespeare, the financially motivated actor-manager without university education or formal credentials, did not reflect the image of a bold leader of democratic and republican revolution idealised by nineteenth-century American intellectuals and politicians.

Bacon set out to prove that the plays were in fact written by an Anglo-Saxon revolutionary and social visionary who, despite state oppression, strove to inspire a new world. For Bacon, this 'new world' was founded in what had become the United States of America, and if the link to the works of Shakespeare could be legitimised through scholarly endeavour, then an inheritance that would inspire, unite and elevate Americans would be revealed and serve as her personal patriotic contribution.

Bacon chose to refer to the author of the plays as 'the scholar' or 'the philosopher'. Her interest in rejecting the authorship of William Shakespeare appears to have been not to unmask a case of Elizabethan fraud but rather to reveal the link between the plays and an 'immortal group of heroes'[14] that in her later work were to be called 'the Elizabethan men of letters'. She believed that this group of anonymous men, perhaps akin to the influential American writers known as 'Publius' who were responsible for the famous *Federalist* papers,[15] were behind the enlightened train of thought that resulted in the foundation of the colony of Virginia and subsequently the United States of America. Throughout the article Bacon makes it clear that she does not seek to remove the name of Shakespeare from the plays and poems. Her more weighty argument was that the name 'Shakespeare' was the collective noun that described a moment in history when a group of men, all 'subject to an oppressive and despotic censorship [and threatened with] cruel maimings and tortures old and new', sought to promote 'the freedom of the new ages that were then beginning'.[16] With this assertion, Bacon sought not a new personal name for Shakespeare but a new ownership of the name and the 'moment'. If Shakespeare could be identified as the collective voice of a struggle for republican freedom then the owner of this important heritage was now the America nation. Bacon passionately informed her readership 'That [the] moment was there; it is chronicled; we have one word for it; we call it – Shakespeare!'[17]

Bacon had now restated the aspect of appropriation that had been visible in so many poems and orations throughout the early nineteenth century. Her impassioned argument can be seen as an appeal to American readers to acquire the works of Shakespeare, not just as a collection of entertaining plays, but, more importantly, as prophetic text intended for the ethnic group who were destined to civilise the continent of North America. Bacon continued to create the links between the American nation and Shakespeare with her rhetorical question 'Which of our statesmen, our heroes, our divines, our poets, our philosophers, has not learned of him; and in which of all their divergent and multiplying pursuits and experiences do they fail to find him still with them, still before them?'[18] This political and cultural link between the plays collectively known as 'Shakespeare' and America was made even more pronounced with a powerful, if slightly enigmatic, passage designed to link the prevailing spirit of American manifest destiny with a suggestion that both the continent named after an explorer and the plays named after the 'poacher' should have been named differently:

You cannot christen a world anew, though the name that was given to it at the font prove an usurper's. With all that we now know of that heroic scholar, from whose scientific dream the New World was made to emerge at last, in the faces of the mockeries of his time, with all that appreciation of his work which the Old World and the New alike bestow upon it, we cannot yet separate the name of his rival from his hard-earned triumph. What name is it that has drunk the melody, forever, all the music of that hope and promise, which the young continent of Columbus still whispers – in spite of old European evils planted there – still whispers in the troubled earth? Whose name is it that stretches its golden letters, now, from ocean to ocean, from Arctic to Antarctic, whose name now enrings the millions that are born, and live, and die, knowing no world but the world of that patient scholar's dream – no reality, but the reality of his chimera?[19]

Within this enigmatic passage can be found the suggestion that, though Shakespeare was, in Bacon's opinion, a 'usurper' not unlike Amerigo Vespucci, his name was already celebrated in the Americas from 'Arctic to Antarctic'.

While Delia Bacon was later to overtly champion Sir Francis Bacon as the leader of the 'men of letters', she resisted the temptation to dwell on the sensational, preferring to argue that the name 'Shakespeare' represented a group of men and a 'moment'.[20]

Bacon followed her *Putnam's Monthly* article with work on a substantial book of 675 pages. With enthusiastic support and several letters of introduction (one of them to Thomas Carlyle) from none other than Ralph Waldo Emerson, she had, since 1853, been in her temporary base in England preparing the evidence to support her provocative claim. It was Emerson who introduced George Putnam to her work,[21] having written to Bacon after receiving her article in manuscript that 'The account of Englishmen, and what is servile in them, and the prophetic American relations of the poetry, struck me much.'[22] His identification with the idea of the 'prophetic' nature of Shakespeare for America, so important to Bacon's thesis, must have been great encouragement. Emerson had the credentials of a respected American intellectual, and support from him in nineteenth-century America was, as Walt Whitman demonstrated with early editions of *Leaves of Grass*, very valuable.[23] While Emerson did not necessarily accept Bacon's 'proof' for her theory, the idea of a 'hero' philosopher with a dream or 'chimera' that would result in the foundation of the United States proved to be very attractive. It is easy to speculate that Emerson supported Bacon in her literary endeavours because she personally represented 'The American Scholar' and because her thesis, if true, would provide the American nation with a more secure claim to this 'representative man'.

Emerson's letter of introduction to Carlyle ensured that another person sympathetic to Bacon's cause, if not to her thesis, would be able to provide assistance. Carlyle's writings had been well received in the United States during the 1840s, and the *North American Review* had suggested that, despite his writing style and 'ways of thinking', Carlyle was admired in America because 'he manifests a strong friendship for his race'.[24] The *Southern Quarterly Review* supported his supremacist views more enthusiastically, claiming 'the spirit of Thomas Carlyle is abroad in the land. The strong thinker, the earnest soul, is making an impress wherever the Saxon tongue and Saxon blood prevail.'[25] Bacon, who was on a quest to associate America with the 'Saxon blood' and 'Saxon tongue' of the 'prophetic poetry' of Shakespeare, received vital moral support from both men.

When *The Philosophy of the Plays of Shakspere Unfolded* finally appeared in April 1857, it proved to be a development of the earlier narrative of the struggle for freedom and the attempt to establish a new social order in Elizabethan England. However, whether because of her passionate commitment to her cause, her possibly deteriorating mental condition,[26] or her anguish that another person (in England) was about to usurp her thesis, what had previously been coherently argued in *Putnam's Monthly* had now become a rambling and difficult text. Once more, as the title of the book indicates, the key issue for Bacon was not the claimed new identity of the previously hidden writer of the plays. Rather than any single author, it was the philosophy that Bacon intended to 'unfold'.

In her book Bacon analysed passages from several plays including *King Lear, Hamlet, Julius Caesar* and *Coriolanus,* offering the generalised conclusion that the philosopher behind the plays intended to challenge 'the expediency and propriety of permitting *any one man* to impose his individual will on the nation'.[27] Connecting America with the philosophy of the plays, Bacon remarked,

That great question, which was so soon to become the outspoken question of the nation and the age, could already be discussed in all its vexed and complicated relations, in all its aspects and bearings, as deliberately as it could be today; exactly as it was, in fact, discussed not long afterwards in swarms of English pamphlets . . . exactly as it was discussed when that 'lofty Roman Scene' came 'to be acted over' here, with the cold-blooded prosaic formalities of an English Judicature.[28]

Bacon demonstrated that she was fully aware of and engaged with contemporary political developments in America by referring to her group of Elizabethan reformers as 'Know-Nothings', who adopted secrecy to avoid punishment for the 'crime' of asking a 'forbidden question'.[29] Bacon also appeared to address her various compatriots who, rather like the transcendentalists, attempted to find new philosophies. Her message on philosophy to these people was, 'We have had them; we need not look to a foreign and younger race for them; we have them, fruit of our own stock; we have had them not cloaked in falseness, but exposed in the searching noon-day glare of our western science.'[30]

The preface to the book was written by novelist Nathaniel Hawthorne, who was at that time United States consul in Liverpool. Bacon had requested his assistance in May 1856, when her financial difficulties worsened. Again the issue of American 'national interest' is evident in the manner of Bacon's appeal to Hawthorne. Her letter to him closes as follows:

This is not *Consular* business exactly, I suppose . . . But I think when President Pierce appointed one so eminent as yourself in the world of letters, to represent him in this country, he deserved the return which he will have if through your aid this discovery should be secured to the country to which it properly belongs instead of being appropriated here – or instead of being lost rather as it is more likely to be.[31]

Hawthorne naturally responded to this appeal to his personal and official patriotism. In the preface he revealed that he wrote his contribution largely on the strength of his reaction to the *Putnam's Monthly* article, as he had not been able to read the complete book prior to its publication. It is perhaps significant that he felt prepared to endorse this large work on the strength of so short an article and a single meeting of 'above an hour'.[32] Hawthorne acknowledged the possible reaction of some contemporary Shakespeare 'idolaters':

The first feeling of every reader must be one of absolute repugnance towards a person who seeks to tear out of the Anglo-Saxon heart the name which for ages it has held dearest, and to substitute another name, or names, to which the settled belief of the world has consigned a very different position.[33]

But any 'repugnance' felt by Hawthorne himself was put aside as he adopted Bacon's main thesis, that there was a single unifying 'new philosophy' contained within the plays, which 'no professor could have ventured openly to teach in the days of Elizabeth and James'.[34] The illusion to the struggle for freedom and the association with America is again made clear when Hawthorne suggests that 'the great secret of the Elizabethan age was inextricably reserved by the founders of a new learning, the prophetic and more nobly gifted minds of a new and nobler race of men'.[35] As Hawthorne wrote this sentence, the 'nobler race' he appeared to have in mind, which would benefit from this 'great secret', was his own Anglo-American 'race'.

Hawthorne provided a partial explanation to a question that might have been posed by readers of *Putnam's Monthly*. He stated that 'unexpected obstacles prevented further publication' of Bacon's thesis in a serialised form of journal articles.[36] The 'obstacles' appear to have been an editorial decision to reject the next three articles on account of the perceived lack of 'proof' for Bacon's claims.[37] Additionally, the manuscripts of the three articles were inexplicably 'lost' by William Emerson and Sophia Ripley while in transit to the home of Ralph Waldo Emerson.[38]

Hawthorne also hints in the preface that 'another evil followed' this misfortune.[39] The particular new 'evil' was that Bacon and Hawthorne were both aware that a non-American was about to publish a book suggesting the name of an alternative author of the works of Shakespeare.[40] The implied sensitivity to, and awareness of, the issue of nationality was emphasised further when Hawthorne stated that 'it had been the author's original purpose to publish [the book] in America; for she wished her own country to have the glory of solving the enigma of those mighty dramas'.[41] Hawthorne again stressed the importance of American 'ownership' by informing the readers that 'it was [however] written . . . in the land of *our own* PHILOSOPHERS and POETS' (italics and capitals are Hawthorne's).[42]

Delia Bacon's *Putnam's Monthly* article and her subsequent book, while perhaps not finding a large readership in the United States, did provoke both widespread comment and review in the 'popular press'. Newspaper and magazine editors, hungry for copy, selectively quoted passages that allowed them to communicate the main points of interest to their readers; namely that 'Shakespeare' was written by either Sir Francis Bacon or Sir Walter Raleigh and that both men shared a proto-American ideology. One such periodical was the *Daily Picayune*. After satirising the question of 'Who Wrote Shickspur?', the editor referred to both a *Boston Post* review and the earlier article in *Putnam's Monthly*. The main comment about Bacon's 675-page text was that

Miss Bacon makes a careful and close examination into the life and writings of the great men of that time – Lord Bacon, Sir Walter Raleigh, and others. She appears to consider them as a band of reformers, for whom the world was not prepared, and who were compelled to conceal their plans of reform; and that they were the real authors of the plays which were brought out in the name of Shakespeare.[43]

This concise summary encapsulated Delia Bacon's self-declared life's work in a manner that allowed the American reader to simultaneously ridicule the English and celebrate American progress.

While Hawthorne's preface to the book could be considered a public endorsement, several years after her death, in the form of a sketch and partial eulogy, he broadly condemned her authorship theory as a 'despotic idea', suggesting that it ultimately caused her decline.[44] However, while he now publically rejected her thesis he described Bacon as a 'gifted woman'. He omitted any mention of his original preface to her book.

MORE WRITERS ON THE AUTHORSHIP QUESTION

Since the publication of Bacon's book, writers on the subject of Shakespeare have often appeared preoccupied with the identity of the playwright. Bacon's argument that the author of Shakespeare was proto-American in character and that he/they shared American democratic ideals has largely been ignored in favour of the sensationalism that surrounds the names of the various candidates proposed as author of the plays. However, while the quest for the identity of the playwright has occupied scholars from various countries, Americans in particular have been motivated to pursue this line of enquiry. Between 1857 and 1884 more than 255 books, pamphlets, essays and articles were published in America on the subject of possible Baconian authorship.[45] While for Peter Rawlings 'The widespread appetite for the Baconian hypothesis in America is easier to dismiss than to take into account',[46] the desire to associate the plays known as 'Shakespeare' with a republican revolutionary playwright provides one possible answer.

Perhaps influenced by this tide of publications, even Walt Whitman felt the need to comment on the subject. In an article first published in 1884 but later included in his *Democratic Vistas*, Whitman suggested that 'it is possible [that] a future age of criticism, diving deeper, mapping the land and lines freer, completer than hitherto, may discover in the plays named the scientific (Baconian?) inauguration of modern Democracy'.[47]

While Whitman's piece did not mention Delia Bacon or other theorists, it can be supposed that he intended the article to be his comment on the authorship debate. The acceptance by Whitman of the idea that Shakespeare could have been a proto-American may explain why, now in his 'dotage', he appears here and elsewhere to have softened his previously expressed hostile opinion on the possible 'undemocratic' nature of Shakespeare's plays. The fact that Whitman was in some small way engaged with this authorship issue can be seen again in the 1891 'death-bed' edition of *Leaves of Grass*, where he included a short poem entitled 'Shakspere – Bacon's Cipher', a reference to a book by Ignatius Donnelly.

Philadelphia-born Donnelly, to further exploit American public interest in the authorship story, published evidence suggesting that within Shakespeare's plays lay 'The Great Cryptogram',[48] its existence providing proof that Sir Francis Bacon was the true author of the plays. Donnelly's thesis was later substantially recycled in a book by Sir George Greenwood, and it was this book that reportedly inspired Mark Twain's subsequent enthusiastic mock autobiography, provocatively entitled *1601, and Is Shakespeare Dead?* Writing about his own early apprenticeship as a Mississippi riverboat pilot in 1857, Twain described how he took part in heated debates with his instructor about the Shakespeare–Bacon controversy.[49] The fact that two professional sailors (one a high-school 'drop out'), both working in the harsh environment of the Middle West more than eleven hundred miles from any east-coast metropolitan city, felt motivated to debate the authorship of Elizabethan drama suggests how widespread the American interest in the Shakespeare–Bacon controversy became.

Behind what could be described as the journalistic desire of some American scholars to unmask a 'secret' person behind the plays of Shakespeare lay a more politicised agenda. Some American scholars saw the benefit of strengthening the association between the most renowned literary works in the English language and the ideological quest for democratic republican reform. Once the association had been legitimised by the 'discovery' of a secret political reformer playwright then the plays and philosophy would become more fully part of American heritage.

For Delia Bacon, reflecting the pervasive nationalistic spirit of the mid-nineteenth century, what was of primary importance was not merely a new name for the author of Shakespeare's plays but that an American scholar should unmask an irrevocable link between the works of the pre-eminent writer in the English language and a philosophy that was to lead to the establishment of the United States.

NOTES

1. Hart had previously written a novel entitled *Miriam Coffin or The Whale Fisherman* (1834), notable for being the first published account of the American whaling industry.
2. Joseph C. Hart, *The Romance of Yachting: Voyage the First* (New York: Harper & Bros., 1848), p. 7. It has been suggested that Shakespeare's authorship may have been challenged in private before Hart's book appeared in America in 1848. However, both Hart and Delia Bacon are generally accepted to be the first two writers to publish their theories.
3. Ibid., p. 11.
4. Ibid., p. 42.
5. Ibid., p. 216.
6. Ibid., p. 242.
7. See letter from Melville to Duyckinck, 14 November 1848, in Jay Leyda, ed., *The Melville Log: A Documentary Life of Herman Melville, 1819–1891*, 2 vols. (New York, 1951), vol. 1, pp. 282–3. Melville's final cruel comment was 'the book is an abortion'.
8. Delia Bacon, 'William Shakespeare and His Plays: An Inquiry Concerning Them', *Putnam's Monthly*, 7 (January 1856), p. 1. Despite the editor's 'hopes', no further articles by Bacon were accepted for publication by *Putnam's Monthly*.
9. Ibid., p. 15.
10. Ibid., p. 2.
11. Ibid.
12. Ibid., p. 1.
13. Ibid., p. 12.
14. Ibid., p. 4.
15. Between October 1787 and August 1788 a series of eighty-five essays addressed 'To the People of the State of New York' and signed by 'Publius' were published in support of the proposed Constitution. The three writers who were collectively responsible for these essays were Madison, Hamilton and Jay. See Alexander Hamilton, John Jay and James Madison, *The Federalist*, ed. Henry Cabot Lodge (New York: G. P. Putnam's Sons, 1900).

16. Bacon, 'William Shakespeare and His Plays', p. 17.
17. Ibid.
18. Ibid., p. 10.
19. Ibid.
20. See Bacon, *The Philosophy of the Plays of Shakspere Unfolded*. Bacon was also to refer to Raleigh as being the 'projector and founder of the liberties of the New World'. See ibid., p. xxv.
21. See letter from Emerson to George Putnam, 19 October 1855, in Ralph Waldo Emerson, *The Letters of Ralph Waldo Emerson*, ed. Eleanor M. Tilton, 10 vols. (New York: Columbia University Press, 1991), vol. VIII, p. 457.
22. See letter from Emerson to Delia Bacon, 23 June 1856, in ibid., pp. 490–2.
23. Whitman used a letter of support from Emerson to promote the sale of the 1855 edition of *Leaves of Grass*.
24. *North American Review*, 62 (April 1846), p. 382. See also Horsman, *Race and Manifest Destiny*, chapter 9, 'Romantic Racial Nationalism'.
25. *Southern Quarterly Review*, 14 (July 1848), p. 77.
26. In 1858 Delia Bacon was committed by her family to the care of a mental asylum in Hartford, Connecticut, where she died on 2 September 1859.
27. Bacon, *The Philosophy of the Plays of Shakspere Unfolded*, p. 326.
28. Ibid., p. 332.
29. Ibid., p. xx. The political Know-Nothing party gained rapid popularity in 1854, promoting nationalist or nativist policies in favour of the Anglo-American population. See Anbinder, *Nativism and Slavery*.
30. Bacon, *The Philosophy of the Plays of Shakspere Unfolded*, p. 566.
31. Letter from Bacon to Nathaniel Hawthorne, 8 May 1856. Quoted here from an editorial note in Hawthorne, *The Letters*. See also Vivian Hopkins, *Prodigal Puritan: A Life of Delia Bacon* (Cambridge MA: Belknap Press, 1959), p. 200.
32. Nathaniel Hawthorne, 'Recollections of a Gifted Woman', *Atlantic Monthly*, 11/63 (January 1863), p. 53.
33. Bacon, *The Philosophy of the Plays of Shakspere Unfolded*, p. xv.
34. Ibid., p. ix.
35. Ibid., p. xi.
36. Ibid., p. xii.
37. *Putnam's Monthly* was then owned by publisher Dix & Edwards and disagreements over fees and academic objections from respected Shakespearean scholar Richard Grant White appear to have stopped further publication. See Hopkins, *Prodigal Puritan*, pp. 197–8.
38. See letter from Emerson to Bacon, 23 June 1856, in Emerson, *The Letters of Ralph Waldo Emerson*, vol. VIII, pp. 490–2.
39. Bacon, *The Philosophy of the Plays of Shakspere Unfolded*, p. xii.
40. William Henry Smith, by privately circulating a fifteen-page pamphlet in late 1856, had announced his intention to publish a book containing his thesis. This pamphlet, *Was Lord Bacon the Author of Shakespeare's Plays? A Letter to Lord Ellesmere*, did not mention Delia Bacon or her *Putnam's Monthly* article. A book was published the following year, *Bacon and Shakespeare: An Enquiry*

Touching Players, Playhouses, and Play-Writers in the Days of Elizabeth (London: John Russell Smith, 1857). As the title suggests, Smith was more concerned with 'authorship' than with the reformist 'philosophy . . . unfolded' as presented by Delia Bacon.

41. Bacon, *The Philosophy of the Plays of Shakspere Unfolded*, p. xiii.
42. Ibid., p. xiv.
43. 'Who Wrote Shickspur?', *Daily Picayune* (New Orleans), 11 June 1857, p. 4.
44. Hawthorne, 'Recollections of a Gifted Woman'.
45. William Henry Wyman, *The Bibliography of the Bacon–Shakespeare Controversy, with Notes and Extracts* (Cincinnati: Cox & Co., 1884).
46. Rawlings, ed., *Americans on Shakespeare*, p. 14.
47. Whitman, 'What Lurks behind Shakspeare's Historical Plays?'.
48. Ignatius Donnelly, *The Great Cryptogram: Francis Bacon's Cipher in the So-Called Shakespeare Plays* (London: Samson, Low, Marston, Searle & Rivington, 1888). A study in two volumes using extensive quotations chiefly from American scholars to support his cryptogram thesis. Donnelly includes a chapter in praise of Delia Bacon.
49. Mark Twain, *1601, and Is Shakespeare Dead?* (New York: Oxford University Press, 1996), p. 4. First published 1909.

CHAPTER 9

Last scenes in the final act of appropriation

Blazon'd with Shakspere's purple page

Walt Whitman

As Shakespeare became part of the cultural language of America, a lingua franca, there began a series of actions that ultimately led to a national shrine to Shakespeare being established in the USA. Americans began to express their interest in and celebration of Shakespeare in a manner that went beyond the printed page or theatre stage. However, few citizens were aware that nationalism, commercial opportunity and Shakespeare had been combined in a manner that reflected American enterprise culture.

IN STRATFORD-UPON-AVON

In 1875, a letter published in the *New York Times* revealed that some Americans had been working to provide their nation with a greater share of the Shakespeare heritage. Writing in support of a campaign to encourage American financial involvement in the building of a theatre in Stratford-upon-Avon in England, Mark Twain demonstrated his admiration for his countrymen and his continued ambivalence towards England and Shakespeare.[1] The letter informed readers that a committee had already been established in the rural Warwickshire town with the specific purpose of raising the necessary funds to build a memorial theatre. Twain had been asked by a friend to organise a collection of subscriptions from American citizens who, in return for their donation of one hundred pounds, would each become a 'governor' of the completed theatre.

Twain, the consummate storyteller, managed to convert this simple appeal for donations into a piece of 'entertainment' and an opportunity to celebrate American character, enterprise and vision. Americans, he pointed out, had 'already subscribed $1000 for an American memorial window to be put in the Shakespeare church at Avon'. This, he insisted, was evidence that 'Americans of every walk in life will cheerfully subscribe to this [new] Shakespeare memorial.' Twain's letter to the editor then recounted the story of how P. T. Barnum, the American circus owner and showman, had attempted to purchase the house where Shakespeare was born and transport it across the Atlantic to America:

> Imagine the house that Shakespeare was born in being brought bodily over here and set upon American soil! That came within an ace of being done once. A reputable gentleman of Stratford told me so. The building was going to wreck and ruin. Nobody felt quite reverence enough for the dead dramatist to repair and take care of his house; so an American came along ever so quietly and bought it. The deeds were actually drawn and ready for the signatures. Then the thing got wind and there was a fine stir in England! The sale was stopped. Public-spirited Englishmen headed a revival of revenue for the poet, and from that day to this every relic of Shakespeare in Stratford has been sacred, and zealously cared for accordingly.[2]

The appeal for donations was supported by an editorial in the *New York Times*, and Twain's letter was later to appear in several newspapers across America. What Twain's appeal illustrates is the gradual involvement of the American people in the material ownership of Shakespeare. It was now not enough to read or listen to the plays. The 'relics' had to be secured and offered to the American public.

Unlike many English businessmen, Barnum recognised the commercial opportunity presented by Shakespeare's birthplace, being aware that millions of Americans were likely to be prepared to pay to see a genuine Shakespeare artefact. Shakespeare was now so much a part of American national culture that Barnum felt confident that his fellow citizens would make their pilgrimage wherever the playwright's birthplace was sited. As Twain pointed out, 'About three-fourths of the visitors to Shakespeare's tomb are Americans. If you will show me an American who has visited England and has not seen that tomb, Barnum shall be on his track next week.'[3]

Twain's *New York Times* letter also implied that there was a competitive motive behind some American expressions of interest in Shakespeare, and this is characteristic of the long-running rivalry between America and England. Echoing the sentiment of the preface of the 1795 'First American Edition' of Shakespeare, Twain suggested that Americans valued Shakespeare more than the English and that it was only American interest that had led to England's recognition of the true potential of the then undervalued cultural icon. It is an assertion that deserves serious consideration. The story of the American attempt to buy Shakespeare's birthplace has often been trivialised; however, closer study suggests that it was indicative of

American appropriation and of American influence on what was to become the Shakespeare industry in England.

SHAKESPEARE'S BIRTHPLACE

When Shakespeare's birthplace and the attached buildings were put up for sale in 1805, the advertisement did not mention Shakespeare or any historic association. The property was sold simply as a collection of buildings. Hence, Thomas Court bought the property from a William Shakspeare Hart for just £210.[4] In 1809, *The Times* carried just two lines informing its readers that the house where Shakespeare had been born was now a butcher's shop.[5] No comment was made about the fact and it was another thirty-eight years before the British newspaper mentioned the house again.

P. T. Barnum, showman, playwright and author, visited Stratford-upon-Avon in September 1844 at the start of a tour of Europe that would last until his return to New York in February 1847. His autobiography recounts how he arrived at a hotel in Stratford accompanied by his friend Albert Smith. When he asked for a guidebook to the local sights, Barnum was both pleased and surprised to be given a copy of 'the Sketch-Book by our illustrious countryman, Washington Irving'.[6] What delighted and perhaps inspired Barnum was that here was tangible proof that Americans recognised the town of Shakespeare's birth and death as a place of pilgrimage whereas the English largely demonstrated apathy. The guidebook offered to tourists was the work of an American, not an Englishman. Perhaps it was this suggestion of the lack of cultural and commercial interest shown by the English that inspired Barnum to consider adding the house to the list of exhibits at his American Museum in New York, where he felt his fellow citizens would be more appreciative.

Barnum's autobiography continued with the narrative of the rest of his European tour, but he returned to the story of Shakespeare's birthplace later in the book. Barnum informed his readers that he

obtained verbally through a friend the refusal of the house in which Shakspeare was born, designing to remove it in sections to my museum in New York; but the project leaked out, British pride was touched, and several English gentlemen interfered and purchased the premises for a Shakspearian Association.[7]

The suggestion of 'British pride' as a possible motive for the formation and actions of this 'association' cannot be proven. However, the house known as 'the Birthplace' was indeed purchased at auction for the sum of three thousand pounds on 16 September 1847 by the 'United Committee' made up of interested persons from both Stratford and London.[8]

'British pride' and English rivalry with America could very well have provoked members of the English public to reassess the importance of Shakespeare and the physical remains of his life and death. It has been suggested that William Makepeace Thackeray and other members of the London Garrick Club were instrumental in the campaign to raise funds to purchase the house and it is clear that it was known in some circles that an American wanted to buy the Birthplace.[9] Evidence of American interest, and the fact that this was perceived to be a 'threat', is indicated by a flurry of letters and editorials published in *The Times*, then considered a symbol of the British Establishment.

The first mention of 'foreign' interest in the sale of the Birthplace appeared as early as October 1846. Under the headline 'Probable Sale of Shakspeare's Birthplace', *The Times* informed its readers that 'The idea which has more than once been named, of removing the house to another site – perhaps a strange country . . . such a desecration will no doubt never be permitted.'[10] One man's indignant response to this suggestion of the threat of 'desecration' by nationals from a 'strange country' subsequently appeared in a letter to the editor:

It is with the greatest indignation that I have this day heard from a very good authority that the house in which Shakspeare was born . . . which was advertised for sale, – which implied, as everyone thought, merely a change of housekeepers, has been purchased for the purpose of its being removed to America, and that its removal is a about to take place. Need I add another word to excite in the breast of every Englishman as much indignation as it does, Sir.[11]

The executor of the estate denied that any such sale had been agreed in *The Times* on 8 December, but the letter from 'An Englishman' had for the first time made the connection between foreign threat and America, and, even though Barnum is not named, it would appear to confirm the story contained in his autobiography.

Although no formal announcement of an auction had been made, in April 1847 another letter to *The Times* stressed the importance of the increasing rivalry between the USA and England over the relics of Shakespeare:

Is the house which is to be bought to the hammer! to be sold by some prattling auctioneer to whoever chooses to speculate in these universal associations! – perhaps to be plundered for curiosity shops, or even transported to the United States to amuse a people who are as proud of their descent from the race of Shakespeare as we are ourselves . . . Such a consummation would be an intolerable disgrace and affliction.[12]

As the characteristically reserved English started to become aware that their playwright and poet was now considered part of American heritage, civic-minded people began to organise themselves. The first public meeting to raise funds for the purchase of the Birthplace took place on 26 April 1847. Two months later, clearly deciding that this was now a matter of public interest, *The Times* carried a report on the progress made towards securing the Birthplace from foreign buyers. The report acknowledged the fact that the Birthplace had a commercial value far beyond the level suggested by the run-down Warwickshire building:

The house is a freehold, and is valued at something like £2,000. This valuation has been formed on the number of visitors. In 1846 it was calculated that something like 8,000 people had visited the house, though not more than 2,500 had entered their names in the book.[13]

Once again the issue of America was raised, and the report mentioned that 'One or two Jonathans have already arrived from America, determined to see what dollars can do in taking it away . . . and it would be no very difficult matter to get it on wheels and make an exhibition of it.' More letters followed on 16 and 17 June, both referring to the threat posed by foreign interest in the Birthplace.

On 21 July 1847, the editor of *The Times*, responding to a property auction announcement published the preceding day, appealed for an 'Archaeological Association' to be formed to 'prevent . . . the house being moved from the country by passing into the hands of some foreign showman', a clear reference to Barnum.[14] The editor went on to suggest that Shakespeare's Birthplace must be secured against 'the desecrating grasp of those speculators who are said to be desirous of taking it from its foundations, and trundling it about on wheels like a caravan of wild beasts, giants, or dwarfs, through the United States of America'. Even the auction announcement, placed by 'Mr Robins of Covent Garden', carried the suggestion of a 'foreign threat' to the house at Stratford-upon-Avon. Perhaps in an attempt to stimulate the spirit of competition within potential buyers, the announcement recommended that the house should be purchased by persons who would assure its 'continuance at the birth and burial-place of the poet'.[15]

Responding to the growing furore, George Jones, the author of that Anglo-American poem written in the visitor book of Holy Trinity Church, wrote to Walter Jessop, the executor, on 22 July. Jones personally offered two thousand pounds for the Birthplace, on condition that the house was immediately withdrawn from public auction. Jones claimed the Stratford house was worth no more than two hundred pounds without the benefit of the association with Shakespeare.[16] The offer was declined. Jones was later to place an advertisement announcing yet another public meeting for the purpose of forming a committee to purchase the Birthplace, to stop what he described as the 'threatened destruction'.[17]

It is clear that the national interest had been successfully invoked and the broader public aroused, and, suitably, the British monarchy reacted to the mood of the people. Queen Victoria's husband Prince Albert now became patron of the Royal Shakspeare Club and *The Times* reported that he had personally donated £250 in order to secure the Birthplace for the nation.[18]

In a final bizarre step prior to the public auction, a letter in *The Times* on 11 September decried 'Yankee speculators', whose existence threatened to drive the price of the house up beyond the funds donated for the purchase. The letter went on to state that the Shakespeare 'committee' would pay no more than three thousand pounds for the house.[19] The house was subsequently bought for the English nation by the members of the joint committee and ownership was immediately transferred to the 'Shakespeare Birthplace Trust', set up specifically to manage and administer the house.

Barely disguised nationalism, on the part of both the American show-man Barnum and the members of the English public, press and theatre establishment, can be seen as a large factor in the episode. The recognition of what can be seen as the competitive national interest in Shakespeare, as demonstrated first by the increasing numbers of Americans visiting the Birthplace and Washington Irving's book and later by Barnum's pur-chase attempt, helped to provoke the English to appreciate the cultural heritage and commercial opportunity presented by Shakespeare. Twain had suggested that 'It was an American who roused into its present vigorous life England's dead interest in her Shakespearean remains',[20] and there is evidence to suggest that he was more than justified in his claim. In England it was finally recognised that a rival nation thought Shakespeare valuable.

Once the Birthplace had been purchased for the nation and there was professional management of the house, the quality of the visitor records improved. Yet while the number of tickets sold was recorded, the nationality of the visitors was not. Twain's claim of 'three-fourths' being from America cannot be verified. As explained in chapter 6, however, American visitors often chose to sign the visitors' book, and it is interesting to note that in the first decade of the existence of the Birthplace Trust the number of American names in the visitors' book represented 32 per cent of the total tickets sold.[21]

FURTHER INFLUENCE ON STRATFORD-UPON-AVON

Twain's attempt at fundraising did succeed in marshalling American enthusiasm, and some financial support was given to erect a physical 'shrine' to Shakespeare, albeit in England rather than America. At the dedication ceremony of the Shakespeare Memorial Theatre on 23 April 1879 the financial contributions from American citizens were formally acknowledged. Just over one hundred years after America had declared its independence from England, England formally acknowledged that America now shared spiritual ownership of Shakespeare. With the Birthplace Trust established, a new theatre opened,[22] and with good rail links from London, Stratford-upon-Avon, more than ever before, became a place of pilgrimage for Americans visiting Europe.

The first Shakespeare Memorial Theatre was later destroyed by fire, but once again there was an appeal for American support to raise funds for a replacement. Once more there was American involvement. The New Shakespeare Memorial Theatre opened on 23 April 1932. The dedication ceremony was attended by Andrew W. Mellon, the United States ambassador to Britain. Mellon made a speech on behalf of Thomas Lamont, chairman of the American Shakespeare Foundation, the American group that had made a contribution to the rebuilding costs. Sir Archibald Flower, speaking on behalf of the Prince of Wales, acknowledged 'the generous help which has been forthcoming from America',[23] the new theatre helping to cater for the entertainment of the more than 169,000 American visitors who had signed the Birthplace visitors' book in the preceding decade.

There was another physical symbol of American interest in Stratford. Wealthy Philadelphia newspaper owner George W. Childs donated the funds for the design and construction of the American Fountain. This public drinking fountain, bearing the symbol of the American eagle and the Stars and Stripes, was dedicated at a lavish civic ceremony on 17 October 1887. The dedication and the formal lunch that followed were attended by the American ambassador Edward John Phelps, actor Henry Irving and a large number of dignitaries. Along with speeches celebrating both Shakespeare and American interest in the playwright, the 'Shakspeare Ode' written by Charles Sprague, originally used at the opening of the Boston Theatre in 1823, was recited, and the band played Joseph Hopkinson's nationalist anthem *Hail Columbia*. A full report of the event carried by *The Times* reprinted the words of the 'Shakspeare Ode' and emphasised that America and Britain were now reunited by a shared appreciation of Shakespeare.[24]

While the fountain may seem to represent no more than an expression of sentimental affection by Childs, the dedication ceremony itself reflected the wider appropriation of Shakespeare. Ambassador Phelps was to echo the ownership issue that had already been voiced by many commentators. In his speech to the Stratford audience Phelps referred to the town as 'A place to which Americans, by the pilgrimage of successive generations, have established a title as tenants in common with Englishmen by right of possession',[25] a point that was to be supported by Irving when he claimed that 'On this spot of all others Americans cease to be aliens, for here they claim our kinship with the great master of English speech.'[26]

Irving also commented on the hitherto thorny problem of rivalry as to who spoke the 'purest' English. He remarked that for him it was the Americans, 'whose colloquial speech still preserves phrases which have come down from Shakespeare's time'. He added, 'Some idioms, which are supposed to be racy of American invention, can be traced back to Shakespeare.'[27] Irving also flattered the pride of the American visitors by alluding to the original colonists who had established Jamestown, Virginia:

we can imagine that in the audience at the old Globe Theatre there were ignorant and unlettered men who treasured up something of Shakespeare's imagery and vivid portraiture, and carried with them over the ocean thoughts and words . . . which helped to nurture their transplanted stock.[28]

The dedication of the American Fountain, the design of which later made it controversial, was an occasion on which many aspects of appropriation, familiar to newspaper readers in America, were presented to the English public gathered in the rural town most associated with the playwright.

AMERICAN BARDOLOGY IN OTHER FORMS

As America welcomed the arrival of the twentieth century, now a major world power, the success of the nineteenth-century appropriation of Shakespeare resulted in several 'material' manifestations confirming his unique position in American culture.

The first American cinema film of a play by Shakespeare was *Macbeth*, entered on the copyright register on 17 April 1908. Perhaps surprisingly, given the nature of nineteenth-century frontier society, the Chicago police censor objected to the visual representation of violence in this 'single-reel' silent film from the Vitagraph Company. Despite this small problem, however, favourite plays of American audiences, such as *Othello*, *Richard III* and *Julius Caesar*, were quickly appropriated by directors who recognised Shakespeare's position as an American cultural icon.[29]

One reason for Shakespeare's popularity with America's new entertainment industry lay in the fact that the plays lent themselves to the melodramatic treatment favoured by the silent film studios. Another reason why film producers and directors turned so quickly to Shakespeare, however, was 'the need for respectability' for this new form of popular culture.[30] Shakespeare supplied this, in addition to a means of attracting audiences still unsure of what to expect from cinema. Before the year closed a further nine cinema films of plays by Shakespeare were produced and screened before American audiences.

Silent Shakespeare, while not quite an oxymoron, does present the audience with at least one significant problem. The success of Shakespeare on the silent screen relied on the audience's familiarity with the essential dramatic moments of each play and perhaps on their ability to silently declaim key passages to themselves. Like Mark Twain, with his parody of Shakespeare in *Huckleberry Finn*, the directors of these silent films felt confident enough that the audience would instantly recognise the plots and characters, helping to ensure appreciation of their films. 'Silent Shakespeare' was made possible partly because the themes of the plays were now so much a part of popular culture.

Another Shakespeare title offered to the American cinema audience in 1908 was *The Taming of the Shrew*. This was directed by the Kentucky-born filmmaker D. W. Griffith.[31] Griffith was later to demonstrate the link that had been forged between Shakespeare and suggestions of Anglo-American ethnic, if not racial, supremacy. In the opening frame of his epic film *The Birth of a Nation*, the audience was informed that, 'The same liberty that is conceded to the art of the written word – that art to which we owe The Bible and The Works of Shakespeare' – should be afforded to this film.[32] The film was completed in 1915, during a period in which there was debate about America's entry to the First World War, and it promoted American nationalism and Anglo-American ethnocentric supremacism. In addition to the opening frame that links the film with art, the Bible and Shakespeare, the narrative also included the by then familiar visual allusion to *Othello* and a scene that portrayed the assassination of Abraham Lincoln by John Wilkes Booth, complete with its Shakespearean imagery.

THE EVACUATION OF SHAKESPEARE'S TEXT TO THE 'NEW WORLD'

As Americans increasingly regarded Shakespeare as part of American tradition, the text itself became the focus for attention. The reliance on English scholars or libraries to safeguard Shakespeare's first printed texts was an anathema to some people, who looked on Shakespeare as a philosophical prophet of the American nation. During the nineteenth century wealthy American collectors and scholars started to seek out copies of the 1623 First Folio, later folios and the various quartos. Whenever and wherever they found these items, nothing could deter them from buying the books and transporting them to the United States. In a study of American Shakespeare libraries, Robert Smith suggested that American influence on the book trade in England 'made itself felt' around the middle of the nineteenth century.[33] The actions of New Yorker James Lenox, who in 1854 paid £163 for a copy of the First Folio, both fuelled interest in early copies of Shakespeare and drove up the price of any volume offered for sale. Over the next twenty years, Lenox bought thirteen folios and twenty-nine quartos, and Smith identified a further thirteen American collections that had been purchasing rare editions of Shakespeare from England and transporting them to America. Smith commented that 'This great flow of Shakespeare rarities into America since the middle of the nineteenth-century has not taken place without some loud protests from patriotic Englishmen.'[34]

Perhaps in recognition of increasing 'foreign' acquisition, in 1902 Sidney Lee prepared a census to identify the whereabouts of each known copy of the First Folio. He published his data for 156 extant copies and suggested that there were then 101 copies in Britain and 50 in the USA.[35] It is possible that the level of American ownership was already understated, however, and that some of the many untraced copies had already left Britain for the USA but were as yet undeclared. Lee quickly recognised certain errors and updated his work with a revision published in 1906. This time greater prominence was given to references to American ownership. Lee noted that 'the American demand for First Folios, which has long been the dominant feature in their history, has shown . . . no sign of slacking'.[36] He revealed that American ownership of copies of the First Folio had increased to sixty-two, with a pro-rata decrease in numbers held in Britain.

Two comments by Lee portend the next stage in the appropriation process that had begun so many years before. He concluded his published census by stating that 'Mr Folger is to be congratulated on having acquired . . . as many as eight copies of the First Folio in all – a record number for any private collector.'[37] Lee's final words were offered as a kind of prophecy: 'The chances are that at the close of [the twentieth century] the existing ratio of American and British copies, sixty-two to one hundred and five, will be exactly reversed.'[38]

Nearly a hundred years later, when Anthony West completed the next census, his data confirmed what Lee had predicted.[39] The world centre for ownership of original Shakespeare texts had moved from Britain to the USA. The West census showed that there are 228 surviving copies of the important 1623 edition of Shakespeare's First Folio. Libraries in the USA hold at least 145 of them. Twenty-seven are located in the 'rest of the world' or are as yet 'unfound'. In the whole of Britain, libraries and collectors hold just forty-three copies of this book published in London in 1623. As a consequence of appropriation and the efforts of Americans during the late nineteenth century, 64 per cent of the extant copies of this book of plays by an English playwright have been acquired and are now available to American scholars and enthusiasts.

'AN AMERICAN SHRINE IN MEMORY OF SHAKESPEARE'[40]

While the position of Shakespeare within American popular culture and tradition was consolidated, the most prestigious 'manifestation' of Shakespeare was reserved for the American capital city. When in the mid-nineteenth century Mary Cowden Clarke wrote in her preface that Shakespeare's plays were a 'library in themselves', she could not have guessed that the grand scale of Shakespeare consumption in America would result in a permanent monument on Capitol Hill, Washington DC, dedicated to the study of the playwright and his work. In a final act of appropriation, Shakespeare and the American nation were united in real estate and stone.

An unrivalled collection of Shakespearean texts had been assembled and presented to the American nation by lawyer and ex-president of Standard Oil of New York Henry Clay Folger. While Folger undoubtedly shared the scholarly interest of Americans such as Richard Grant White and Horace Howard Furness, Michael D. Bristol has suggested that his '*motives*... lean more towards nationalistic sentiments'.[41] The scale and quality of this collection provided a resource for America that was unmatched anywhere in the world and that 'freed American Shakespeare scholars from the dependency on England'.[42]

The Washington Folger Shakespeare Library has seventy-nine of the surviving 228 copies of Shakespeare's First Folio. By comparison the largest number of these rare volumes held in a single collection in Britain is just five. The Washington library also has 118 copies of the second, third and fourth folios, 229 quartos and about 7,000 other editions of Shakespeare's works. It would be possible to argue that, rather than just a scholarly resource, the Folger Shakespeare Library represents a national holding or a type of 'bank' to safeguard the future of what has become to the American nation 'a kind of second, or secular Bible'.[43]

The collection of play scripts by Shakespeare is housed in the city chosen by Congress to preserve and display the symbols of the American nation. Within walking distance of the public exhibition of the Declaration of Independence, the United States Constitution and the Bill of Rights, the work of an English playwright is enshrined as an American treasure. The importance of America's naturalisation of Shakespeare had been made manifest and the permanence of the appropriation was marked by the act of opening the Folger Shakespeare Library.

The importance of the political symbolism of this collection, the building that has become its home and the 1932 dedication ceremony, already highlighted in the work of Michael D. Bristol, more than justifies a second and more detailed examination in this concluding chapter.

Henry Clay Folger spent many years on his book collection and more than nine years acquiring the property necessary for the construction of a library dedicated to the study of Shakespeare. Unfortunately, he was to die before his huge project could be completed, so it was left to his wife and colleagues to tell the story of the library that bore his name.

In a presentation given in 1933, Emily Jordan Folger recalled that her husband had been inspired to study and collect Shakespeare by an address he heard in the spring of 1879 when he was a senior at Amherst College. The address was delivered by Ralph Waldo Emerson, the man who, as we have already seen, influenced so many of his fellow citizens. Mrs Folger stated that her husband 'understood the relation of Shakespeare to the Bible and to English literature in general and to American idealism in particular. It fascinated him, just as it had fascinated George Washington and Lincoln.'[44] His study of Shakespeare was not just an expression of an interest in dramatic art. For Folger, like so many in the nineteenth century, Shakespeare was connected to the American nation and the American character. Mrs Folger echoed the feelings of many when she added, 'the poet is one of our best sources, one of the wells from which we Americans draw our national thought, our faith and our hope'.[45]

The patriotism demonstrated by the choice of city for the location of the library was confirmed by Folger's explanation as to why he had not placed his great collection in Stratford-upon-Avon. He answered that he had considered placing it 'near the bones of the great man' but resolved to 'give it to Washington; for I am an American'.[46]

But despite his patriotism there were difficulties in securing such a prestigious site for the library. The land had been destined for compulsory purchase to allow for the expansion of the Library of Congress. When Folger became aware that his still confidential plans were in jeopardy, he contacted Dr Herbert Putnam at the Library of Congress, and once 'The cultural purpose of [the] plan was explained . . . the site providentially was saved for the library'.[47] It was not quite that easy, however, as a special amendment to the existing compulsory purchase Bill had to be negotiated and passed by Congress to allow the federal government plans to be changed in deference to the wishes of a private collector of Shakespeariana. A Congressional Bill was duly debated and passed in May 1928, authorising funds to purchase and clear the land of buildings prior to construction of two further libraries but allocating space for the Folger building.[48] The importance placed on both the project and the land is indicated by the fact that 'a commission' of five senators had been formed, with the then United States president, John Calvin Coolidge, taking interest in the project, to develop the Capitol Hill site for the Library of Congress.

Once government plans had been changed in favour of the proposed Shakespeare library, fourteen buildings had to be demolished before construction could commence. A modern-day site plan clearly indicates how the John Adams Building (completed in 1939) had to be reduced in size and designed 'offset' within the block to allow for the siting of the Folger Shakespeare Library on such an important piece of Washington soil.[49] Libraries dedicated to Thomas Jefferson and James Madison complete the Library of Congress development.

In July 1930, as part of a funeral eulogy for Henry Clay Folger, William Adams Slade drew attention to the symbolism of the location of the still to be completed library. For Slade, who used language and imagery that was both nationalistic and heroic, there had been a 'historical movement' in England around the time of Shakespeare, and 'lines' from this movement could be traced,

taking new directions, radiat[ing] from a common center, some more and some less, so too, a line drawn from the site of the Folger Shakespeare Memorial through the Capital building and extended onward, will all but touch the monument to Washington and the memorial to Lincoln – the two Americans whose light also spreads across the world.[50]

Echoing the view of Ashley Thorndike, Slade stated that 'Shakespeare, Washington, and Lincoln are at one and at home in a Nation which is one, and which in the idealism of its heroes can find the expression of its own idealism.'[51] Slade was later to carry this message directly to the heart of American democracy, presenting a special report to the elected members of the Seventieth US Congress.

While the morale of the American nation was high in 1928 when the plans were finalised and the construction teams arrived, things were soon to be very different. As building commenced the Great Depression began with the stock market crash of October 1929. By the time of the dedication ceremony for the completed library in April 1932, the American stock market was worth just 20 per cent of its 1929 value; fifteen million people or 30 per cent of the workforce were without jobs and eleven thousand of the twenty-five thousand American banks had failed. As corporate America struggled and a crisis of unprecedented proportions threatened the American population, the nation's leaders gathered together to acknowledge the role played by Shakespeare in promoting national unity and creating American tradition.

The completed Folger Shakespeare Library was dedicated at a lavish ceremony on 23 April 1932, where President Herbert Clark Hoover and the first lady 'sat on the platform surrounded by military and naval aides, [and] representatives of the services'.[52] This was a state occasion boosted by all the trappings of nationhood that would not have been out of place at a ceremony at the Court of St James's, London, and as if to emphasise the point the *Washington Post* of the following day reported that 'King George [had] cabled a greeting from Windsor Castle.'[53] The invited dignitaries heard a member of one of America's most distinguished families deliver an oration that explained the process of appropriation that had occurred throughout the previous century.

The key speaker was Joseph Quincy Adams, namesake of the son of the man who in 1786 had suggested that the 'English fail to . . . care for their own traditions', former professor of English at Cornell University and now Supervisor of Research of the Library. Adams was to repeat several of the main declarations made in 1927 by Ashley Thorndike in his *Shakespeare in America* address. However, whereas Thorndike delivered his words in London to a private audience of British academics, at this later lavish state occasion Adams directly addressed America. Before the president of the United States, the first lady and other gathered dignitaries, he presented a thesis that can be seen to reflect many if not all of the aspects that were central to the appropriation of Shakespeare during the previous century. It was as if the eminent scholar had drawn his argument directly from the newspapers, lectures, sermons and journals of the 1850s. The status of the presenter, the importance of the audience and the grandeur of the location all confirmed that the appropriation of Shakespeare was now complete. Shakespeare had officially been given a home in America.

Adams first re-emphasised the significance of Washington DC as the chosen site for a Shakespeare Memorial:

In its capital city a nation is accustomed to rear monuments to the persons who most have contributed to its well-being. And hence Washington has become a city of monuments. Varied in kind, and almost countless in number, they proclaim from every street, park and circle the affection of a grateful American people. Yet amid them all, three memorials stand out, in size, dignity and beauty, conspicuous above the rest: the memorials to Washington, Lincoln, Shakespeare.[54]

With these words Adams set the tone for his address. It was as if his intention was not to praise Shakespeare but to publicly confirm his status as an American hero and founding father. Adams declared, 'The three monuments thus stand as memorials, and as symbols, of the three great personal forces that have moulded the political, the spiritual, and the intellectual life of our nation.'[55]

Countering the comments voiced by some nineteenth-century British travellers to the United States, Adams rejected any suggestion that the national claim to Shakespeare was less justified than the claim to Americans Washington and Lincoln. His argument echoed that of Joseph Watson in the *New York Herald* in 1877, emphasising that the colonists who arrived in North America from Britain could legitimately claim Shakespeare, 'the finest flower of . . . language and culture, [as their] birth-right'.[56] Ethnocentric philosophy, which had been institutionalised in the nineteenth century, encouraged Adams to regard himself, his audience and Shakespeare as members of an 'Anglo-Saxon race' with a shared 'birth-right'.[57] The report in *The Washington Post* concurred, suggesting that Shakespeare represented the same 'racial stock . . . as the two Presidents who happened to be born on our side of the Atlantic' and that 'Shakespeare was as American as Washington and Lincoln.'[58]

Adams described how copies of Shakespeare had gradually arrived in the homes of prominent Americans and then, via the theatre stage, lecture room and parlour table, became part of American culture. In the words of the *Washington Post*, Shakespeare may not have 'come over on the Mayflower, but he came shortly afterwards'.[59] In anticipation of possible criticism, Adams insisted that he was not 'overemphasizing the influence of Shakespeare in America during this awkward – we might say adolescent – period of growth'.[60] For Adams, as for many other academics, the appropriation of Shakespeare, with the resultant Shakespeare idolatry during the 'American renaissance', was 'one of the astonishing manifestations of our intellectual life'.[61] While not criticising the process responsible for this situation, Adams asked the audience the reasonable question 'How are we to explain this remarkable phenomenon?'[62] Following a line of argument that would perhaps have seemed heretical to some Shakespeare idolaters,

Adams asserted that 'The sheer excellence of Shakespeare as an artist cannot be regarded as adequate to account for the veneration accorded him by the very rank and file of a not over cultivated folk', and that 'another reason must be sought, more tangible in kind, and springing from some fundamental characteristic of the people as a whole'.[63]

The question that Adams now posed was not why the citizens of the educated elite, such as Furness, Grant, Folger, Slade or Adams himself, might recognise the value in Shakespeare. These people might perhaps be considered as members of a discerning and economically privileged group. The 'phenomenon' that Adams wished to explore for his audience was why Americans 'en masse', the demonstrably anti-English citizens and, in Adams's words, 'not over cultivated folk', had, during the past century, embraced an English playwright as a type of American hero.

To answer his rhetorical question Adams acknowledged the service Shakespeare had unknowingly performed in 'preserving in America a homogeneity of English culture when our territory was being rapidly expanded, and [. . .] stretched across a wilderness almost to breaking point'.[64] In the now familiar language that had been a significant part of nineteenth-century political and social discourse, he stated the great importance of Shakespeare 'when foreign immigration, in floodgate fashion, poured into our land to threaten the continued existence of that homogeneity', immigrants who, while 'honest, thrifty, and altogether admirable as citizens . . . began in the big Middle West seriously to alter the solid Anglo-Saxon character of the people'.[65] For Adams, and perhaps for many of the nativists of the nineteenth century, immigrants 'Foreign in their background and alien in their outlook upon life . . . exhibited varied racial characteristics, varied ideals, and varied types of civilization'. Adams pronounced the great fear of nineteenth-century American citizens who benefited from their position of privilege. The fear was that 'America seemed destined to become a babel of tongues and cultures',[66] and in order to preserve the Anglo-American culture that had originated in the thirteen east-coast former colonies, Shakespeare was appropriated to the cause of E Pluribus Unum.

Before the American president and the audience of assembled dignitaries, Adams described how Shakespeare had been increasingly appropriated, 'about the time the forces of immigration became a menace to the preservation of our long established English civilization'.[67] It was to Shakespeare that the nineteenth-century American Establishment turned to unite the population through the adoption of language, culture, symbol and philosophy. As Adams explained,

To young and receptive minds the great English dramatist was held up as the supreme thinker, artist, poet. Not Homer, nor Dante, nor Goethe, not Chaucer, nor Spenser, nor even Milton, but Shakespeare was made the chief object of their study and veneration.[68]

Adams justified the status now formally awarded to Shakespeare in this city of memorials to Americans such as George Washington and Abraham Lincoln. His powerful conclusion was that 'If out of America, unwieldy in size, and commonly called the melting-pot of races, there has been evolved a homogeneous nation, with a culture that is still essentially English, we must acknowledge that in the process Shakespeare has played a major part.'[69]

After more than a century of appropriation, a fitting memorial to another American founding father had been dedicated in the city of American monuments. To the visually impressive if not imperial Mall of Washington DC, grouped together with the United States Capitol, Supreme Court and Library of Congress buildings, was added the Folger Shakespeare Library. Henry Clay Folger had 'founded in America a dwelling place for the spirit of Shakespeare'.[70] The words of the *Washington Post* perhaps captured the belief of many nineteenth-century Americans: 'Shakespeare is here just as certain as God reposes in some of the quieter Churches.'[71] Shakespeare's position at the heart of the American nation had now been confirmed.

This book has provided evidence of the comprehensive appropriation of Shakespeare by a culturally Anglo-Saxon-led American society during the nineteenth century. I have argued that the idea of America was established on an idealised notion of republicanism, in binary opposition to the British Establishment, and that there had been an urgent need to identify accessible symbols that could help to unite the new nation and forge a sense of American tradition. Many in English-speaking America chose to adopt Shakespeare as a national figure and promote his writings as being important to all Americans, whatever their background. During this process of E Pluribus Unum, pride in expressions of American nationalism and ethnic Anglo-Saxonism increased, fostered in part by the appropriation of the cultural icon of Shakespeare.

As Thorndike, Slade and Adams have eloquently argued, without the conditioning effect of Shakespeare on the diverse population of America, the reality of new immigration and the large number of citizens for whom English was not the 'mother tongue' could have combined to threaten the cultural hegemony and version of republicanism preferred by the American elite. In an attempt to counter what many regarded as a danger to the republic in the nineteenth century, Shakespeare was used to promote the cause of American nationalism, to encourage expression of patriotic pride and to teach citizens to read and write American English. This process of appropriation proved to be so successful and wide-ranging that, for many American citizens, Shakespeare had become as American as George Washington.

NOTES

1. *New York Times*, 29 April 1875, p. 6.
2. This Barnum 'story' was to be repeated in Twain's later 'travelogue', *Following the Equator: A Journey around the World*, 2 vols. (New York, 1897), vol. II, pp. 312–17.
3. *New York Times*, 29 April 1875, p. 6.
4. Hart was the fourth member of the family to bear the name 'Shakspeare'. The Hart family inherited the Birthplace property in 1670 following the death of Shakespeare's granddaughter Lady Barnard.
5. *The Times*, 25 October 1809, p. 4.
6. Phineas Taylor Barnum, *The Life of P. T. Barnum, Written by Himself* (London: Sampson, Low & Son, 1855), p. 275.
7. Ibid., p. 344.
8. Levi Fox, *In Honour of Shakespeare* (Norwich: Jarrold & Son, 1972), p. 7.
9. Westfall, *American Shakespearean Criticism*, pp. 203–4.
10. *The Times*, 31 October 1846, p. 6. Reprinted in *The Times* from a story first carried in the *Banbury Guardian*.
11. *The Times*, 5 December 1846, p. 6.
12. *The Times*, 10 April 1847, p. 7.
13. *The Times*, 15 June 1847, p. 7.
14. 'Shakspeare's House', *The Times*, 21 July 1847, p. 5.
15. *The Times*, 20 July 1847, p. 12.
16. Shakespeare Birthplace Trust, Office of Records, Records DR 628/13.
17. See editorial in the *Atlas*, 1106/22 (24 July 1847), p. 506.
18. *The Times*, 6 August 1847, p. 6.
19. *The Times*, 11 September 1847, p. 6. According to Shakespeare Birthplace records, no real bidding took place at the auction. It would appear that the 'combined committee's' offer of three thousand pounds was accepted and the auction immediately closed.
20. *New York Times*, 29 April 1875, p. 6.
21. Between 1852 and 1862 there were 16,188 visitors, while 5,134 Americans chose to sign the visitor book (visitor data taken from the records of the Shakespeare Birthplace Trust).
22. Performing in the first play at the new theatre was eighteen-year-old Sacramento-born Mary Anderson.

23. Sidney Charters, *The Home of Lovely Players* (Birmingham, 1935), p. 19. American money also helped to meet the cost of building the town's Swan Theatre.
24. 'Shakespeare and America', *The Times*, 18 October 1887, p. 6.
25. Ibid.
26. Ibid.
27. Ibid.
28. Ibid.
29. Over four hundred silent films were to be made utilising the plays of Shakespeare before the advent of the 'talkie'. The first film of a play by Shakespeare to have a soundtrack was *The Taming of the Shrew*, directed by Sam Taylor in 1929, just two years after the first 'talkie' was screened. Mary Pickford and Douglas Fairbanks took the lead roles. See Roger Manvell, *Shakespeare and the Film* (New York: A. S. Barnes & Co., 1979), pp. 23–4.
30. Robert Hamilton Ball, *Shakespeare on Silent Film: A Strange Eventful History* (London: George Allen & Unwin, 1968), p. 39.
31. See also *Macbeth*, D. W. Griffith (USA, 1916).
32. *The Birth of a Nation*, D. W. Griffith (USA, 1915).
33. Robert Metcalf Smith, *The Formation of Shakespeare Libraries in America* (New York: Shakespeare Association of America, 1929), p. 66.
34. Ibid., p. 73.
35. Sidney Lee, *Shakespeare's Comedies, Histories and Tragedies, Containing a Census of Extant Copies with Some Account of Their History and Condition* (Oxford, 1902), p. 16.
36. Sidney Lee, *Notes and Additions to the Census of Copies of the Shakespeare First Folio* (London: Oxford University Press, 1906), p. 12.
37. Ibid., p. 30.
38. Ibid.
39. Anthony James West, 'Provisional New Census of the Shakespeare First Folio', *Library*, 17/1 (March 1993), pp. 60–6. The first part of this census has now been published, see West, *The Shakespeare First Folio*.
40. Slade, 'The Significance of the Folger Shakespeare Memorial', p. 70.
41. Bristol, *Shakespeare's America*, p. 73.
42. Ibid., p. 72.
43. Slade, 'The Significance of the Folger Shakespeare Memorial', p. 59.
44. Emily Jordan Folger, *Meridian Club Paper by Mrs Folger, 1933* (privately published and held within the Folger Archive, Folger Shakespeare Library, Washington DC), pp. 13–14.
45. Ibid.
46. S. Parkes Cadman, 'Prayer and Eulogy', in *Henry C. Folger: 18 June 1857–11 June 1930* (New Haven, 1931), p. 17.
47. Folger, *Meridian Club Paper*, p. 18.
48. *Congressional Record*, 70th Congress, 1st session, 1928, 69, part 7, pp. 8004–5, debate on Bill HR 9355. This Bill was debated authorising 'purchase, condemnation or otherwise at a cost not to exceed $600,000, all the privately owned land including buildings and other structures in squares nos. 760 and 762

for the Library of Congress'. See also 'Shakesperiana Collection', *Congressional Record*, 70th Congress, 1st session, 1928, 69, part 7, pp. 7422–3.

49. See appendix 2, below.
50. Slade, 'The Significance of the Folger Shakespeare Memorial', p. 41.
51. Ibid., p. 70.
52. Folger, *Meridian Club Paper*, p. 38.
53. James Waldo Fawcett, 'Dedication of the Folger Shakespeare Memorial Library', *Washington Post*, 24 April, 1932, p. 1. The report continued on pp. 7 and 10.
54. Adams, 'The Folger Shakespeare Memorial', p. 212.
55. Ibid.
56. Ibid., p. 213.
57. Ibid.
58. Fawcett, 'Dedication of the Folger Shakespeare Memorial Library', p. 1.
59. Ibid.
60. Adams, 'The Folger Shakespeare Memorial', p. 229.
61. Ibid.
62. Ibid.
63. Ibid.
64. Ibid., p. 230.
65. Ibid.
66. Ibid.
67. Ibid.
68. Ibid.
69. Ibid., p. 231.
70. George E. Dimock, 'Biographical Sketch', in *Henry C. Folger: 18 June 1957–11 June 1930* (New Haven, 1931), p. 23.
71. *Washington Post*, 24 April 1932, p. 7.

Epilogue

While the ceremony performed to dedicate the Folger Shakespeare Library in Washington DC officially confirmed Shakespeare's important position within American culture, uninterrupted mass consumption of Shakespeare provided the popular endorsement. This acceptance of Shakespeare as an American idol encouraged recognition of the name (now almost a brand) by subsequent generations of young Americans.

Today Shakespeare is still willingly consumed, though very few Americans are likely to consider how or why the plays and imagery seem to fit so easily into their national consciousness. What Glen Loney and Patricia MacKay described as 'the Shakespeare complex' represents an almost religious fervour for Shakespeare and associated imagery.[1] It is as though for many Americans Shakespeare is a 'cultural talisman, [and] to admit a distaste for Shakespeare or his plays is tantamount to blasphemy'.[2]

STAGE AND PARK

In America there are now more than 118 separate Shakespeare festivals and companies catering for the demand from audiences.[3] These festivals allow Americans the opportunity to affirm their adopted cultural association – to offer their 'pledge of allegiance'. Through Shakespeare festivals, American communities celebrate and market the playwright and his dramatic works across the US, in cities as far apart as Montgomery, San Diego, Boulder, Atlanta, Ashland, Dallas and Cedar City.

To qualify for the title 'festival' in *Shakespeare Companies and Festivals: An International Guide* (1995) 'a substantial portion of a company's annual season had to be dedicated to producing Shakespeare's plays'.[4] While perhaps quite broad, it is clear that within America the term 'Shakespeare festival' has the power to attract paying customers, and hence the title is favoured by theatre companies. These celebrations of Shakespeare divide into two general categories, namely 'destination festivals and community festivals'.[5]

The former are fully professional, operating throughout the whole year, sometimes using more than one stage, and attracting visitors to city and region. For example, the festival in Ashland, Oregon (founded in 1935), with its three stages, drew an audience of 400,000 in 2002, while the local population numbered only 30,000.[6] The less formal community festivals are usually run by amateurs over a limited period, and as such attract mostly local audiences.

The *Shakespeare Companies and Festivals* guide includes annual atten-dance figures for 102 of the 118 American entries. This data suggests that the total annual paying theatre audience for Shakespeare in America was, at the time of survey, at least 3,048,270.[7] This figure excludes the many free performances, such as those presented in New York's Central Park and school or college productions, and it includes a number of plays that are not by Shakespeare. Yet while the core data is admittedly a little unrefined, the suggestion of over three million annual ticket sales provides evidence of Shakespeare's continued power to attract an American audience.

This type of mass enthusiasm for Shakespeare and related folk culture has also helped to spawn 149 weekend 'Renaissance Faires'. These fairs, com-bining activities and imagery gleaned from Shakespearean drama and other romantic fiction, are now popular with families throughout the USA. Any Internet search of the World Wide Web will reveal the extent of the com-prehensive calendar of events, the merchandising and the entertainments designed to capitalise on this fervour for a characteristically American leisure activity.[8]

In addition to the festivals and Renaissance Faires in America, there are also 'replica' Shakespearean theatres. The American nineteenth-century acceptance of Shakespeare as popular culture, performed in front of a lively democratic audience, perhaps provided the inspiration for a type of presen-tation largely ignored by members of the theatre establishment in England. The first reconstruction of a Shakespearean 'Globe style' theatre was erected for the Chicago World's Fair of 1933, and an interesting episode from the history of this replica clearly exemplifies American enthusiasm.

Following the close of the Chicago fair, the complete 'Globe' theatre building was moved to Dallas, Texas, and in June 1936, as part of that state's official centennial celebrations, a quasi-religious ceremony 'conse-crated' the newly re-erected stage for the citizens of the Southwest.[9] Earlier that year the American vice consul to the UK and a party of local digni-taries in Stratford-upon-Avon had gathered to collect soil from the garden at Shakespeare's Birthplace and river water from the Avon, in preparation for the Dallas ceremony. The soil was placed in a box made from charred wood saved from the recently destroyed Stratford-upon-Avon theatre and the water secured in a pristine aluminium bottle, ready for shipping across the Atlantic by Cunard liner. On its arrival in New York, a member of the British consulate met the package prior to its final onward journey to Dallas.

The *Dallas Morning News* of 3 June 1936 reported the previous day's 'rites' of sprinkling the earth and water on the replica Globe stage before an invited audience of six hundred, transmitted via a live radio broadcast to the many listeners of station WFAA.[10] With the stage symbolically consecrated, the citizens of Texas were invited to the Globe to watch a Shakespeare play performed 'every hour on the hour' for the next 177 days.[11]

The reverence that had been shown to these 'relics' and the ceremony performed at the opening of Dallas's Globe playhouse provides evidence of the prestige conferred on Shakespeare by Americans living deep in the interior of the US, far from Washington DC with its national monuments and Folger Shakespeare Library.

Following the success of the Chicago and Dallas experiments, at least nine Globe-style theatres were built in cities across America to allow audiences to experience Shakespeare in a more interactive if not authentic setting. England had to wait until 1997 for its single Globe Theatre reconstruction, but again it was largely due to American enthusiasm that this celebration of Shakespearean theatre was completed.[12] Chicago-born actor Sam Wanamaker fought a more than thirty-year campaign to rebuild Shakespeare's Globe Theatre close to its original site, and in the process he overcame the apathy of England's theatre establishment and the opposition of the local authorities.[13] At the age of fifteen Wanamaker had attended the Chicago World's Fair of 1933 with its Globe reconstruction, and he later reflected that it was in Chicago that he first dreamed of rebuilding Shakespeare's Globe.

While Wanamaker was to suggest that his campaign was a case of 'British culture – American money',[14] it can in fact be considered an example of the contrast between American and English attitudes to Shakespeare. While after the successful nineteenth-century appropriation Americans accepted Shakespeare as a key cultural icon, many English academics considered him a worthy playwright but an inconvenient conservative cultural anachronism. As an illustration of this difference in attitude, when Wanamaker asked renowned English actor Sir John Gielgud to be the 'honorary Vice President' of the London Globe project, Gielgud had 'strong misgivings'.[15] Three years after Wanamaker's death, Gielgud confessed that, despite being a London resident during the period in which this American citizen devoted a large part of his energies to the Globe project, he was 'ashamed' to admit that he had not even bothered to have a private meeting with him to offer personal support. As Gielgud observed, it was 'ironic that the conception and funding [of Shakespeare's Globe] should be American'.[16]

Other Americans born into a national culture that so freely celebrates Shakespeare continue Wanamaker's efforts to export the playwright back across the Atlantic to England. At the time of writing, the longest-running comedy show in London consists of a presentation of Shakespeare by a group of American players. The Reduced Shakespeare Company has, since its origins in 1981 as a pass-the-hat act at California Renaissance Faires, offered appreciative audiences in London a vaudeville-burlesque parody presenting thirty-seven Shakespeare plays in just ninety-seven minutes.[17]

SCREENS LARGE AND SMALL

While the growing number of Hollywood film versions of complete plays is obvious to many observers and requires no additional comment, what is more indicative of Shakespeare in modern American culture is the way the plays or the playwright have been introduced into genres far removed from traditional stage drama.[18] In *Shakespeare and Modern Popular Culture*, Douglas Lanier revealed the frequency of Shakespeare appearances across the breadth of entertainment channels. Unsurprisingly although important, the majority of these channels and genres originate in America and are primarily targeted at American consumers. Lanier chose to begin his book with a description of a scene from *Star Trek VI: The Undiscovered Country*.[19] In this film 'product', created to reflect contemporary American social and geopolitical issues, a group of Klingons recommend to the crew of the Star Ship Enterprise that they read Shakespeare in the 'original Klingon'.[20] To make sense of this instalment of the popular science-fiction series, it is necessary to calmly accept the insinuation that Shakespeare first migrated from England to America and then, through American exploration of space, was introduced into the Galaxy with its race and culture of Klingons. Space travel indeed.

Back on earth but firmly anchored in Hollywood's version of the American dream, Arnold Schwartzeneggar briefly played the role of Hamlet. In the *Last Action Hero*, the audience was introduced to a high-school teacher who described Hamlet as the 'first action hero'.[21] In the imagination of the movie's young protagonist, Hamlet is played by Schwartzeneggar, a swaggering, gun-toting, explosive-detonating Dane, who creates mayhem in Elsinore, deciding without hesitation that all around him are 'not to be'.

Lanier provides other examples of Shakespeare's incorporation into modern popular culture. Characteristically American cartoons such as Mr Magoo, the Flintstones, Donald Duck, Bugs Bunny and Mickey Mouse have all included Shakespeare.[22] While not within Lanier's list of animations, even Bart Simpson and the Springfield cartoon cast played a six-minute parody version of *Hamlet* (Lisa as Ophelia and Moe Szyslak as Claudius were particularly successful), and Shakespeare references appear in another fifteen Simpson episodes.[23]

From television to computers, and while at present there is little evidence that 'computer gamers' with their violent cyber world have been offered characters drawn from Shakespeare, *Star Trek VI: The Undiscovered Country* did spawn a computer game entitled 'Klingon Academy', complete with Shakespeare-quoting General Chang. Perhaps *Hamlet* 'the game' is not far away.

Further demonstrating how freely Shakespeare is now incorporated into niche markets in America, Shakespeare even provides inspiration for soft erotica and cult horror videos, titles such as *Live Nude Shakespeare*[24] and *Tromeo and Juliet*[25] demonstrating the extent of the 'cross over'. The latter adaptation of *Romeo and Juliet* is from the New York studio Troma Inc., better known for titles such as the *Toxic Avenger* series of cult 'blood and gore' films. Troma have marketed this youth product to an American audience by proclaiming, 'Body piercing. Kinky sex. Dismemberment. The things that make Shakespeare great!' Examples such as these highlight the way consumer awareness of Shakespeare, in no small part due to the process of appropriation in the nineteenth century, is now enthusiastically exploited for both amusement and financial profit in a manner that reflects the traditional enterprise culture of the US.

BAND OF BROTHERS

A recent episode in the long story of Shakespeare and the American nation serves to combine many aspects of the appropriation and clearly indicates how complete and how significant the process has ultimately become. A news release from the US Department of Defense dated 10 December 2002 announced further distribution of free copies of Armed Services Edition (ASE) books to military personnel serving at the Pentagon, Washington DC, and aboard the USS *Nicholas*.[26] One of the four titles chosen for the up to 100,000 members of 'deployed US forces' was a special edition of Shakespeare's *Henry V* published in an easy-to-carry 'cargo pocket size'. In the opinion of the Pentagon's Chief of Naval Information, Rear Admiral

Stephen R. Pietropaoli, 'Getting quality reading material to our troops on the front lines is a great initiative.'[27]

Widely reported in the media, this idea of the US military carrying pocket-sized editions of Shakespeare, possibly into combat, is of course wholly consistent with the nineteenth-century appropriation of the playwright to the cause of the American nation. And what makes this story more than ordinarily newsworthy and relevant to the epilogue of this book is the timing. In December 2002 the American nation was still in a heightened state of patriotism and, more importantly, US 'troops on the front lines' were at a state of readiness for combat far from the American homeland.

Although US service personnel on overseas deployment doubtless welcomed this free reading material, the idea of Shakespeare possibly inspiring or influencing American troops was too much for some to bear quietly. While several American academics commented publicly on the ASE distribution, one modern-day malcontent, writing for the UK's *Guardian* newspaper (ostensibly about *Henry V* but actually to express his hostility to what was described as the 'illegal invasion of Iraq'), went so far as to specifically blame Shakespeare for the presence of English-speaking American and British military forces in Iraq and for their 'demonstrations of Anglo-Saxon omnipotence'.[28] The writer claimed that the plays of Shakespeare had, 'for more than four centuries', helped to create the shared perceptions that allowed English-speaking people to assert themselves so confidently and forcefully over other nations and cultures.

In the early twentieth century the powerful words of Ashley Thorndike, William Adams Slade and Joseph Quincy Adams formally proclaimed Shakespeare's important role as an American hero and as one of the revered band of brothers helping to unite the American nation. It would appear from recent evidence that their collective appraisal of the relationship between Shakespeare and the American nation still remains as valid and relevant as ever.

NOTES

1. Glen Loney, and Patricia MacKay, *The Shakespeare Complex* (New York: Drama Book Specialists, 1975).
2. Ibid., p. 6.
3. Ron Engle, Felicia Hardison Londré and Daniel J. Watermeier, eds., *Shakespeare Companies and Festivals: An International Guide* (Westport CT: Greenwood Press, 1995), pp. 511–15. For an earlier survey of Shakespeare festivals, see Loney and MacKay, *The Shakespeare Complex*.

4. Engle, Londré and Watermeier, eds., *Shakespeare Companies and Festivals*, p. xvii.

5. Ibid.

6. The audience for the Oregon Shakespeare Festival in Ashland is given as 399,609 for 795 performances of eleven different plays.

7. The tabulated total audience figures exclude school groups (where declared). Data in the guide represents single years between 1989 and 1994.

8. Loney and MacKay, *The Shakespeare Complex*. See also the website for the *Renaissance Magazine*, Bridgeport CT: http://www.renaissancemagazine.com/fairelist.html.

9. Ivor Brown and George Fearon, *Amazing Monument: A Short History of the Shakespeare Industry* (London: William Heinemann, 1939), pp. 9–11. See also chapter 6, 'Hands across the Sea'. An account of this Dallas ceremony can also be found in Graham Holderness, ed., *The Shakespeare Myth* (Manchester: Manchester University Press, 1988), p. 1.

10. 'Earth and Water from Bard's Homeland Is Sprinkled on Stage', *Dallas Morning News*, 3 June 1936, section 1, p. 12.

11. 'Unique Rites Supported by Civic Leaders', *Dallas Morning News*, 31 May 1936, section 2, p. 3.

12. As part of a special event in 1912 at the Earl's Court Exhibition Hall in London, the 'first Globe theatre' since the seventeenth century was opened to the public as part of a feature called 'Shakespeare's England'. This theatre, although designed by Sir Edwin Lutyens, was the result of 'the energy and imagination of a Brooklyn-born lady'. This lady was known in New York, prior to her marriage into the English aristocracy, as Jennie Jerome, but upon marrying became Lady Randolph Churchill, later to be the mother of Sir Winston Churchill. See Loney and MacKay, *The Shakespeare Complex*, p. 26.

13. Barry Day, *This Wooden 'O'* (London: Oberon Books, 1996), p. 19. See also the interview with Sam Wanamaker in Holderness, ed., *The Shakespeare Myth*, pp. 16–23.

14. Day, *This Wooden 'O'*, p. 156.

15. Ibid., foreword by Gielgud, p. ix.

16. Ibid. The difference between American and English attitudes towards memorials to Shakespeare is further demonstrated by the case of the church of St Mary, Aldermanbury, City of London. Heminges and Condel, friends of Shakespeare, shareholders in the Globe and compilers of the First Folio of 1623, were both lifelong members of this church parish and both were buried within its grounds. The church, badly damaged by fire in 1940, was acquired and reassembled in Fulton, Missouri, by Westminster College. The graveyard in London where the church stood until 1966 is now marked by a simple memorial to the two men, who after Shakespeare himself must be the most important figures in Shakespeare 'Bardology'.

17. Douglas Lanier, *Shakespeare and Modern Popular Culture* (Oxford: Oxford University Press, 2002), pp 102–4.

18. For a study of film adaptations, see Manvell, *Shakespeare and the Film*.

19. *Star Trek VI: The Undiscovered Country*, Nicholas Meyer (USA, 1991).
20. Lanier, *Shakespeare and Modern Popular Culture*, p. 2.
21. *Last Action Hero*, John McTiernan (USA, 1993). See also Lanier, *Shakespeare and Modern Popular Culture*, pp. 102–4.
22. Lanier, *Shakespeare and Modern Popular Culture*, pp. 82–109.
23. 'Tales from the Public Domain', *The Simpsons* (USA, 17 March 2002).
24. *Live Nude Shakespeare*, Michael D. Fox and Dale Evans (USA, 1997). See also the description in Lanier, *Shakespeare and Modern Popular Culture*, p. 101.
25. *Tromeo and Juliet*, Lloyd Kaufman (USA, 1996). See also the description in Lanier, *Shakespeare and Modern Popular Culture*, pp. 101–2.
26. 'Major Publishers Begin Massive Distribution of Free Books to US Troops Abroad', United States Department of Defense, News Release no. 627-02. See also http://www.defenselink.mil/news/Dec2002/b12102002_bt627-02.html.
27. Ibid.
28. Gary Taylor, 'Cry Havoc: Shakespeare Saw Henry V's Brutal Strike against the French as a Battle of Good against Evil, of "Plain Shock" and "Awe" ', *Guardian*, 5 April 2003.

The title page and preface from *The Plays and Poems of William Shakespeare... First American Edition* (Philadelphia: Bioren & Madan, 1795). The preface is thought to have been written by the lawyer Joseph Hopkinson.

For this modernised 'facsimile', I have felt it necessary to adjust the spelling and punctuation of the text in certain places.

THE
PLAYS AND POEMS

OF

WILLIAM SHAKSPEARE

CORRECTED FROM THE LATEST AND BEST
LONDON EDITIONS, WITH NOTES, BY

SAMUEL JOHNSON, L.L.D.

TO WHICH ARE ADDED,

A GLOSSARY

AND THE

LIFE OF THE AUTHOR.

EMBELLISHED WITH A STRIKING LIKENESS FROM
THE COLLECTION OF HIS GRACE THE DUKE OF CHANDOS.

FIRST AMERICAN EDITION.

VOL. I.

PHILADELPHIA:

PRINTED AND SOLD BY BIOREN & MADAN.

MDCCXCV.

PREFACE
TO THE
AMERICAN EDITION.

AN Edition of the Works of William Shakspeare is now offered to the citizens of the United States. This poet has always been considered as the father of the English drama, and as, beyond any comparison, the greatest theatrical writer in the English language. Within the last thirty years, we may safely compute that his plays have undergone at least thirty editions. One of these, published about three years ago, by Mr. Boydell of London, was upon a superfine quarto page, and including numerous superb engravings, each copy cost about an hundred guineas. No other English poet has afforded such an inexhaustible harvest for critical illustration. It is indeed hardly possible to open any English book on the Belles Lettres, without meeting a reference to Shakspeare. So incessant is the echo of his name, so tumultuous the admiration of his talents, that a plain reader may be tempted to feel something like that Athenian, who was tired with constantly hearing of ARISTIDES THE JUST. Quintilian tells us that Menander, the ancient comic poet, had so totally surpassed all his competitors in that species of composition, that they served only as foils to reflect his lustre. A remark of this kind may be applied to the plays of Shakspeare; for a jury of critics would agree that they are more truly valuable than all the other productions collectively of the English stage.

An attentive perusal of this author must indeed afford the utmost pleasure, and justify the utmost praise. We have neither inclination, nor time to insert the ponderous dissertations on his merit, that some preceding editors have discharged upon the world. But it will not be unacceptable to hazard a few remarks on the genius and the writings of a poet, as yet but imperfectly known on the western shore of the Atlantic.

The most popular and formidable objection to theatrical exhibitions appears to be, that they have an immoral tendency. The dramatic writers of England afford too much foundation for this remark; and it is worth while to compare Shakspeare in this point of view with some of his successors. Lord Kaimes, in his Elements of Criticism observes, that 'if Congreve's comedies did not rack him with remorse in his last moments, *he must have been lost to all sense of virtue.*' Mr. Pope speaks of another of these dramatic panders, *who fairly puts all characters to bed.* Farquhar may candidly be termed an apostle of adultery. The Country Wife of Wycherly, is one of the most animated comedies imaginable, but it is at the same time a hot bed of prostitution; and some of the other plays of the same author are almost equally exceptionable. Dryden wrote twenty-eight pieces for the stage, and as he frankly declares of some of them, he knew at the time of writing, that *they were bad enough to please*. The Orphan of Otway has many hateful passages; and it is well known in Newgate, that Gay's Macheath has conducted more than one of his imitators to the gibbet. The late Sir John Fielding, sometime before his decease, thought proper to send a message to Mr. Garrick, requesting that he would stop the performance of the Beggar's Opera; as the exhibition was regularly followed by an addition to the catalogue of felons. Lord Gardenstone, when speaking of *The City Wives, or the Confederacy*, a comedy by Vanburgh, has the following passage: 'This is one of those plays which throw infamy on the English stage, and general taste, though it is not destitute of wit and humour. *A people must be in the last degree depraved, among whom such public entertainment are produced and encouraged*. In this symptom of degenerate manners, we are, I believe, *unmatched by any nation that is, or ever was, in the world*.'* Among modern comic writers, Foote is one of the most entertaining and voluminous. The depravity of his writings too often corresponded with that of his life. Of this class of authors Dr. Johnson has given the following character.

> Themselves they studied; as they felt, they writ;
> Intrigue was plot, obscenity was wit.
> Vice always found a sympathetic friend;
> They pleas'd their age, and did not aim to mend.
> Yet bards like these aspir'd to lasting praise,
> And proudly hop'd to pimp on future days.[+]

We have been thus explicit in admitting the frequent immorality of the British stage, because excellence is best known by comparison, and because on this head, Shakspeare has nothing to fear. His text contains indeed a few, and but a few sentences, that the rigour of ecclesiastical discipline would exclude from publicity. Whether they were written by himself it is impossible to guess, on account of the strange condition in which his works have been printed. But one fact is certain, that, in the whole circle of his personages, there is not to be found a Wildair, a Ranger, a Macheath, or a Horner, characters whose accomplishments are calculated to varnish over their vices. The fools of Shakspeare are always despised, and his villains are always hated. His Iago, Edmund, and Richard III possess an un-common degree of cynical pleasantry, and, in a writer of ordinary talents, this quality would have been suffered to overbalance their guilt, and like the heroes of

---

* Miscellanies in prose and verse, printed in Edinburgh, in 1792, second edition, p. 136.
[+] Prologue, at the opening of the Theatre Royal, Drury Lane, 1747.

Gay and Wycherly, they would, in spite of common sense, have become a sort of favourites. But in Shakspeare this dash of humour is merely cast in to relieve the feelings of the reader, that he may without disguise attend them to the completion and the punishment of their crimes. If any one of the vicious characters in this writer can be termed seductive, it must be Falstaff; yet he is, on every occasion, overwhelmed with such ridicule and contempt, that no reader can envy his situation, and Shakspeare, in the sequel, dismisses him to an excess of neglect and ignominy, that may hurt the sensibility even of the severest morality. In Farquhar and other writers of his kind, the laws of marriage are universally despised; their violation is a common jest; and from an attendance on such scenes, young people of both sexes must retire with the most unsuitable impressions. But in no part of Shakspeare will such depravity be found. Doll Tearsheet and Falstaff's Hostess are no formidable advocates of corruption. The leading female personages in Shakspeare, such as Miranda, Isabella, Desdemona, Perdita, Beatrice, Rosalind, the two Portias, Imogen, Ophelia, Juliet, Olivia, and Cordelia, are all equally remarkable for the purity of their manners. Even in the Merry Wives of Windsor, there is not a line ascribed to any female that can hurt delicacy; and while *The Country Wife* concludes with a dance of cuckolds, the abortive gallantry of Falstaff ends with a marriage. The more carefully that we compare Shakspeare with his successors, the more shall we be convinced, that as a moral writer he was infinitely superior to any one of them, and that the reproaches which have been thundered from the pulpit against the stage, cannot reasonably be applied to the stage of Shakspeare.

Even when this author found it requisite to represent female characters as vicious, they are divested of the usual attractions of the sex. Lady Macbeth, and the two elder daughters of Lear, present examples too horrid to be contagious; and each of them meets with the due reward of her merits. Cressida comes nearer than any other of Shakspeare's females to the portrait of a seductive woman of pleasure; but even this character is managed in such a way as affords no promising prospect to her successors. Cleopatra is represented not as an alluring companion, but a repulsive termagant. The desertion of a young woman, by her lover, on the day assigned for marriage, is represented* in a torrent of most pathetic and heart-rending eloquence, as an act of treachery, that can be expiated only by the blood of the criminal. How opposite are the Relapse, the Beaux Stratagem, and fifty other *celebrated* English comedies? Impurity of sentiment is not confined to comedy. In the Fair Penitent, Lothario describes his amour with Calista in terms that one would suppose insufferable to any decent audience. Venice

---

* Much Ado about Nothing, Act IV. Scene I.

Preserved, contains many admirable passages, which only Shakspeare or Otway could have written. Yet this tragedy is, after all, a kind of Beggar's Opera, in blank verse. The heroes of the piece are ruffians and cut-throats; and the buffoonery of the antiquated debauchee is interlarded with the tenderness and heroism of Jaffier and Belvidera.

It would be endless to cite other examples of immoral tragedy. We now return to Shakspeare. It is true that he contains many trifling pages; and many that are entirely beneath his abilities and his fame; an observation which applies in an equal degree to all other English dramatic writers. But we contend that none of his personages are *expressly drawn to recommend vice*, and his plots are never, like those of Farquhar, and others, in a state of opposition to conjugal virtue. His works indeed abound with exquisite maxims of morality. So these great numbers have been quoted hundreds or thousands of times by authors of all classes; so that his plays may be said to be interwoven with the very vitals of English literature.

For the inequality of composition on this poet, a satisfactory apology may be made. His works have descended to posterity without being ever published under his own inspection. Of his thirty-six plays, twenty were never printed, till six years after his death. 'He sold them not to be printed, but to be played. They were immediately copied for the actors, and multiplied by transcript after transcript, vitiated by the blunders of the penmen, or changed by the affectation of the player; perhaps enlarged to include a jest, or mutilated to shorten the representation; and printed at last without the concurrence of the author, without the consent of the proprietor, from compilations made by chance or stealth out of the separate parts written for the theatre; and thus thrust into the world surreptitiously and hastily, they suffered another depravation from the ignorance and negligence of the printers, as every man who knows the state of the press in that age, will readily conceive. It is not easy for invention to bring together so many causes concurring to vitiate the text. No other author ever gave up his works to fortune and time with so little care. No books could be left in hands so likely to injure them, as plays frequently acted, yet continued in manuscript; no other transcribers were likely to be so little qualified for their task as those who copied for the stage, at a time when the lower ranks of the people were universally illiterate; no other editions were made from fragments so minutely broken, and so fortuitously reunited; and in no other age was the art of printing in such unskilful hands.'*

---

* Proposals for printing the works of Shakspeare, by Dr. Samuel Johnson. The Doctor should have said in the last line '*more* unlikely hands', for surely the printers of the sixteenth century were equal to their predecessors.

Mr. Pope was the first critic who attempted to correct the text of Shakspeare. He did much, but he left much more undone. Theobald was the next editor of this kind; and his notes and corrections are still among the most useful in the collection. Sir Thomas Hanmer then followed, and he was succeeded by Dr. Warburton. In 1756, Dr. Johnson printed his *Proposals* for an edition; and in October 1765, it was published. These critics have treated each other with very little ceremony, and sometimes with positive rudeness. Dr. Johnson, for instance, tells us that Theobald was *weak* and *ignorant, mean* and FAITHLESS, *petulant* and *ostentatious*. A person having published a book entitled *The Revisal of Shakspeare's Text*, Johnson says that *he bites like a viper, and would be glad to leave inflammations and gangrene behind him.* In politeness of style, Theobald and Warburton rival Johnson. Pope, as we learn from his Dunciad, felt the most implacable rancour against Theobald, for having detected some of his mistakes. It is not worth while to say more about these gentlemen. If the western continent shall ever have the glory to produce a Shakspeare, it is to be hoped that *his* commentators will not rake for distinction through the kennels of Billingsgate. Since the year 1765, the editors and correctors of this poet have multiplied in at least a tenfold proportion. Their notes have swelled Shakspeare to an inconvenient bulk. Of the value of some of these notes, the reader may form a judgement from the following. There is a line in Othello which says

A fellow almost damn'd in a fine face.

In one of the late London editions, this important line is clogged with *ten* successive explanations, each of which is accompanied by the name of its inventor. The present edition contains no notes of any kind, except one by Dr. Johnson, at the end of each play. In place of notes, a glossary of obsolete words will be given in the first volume of the work, and will be found sufficient for every substantial purpose of elucidation. An American reader is seldom disposed to wander through the wilderness of verbal criticism. An immense tract of excellent land, uncultivated, and even unexplored, presents an object more interesting to every mind than those ingenious literary trifles, that in Europe are able to command so much attention. The text of our author, as mentioned in our title page, is taken from the latest and most approved London editions.

It is pleasing to remark the progress of typography, and of general knowledge. 'The nation had been satisfied, from 1623, to 1664, that is forty-one years, with only two editions of Shakspeare, which probably did not together make one thousand copies.'* Within the last forty years, the sale has been at least an hundred and fifty times more extensive.

'If to feel strongly, and to describe naturally, be the two chief ingredients in poetical genius, Shakspeare must, after a fair examination, be allowed to possess that genius in a high degree. The question is not *whether a few improprieties may be pointed out in his works*; whether this, or that passage might not have been worked up with more art and skill, by some writer of happier times? A thousand such cold and frivolous criticisms are altogether indecisive as to his genuine merit. But, has he the spirit, the fire, the inspiration of a poet? Does he utter the voice of nature? Does he elevate by his sentiments? Does he interest by his descriptions? Does he paint to the heart as well as the fancy? Does he make his readers glow, and tremble, and weep? These are the great characteristics of true poetry. Where these are found, he must be a minute critic indeed, who can dwell upon slight defects. A few beauties of this kind transcend whole volumes of faultless mediocrity. Uncouth and abrupt, Shakspeare may sometimes appear. – But he is sublime, he is pathetic, in an eminent degree. If he flows not always a clear stream, he breaks forth often like a torrent of fire. Of art too, he is from being destitute, and his imagination is remarkable for delicacy as well as strength. – Though his merit were in other respects much less than it is, this alone ought to entitle him to high regard, that his writings are remarkably favourable to virtue. They awake the tenderest sympathies and inspire the most generous emotions.'** These remarks, though made upon a very different poet, apply with equal justice to Shakspeare.

That no part of this author may be lost, we have added to the present Edition his poems. Though not destitute of merit, they are confessedly inferior to his dramas. Their authenticity is not questioned, and they possessed one particular advantage. Some of them were published by the Author himself, and all of them, the two last excepted, in his lifetime.

In preparing this work for publication, the editors have exerted themselves as much as possible, by an elegant type and good paper, to do credit to the American press. Conscious of their solicitude to deserve approbation, they hope that their efforts have not been entirely unsuccessful; and it will be admitted that he merits forgiveness at least, if not gratitude, who has honestly done his utmost.

Philadelphia, July
1st, 1795.

---

* Johnson's Life of Milton.
** Critical Dissertation on the Poems of Ossian, by Dr. Blair.

Position of the Folger Shakespeare Library, Washington DC.

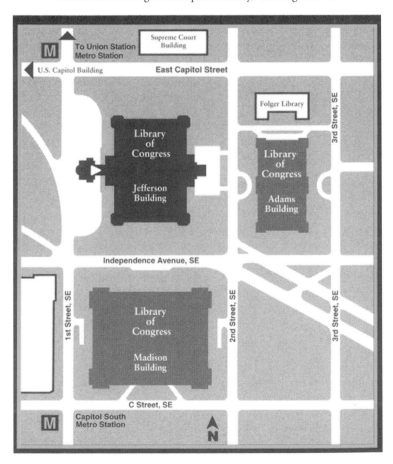

Bibliography

EDITIONS OF SHAKESPEARE

The Tragic History of King Richard III, Altered from Shakespear by Colley Cibber (London: J. & R. Tonson, 1766).

The Plays and Poems of William Shakespeare: Corrected from the Latest and Best London Editions, with Notes, by Samuel Johnson, L.L.D. To Which Are Added, a Glossary and the Life of the Author . . . First American Edition (Philadelphia: Bioren & Madan, 1795).

The Dramatick Works of William Shakespeare, Printed Complete (Boston MA: Munroe & Francis, 1802).

The Dramatic Works of William Shakspeare; with a Life of the Poet, Original and Selected, 7 vols. (Boston MA: Hilliard, Gray & Co., 1836).

The Complete Works of Shakspere: Revised from the Original Editions, with Historical Introductions, and Notes Explanatory & Critical; a Life of the Poet, and an Introductory Essay on His Phraseology & Metre. By J. O. Halliwell, Esq. F.R.S. F.S.A. (New York: Tallis, Willoughby & Co., 1850), vol. 1.

The Comedies, Histories, Tragedies and Poems of William Shakspere, ed. Charles Knight (Boston MA: Little, Brown & Co., 1853).

The Works of Shakespeare, ed. J. Payne Collier (New York: Redfield, 1853).

Shakespeare's Works, ed. Mary Cowden Clarke (New York: D. Appleton & Co., 1859).

The Complete Works of Shakspeare (Cincinnati: Rickey & Carroll, 1864).

The Works of William Shakespeare, ed. Richard Grant White (Boston MA: Little, Brown & Co., 1865).

The Complete Works of William Shakespeare (Philadelphia: J. P. Lippincott & Co., 1875).

The Complete Works of William Shakespeare: American Standard Edition, Carefully Collated and Compared with the Editions of Halliwell, Knight, Collier, and Others, with a Comprehensive Life of the Great Dramatist, by Charles Knight; Beautifully Illustrated with Numerous Steel Engravings, from Original Drawings, Chiefly Portraits in Character of the Most Distinguished American Actors (Philadelphia: William T. Amies, 1878). Also published by Baird & Dillon, Philadelphia, 1878.

King Richard III, as Presented by Edwin Booth, ed. William Winter (New York: Francis Hart & Co., 1881). Adapted from Colly Cibber.
The Complete Works of Shakespeare, ed. William Cullen Bryant (Philadelphia: Carson & Simpson, 1886).
The Complete Works of William Shakespeare (Chicago: Morrill, Higgins & Co., 1892).

BOOKS AND PAMPHLETS

Adams, John, *The Works of John Adams, Second President of the United States*, 10 vols. (Boston MA: Little, Brown & Co., 1856).
Adams, John Quincy, *An Oration Addressed to the Citizens of the Town of Quincy, on the Fourth of July, 1831, the Fifty-Fifth Anniversary of the Independence of the United States of America* (Boston MA: Richardson, Lord & Holbrook, 1831).
Alcott, Louisa May, *Little Women* (New York: Penguin, 1989). First published 1869.
Alter, J. Cecil, *James Bridger, Trapper, Frontiersman, Scout and Guide; a Historical Narrative* (Salt Lake City UT: Shepard Book Co., 1925).
Anbinder, Tyler, *Nativism and Slavery: The Know Nothings and the Politics of the 1850s* (New York: Oxford University Press, 1992).
Anderson, Charles, *An Address on Anglo Saxon Destiny: Delivered before the Philomathesian Society, of Kenyon College, Ohio, August 8th, 1849: and Repeated before the New England Society of Cincinnati; December 20th, 1849* (Cincinnati: John D. Thorpe, 1850).
Bacon, Delia, *The Philosophy of the Plays of Shakspere Unfolded* (London: Groombridge & Sons, 1857).
Ball, Robert Hamilton, *Shakespeare on Silent Film: A Strange Eventful History* (London: George Allen & Unwin, 1968).
Barlow, Joel, *The Columbiad, a Poem* (Philadelphia: C. & A. Conrad & Co., 1807).
Barnum, Phineas Taylor, *The Life of P. T. Barnum, Written by Himself* (London: Sampson, Low & Son, 1855).
Beaumont, Gustave de, *Marie or Slavery in the United States*, trans. Barbara Chapman (Baltimore: Johns Hopkins University Press, 1999) First published 1835.
Beecher, Lyman, *A Plea for the West*, 2nd edn (Cincinnati: Truman & Smith, 1835).
Bercovitch, Scavan, ed., *The Cambridge History of American Literature*, 7 vols. (Cambridge: Cambridge University Press, 1994).
Berrian, Samuel, *An Oration Delivered before the Tammany Society or Columbian Order . . . in the City of New-York, on the Fourth Day of July, 1815* (New York: John Low, 1815).
Bevington, David, and Jay L. Halio, eds., *Shakespeare, Pattern of Excelling Nature* (London: Associated University Press, 1978).
Bloom, Allan, *The Closing of the American Mind* (New York: Simon & Schuster, 1987).
Bode, Carl, *The Anatomy of American Popular Culture 1840–1861* (Berkeley: University of California Press, 1959).

Booth Grossman, Edwina, *Edwin Booth, Recollections by His Daughter, Edwina Booth Grossmann, and Letters to Her and to His Friends* (New York: Century Co., 1894).

Boudinot, Elias, *An Oration, Delivered at Elizabeth-Town, New Jersey, Agreeably to a Resolution of the State Society of Cincinnati, on the Fourth of July, 1793* (Elizabeth-Town NJ, 1793).

Bristol, Frank M., *Shakespeare and America* (Chicago: Hollister & Bros., 1898).

Bristol, Michael D., *Shakespeare's America, America's Shakespeare* (New York: Routledge, 1990).

Brown, Ivor, and George Fearon, *Amazing Monument: A Short History of the Shakespeare Industry* (London: William Heinemann, 1939).

Brown, Jared, *The Theatre in America during the Revolution* (Cambridge: Cambridge University Press, 1995).

Brown, William Wells, *Clotel; or The President's Daughter: a Narrative of Slave Life in the United States. With a Sketch of the Author's Life* (London: Partridge & Oakey, 1853).

Bryant, William Cullen, *Orations and Addresses* (New York: G. P. Putnam's Sons, 1878).

Buchanan, Archibald, *An Oration Composed and Delivered at the Request of the Republican Society of Baltimore, on the Fourth of July, One Thousand Seven Hundred and Ninety-Four* (Baltimore: Clayland Dobbin & Co., 1794).

Bulwer-Lytton, Edward, *The Lady of Lyons or, Love and Pride* (New York: T. H. French, 1838).

Calvert, George Henry, *Cabrio: A Poem* (Baltimore: N. Hickman, 1840).

Carlyle, Thomas, *On Heroes, Hero Worship and the Heroic in History* (London: James Fraser, 1841).

Channing, William E., *The Works of William Channing* (Boston MA: American Unitarian Association, 1866).

Charters, Sidney, *The Home of Lovely Players* (Birmingham, 1935).

Clarke, Mary Cowden, *The Complete Concordance to Shakespeare* (London: Bickers, 1886). First published 1845.

Conrad, Robert, *Jack Cade* (New York, 1841).

Cooper, James Fenimore, *Notions of the Americans: Picked up by a Travelling Bachelor* (Philadelphia, 1828).

Cornerstones of American Democracy (Washington DC: National Archives Trust Fund Board, 1995).

Cowell, Joe, *Thirty Years Passed among the Players: Interspersed with Anecdotes and Reminiscences of a Variety of Persons, Directly or Indirectly Connected with the Drama during the Theatrical Life of Joe Cowell, Comedian* (New York: Harper & Bros., 1844).

Crapol, Edward P., *America for Americans: Economic Nationalism and Anglophobia in the Late Nineteenth Century* (Westport CT: Greenwood Press, 1973).

Cushing, Caleb, *An Oration on the Material Growth and Territorial Progress of the United States, Delivered at Springfield, Mass., on the Fourth of July, 1839* (Springfield MA: Merrian, Wood & Co., 1839).

Dawson, Giles Edwin, *Four Centuries of Shakespeare Publication* (Lawrence KA: University of Kansas Libraries, 1964).

Day, Barry, *This Wooden 'O'* (London: Oberon Books, 1996).

Denning, Michael, *Mechanic Accents, Dime Novels and Working-Class Culture in America* (New York: Verso, 1987).

Dickens, Charles, *American Notes for General Circulation*, ed F. S. Schwarzbach (London: Everyman, 1997).

Diebals, Mary C., *Peter Markoe (1752?–1792): A Philadelphia Writer* (Washington DC: Catholic University American Press, 1944).

Dollimore, Jonathan, and Alan Sinfield, eds., *Political Shakespeare: Essays in Cultural Materialism* (Manchester: Manchester University Press, 1994).

Donnelly, Ignatius, *The Great Cryptogram: Francis Bacon's Cipher in the So-Called Shakespeare Plays* (London: Samson, Low, Marston, Searle & Rivington, 1888).

Drayton, Michael, *The Ballad of Agincourt and the Ode to the Virginian Voyage* (London, 1606).

Dukes, Joseph H., *An Oration Delivered before the Firemen of Charleston, on the Fourth of July, 1844* (Charleston: Walker & Burke, 1844).

Dunlap, Andrew, *An Oration Delivered at Salem on Monday July 5, 1819* (Salem MA: Warwick Palfrey Jr, 1819).

Dunlap, William, *The Glory of Columbia: Her Yeomanry!* (New York: David Longworth, 1817).

    History of the American Theatre (New York, 1832).

    Memoirs of George Fred Cooke (London: Henry Colburn, 1813).

    Yankee Chronology; or a Huzza for the Constitution! (New York: David Longworth, 1812).

Dunn, Esther Cloudman, *Shakespeare in America* (New York: Benjamin Blom, 1939).

Elson, Ruth Miller, *Guardians of Tradition* (Lincoln NE: University of Nebraska Press, 1964).

Emerson, Ralph Waldo, *The Collected Works of Ralph Waldo Emerson*, ed. Alfred R. Ferguson (Cambridge MA: Belknap Press, 1971).

    The Correspondence of Emerson and Carlyle, ed. Joseph Slater (New York: Columbia University Press, 1964).

    English Traits, ed. Howard Mumford Jones (Cambridge MA: Belknap Press, 1966).

    The Letters of Ralph Waldo Emerson, ed. Eleanor M. Tilton, 10 vols. (New York: Columbia University Press, 1991).

    Nature Addresses and Lectures (Cambridge MA: Houghton, Mifflin Co., 1883).

    Representative Men (Philadelphia: David McKay, 1892).

    Selected Essays, ed. Larzer Ziff (Harmondsworth: Penguin, 1985).

Engle, Ron, Felicia Hardison Londré and Daniel J. Watermeier, eds., *Shakespeare Companies and Festivals: An International Guide* (Westport CT: Greenwood Press, 1995).

Fearon, Henry Bradshaw, *Sketches of America. A Narrative of a Journey of Five Thousand Miles through the Eastern and Western States of America* (London: Longman, Hurst, Rees, Orner & Brown, 1818).

Ferington, Esther, ed., *Infinite Variety: Exploring the Folger Shakespeare Library* (Washington DC: Folger Shakespeare Library, 2002).

Fisher, Judith L., and Stephen Watt, eds., *When They Weren't Doing Shakespeare: Essays on Nineteenth-Century British and American Theatre* (Athens GA: University of Georgia Press, 1989).

Folger, Emily Jordan, *Meridian Club Paper by Mrs Folger, 1933* (privately published and held within the Folger Archive, Folger Shakespeare Library, Washington DC).

Forrest, Edwin, *Oration Delivered at the Democratic Republican Celebration of the Sixty-Second Anniversary of the Independence of the United States in the City of New-York, Fourth July, 1838* (New York: J. W. Bell, 1838).

Fox, Levi, *In Honour of Shakespeare* (Norwich: Jarrold & Son, 1972).

Franklin, Benjamin, *The Interests of Great Britain with Regard to her Colonies, and the acquisitions of Canada and Guadaloupe: to Which Are Added, Observations Concerning the Increase of Mankind, Peopling of Countries* (London, 1761).

Frantzen, Allen J., *Desire for Origins* (New Brunswick NJ: Rutgers University Press, 1990).

Frantzen, Allen J., and John D. Niles, *Anglo-Saxonism and the Construction of Social Identity* (Gainesville FL: University Press of Florida, 1997).

Freneau, Philip Morin, *A Voyage to Boston. A Poem* (New York, 1775).

Fuller, S. Margaret, *At Home and Abroad* (Boston MA: Roberts Bros., 1874).

Garrison, Webb, *Lost Pages from American History* (Harrisburg PA: Stackpole Books, 1976).

Gayley, Charles Mills, *Shakespeare and the Founders of Liberty in America* (New York: Macmillan, 1917).

Gilpin, William, *Mission of the North American People, Geographical, Social, and Political* (Philadelphia: J. B. Lippincott, 1873). First published 1860 as *The Central Gold Region: the Grain, Pastoral, and Gold Regions of North America*.

Gjerde, Jon, ed., *Major Problems in American Immigration and Ethnic History* (Boston MA: Houghton, Mifflin Co., 1998).

Goldberg, Isaac, *Major Noah: American-Jewish Pioneer* (New York: Alfred A. Knopf, 1937).

Granqvist, Raoul, *Imitation as Resistance: Appropriations of English Literature in Nineteenth-Century America* (Madison NJ: Fairleigh Dickinson University Press, 1995).

Griffin, G. W., *Hamlet the Dainty, an Ethiopian Burlesque on Shakespeare's Hamlet* (n.p., 1870).

Grimsted, David, *Melodrama Unveiled: American Theater and Culture, 1800–1850* (Los Angeles: University of California Press, 1968).

Hamilton, Alexander, John Jay and James Madison, *The Federalist*, ed. Henry Cabot Lodge (New York: G. P. Putman's Sons, 1900).

Harding, Walter, *The Days of Henry Thoreau* (New York: Alfred A. Knopf, 1966).

Harrison, Gabriel, *Edwin Forrest: the Actor and the Man, Critical and Reminiscent* (Brooklyn, 1889).

Hart, Joseph C., *The Romance of Yachting: Voyage the First* (New York: Harper & Bros., 1848).

Hase, Ragnhild Fiebig-von, and Ursula Lehmkuhl, eds., *Enemy Images in American History* (Providence RI: Berghahn Books, 1997).

Hawthorne, Nathaniel, *The English Notebooks*, ed. Randall Stewart (New York: Modern Language Association of America, 1941).

The Letters, 1853–1856, ed. Thomas Woodson et al. (Columbus OH: Ohio State University Press, 1987).

Hildreth, Richard, *History of the United States of America, from the Discovery of the Continent to the Organization of Government under the Federal Constitution* (New York: Harpers & Bros., 1849).

Hobsbawm, Eric, and Terence Ranger, eds., *The Invention of Tradition* (Cambridge: Cambridge University Press, 1983).

Holderness, Graham, ed., *The Shakespeare Myth* (Manchester: Manchester University Press, 1988).

Hone, Philip, *The Diary of Philip Hone 1828–1851*, ed. Baynard Tuckerman, 2 vols. (New York: Dodd, Mead & Co., 1889).

Hopkins, Vivian, *Prodigal Puritan: A Life of Delia Bacon* (Cambridge MA: Belknap Press, 1959).

Hopkinson, Joseph, *Hail Columbia* (Philadelphia: J. Ormrod, 1798).

What Is Our Situation and What Our Prospects? (Philadelphia, 1798).

Horsman, Reginald, *Race and Manifest Destiny: The Origins of American Anglo-Saxonism* (Cambridge MA: Harvard University Press, 1981).

Howe, Daniel Walker, ed., *Victorian America* ([Philadelphia]: University of Pennsylvania Press, 1976).

Howells, William Dean, *My Literary Passions* (New York: Harper & Bros., 1895).

Hughes, Glenn, *A History of the American Theatre, 1700–1950* (New York: Samuel French, 1951).

Hunt, Benjamin Faneul, *An Oration, Delivered by Their Appointment, before the Washington Society, in Charleston, South-Carolina, on the 4th of July, 1839* (Charleston: S. S. Miller, 1839).

Hutton, Laurence, *Edwin Booth* (New York: Harper & Bros., 1893).

Irving, Washington, *The Sketch Book of Geoffrey Crayon, Gent.* (New York: Penguin Classics, 1988).

Jaggard, William, *Shakespeare Bibliography* (Stratford-upon-Avon, 1911).

James, Henry, 'The Birthplace', in James, *The Better Sort* (New York: C. Scribner's Sons, 1903).

Jefferson, Thomas, *The Papers of Thomas Jefferson*, ed. Julian P. Boyd et al. (Princeton: Princeton University Press, 1955).

Writings, ed. Merrill D. Peterson (New York: Library of America, 1984).

Johannsen, Albert, *The House of Beadle and Adams and Its Dime and Nickel Novels: The Story of a Vanished Literature*, 3 vols. (Norman OK: University of Oklahoma Press, 1962).

Jones, George, *The First Annual Jubilee Oration upon the Life, Character and Genius of Shakspeare, Delivered at Stratford-upon-Avon, April 23rd, 1836, before the Royal Shakspearian Club* (London: Edward Churton, 1836).

Oration on the National Independence, Richmond, Va., July 4, 1840 before the Franklin Society at the City-Hall, Written and Pronounced by George Jones, Tragedian (Richmond VA: Franklin Society, 1840).

Kelly, Mary Gilbert, *Catholic Immigration Colonization Projects in the United States, 1815–1860* (New York: United States Catholic Historical Society, 1939).

Kendall, John Smith, *The Golden Age of the New Orleans Theater* (Baton Rouge LA: Louisiana State University Press, 1952).

Shakespeare in Amerika (Berlin: Theodor Hofmann, 1882).

Kohn, Hans, *American Nationalism: An Interpretive Essay* (New York: Macmillan, 1957).

Kolin, Philip C., ed., *Shakespeare and Southern Writers: A Study in Influence* (Jackson MS: University Press of Mississippi, 1985).

Shakespeare in the South: Essays on Performance (Jackson MS: University Press of Mississippi, 1983).

Konkle, Buton Alva, *Joseph Hopkinson, 1770–1842: Jurist, Scholar, Inspirer of the Arts* (Philadelphia: University of Pennsylvania Press, 1931).

Koon, Helene Wickham, *How Shakespeare Won the West* (Jefferson WI: McFarland & Co., 1925).

Lanier, Douglas, *Shakespeare and Modern Popular Culture* (Oxford: Oxford University Press, 2002).

Lee, Charles, *Strictures on a Pamphlet Entitled a 'Friendly Address to All Reasonable Americans, on the Subject of Our Political Confusions,' Addressed to the People of America* (Philadelphia: T. Green, 1775).

Lee, Sidney, *Notes and Additions to the Census of Copies of the Shakespeare First Folio* (London: Oxford University Press, 1906).

Shakespeare's Comedies, Histories and Tragedies, Containing a Census of Extant Copies with Some Account of Their History and Condition (Oxford, 1902).

Levine, Lawrence W., *Highbrow/Lowbrow: The Emergence of Cultural Hierarchy in America* (Cambridge MA: Harvard University Press, 1988).

The Unpredictable Past (New York: Oxford University Press, 1993).

Lewis, Richard W. B., *The American Adam: Innocence, Tragedy and Tradition in the Nineteenth Century* (Chicago: University of Chicago Press, 1955).

Livermore, Abiel Abbot, *The War with Mexico Reviewed* (Boston MA: W. Crosby & H. P. Nichols, 1850).

Loney, Glen, and Patricia MacKay, *The Shakespeare Complex* (New York: Drama Book Specialists, 1975).

Louisiana Native American Association, *Address of the Louisiana Native American Association, to the Citizens of Louisiana and the Inhabitants of the United States* (New Orleans: D. Felt & Co., 1839).

Manvell, Roger, *Shakespeare and the Film* (New York: A. S. Barnes & Co., 1979).

Marble, Annie Russell, *Heralds of American Literature* (Chicago: University of Chicago Press, 1907).

Marder, Louis, *His Exits and His Entrances: The Story of Shakespeare's Reputation* (Philadelphia: J. B. Lippincott, 1963).

Markoe, Peter, *Miscellaneous Poems* (Philadelphia, 1787).

Marryat, Frederick, *Diary in America with Remarks on Its Institutions* (New York: William H. Colyer, 1839).

Marsden, Jean I., ed., *The Appropriation of Shakespeare* (New York: Harvester Wheatsheaf, 1991).

Marshall, Herbert, and Mildred Stock, *Ira Aldridge, the Negro Tragedian* (London: Rockliff, 1958).

Matthiessen, Francis Otto, *American Renaissance: Art and Expression in the Age of Emerson and Whitman* (New York: Oxford University Press, 1941).

Melville, Herman, *The Complete Shorter Fiction* (London: Everyman, 1997).

The Confidence-Man (Oxford: Oxford University Press, 1989). First published 1856.

Journal of a Visit to Europe and the Levant, October 11, 1856–May 6, 1857, ed. Howard C. Horsford (Princeton: Princeton University Press, 1955).

Moby-Dick; or, The Whale (London: Penguin, 1986). First published 1851.

Michel, Lou, and Dan Herbeck, *American Terrorist: Timothy McVeigh and the Oklahoma City Bombing* (New York: Regan Books, 2001).

Moody, Richard, *The Astor Place Riot* (Bloomington IN: Indiana University Press, 1958).

Morse, Samuel, *Imminent Dangers to the Free Institutions of the United States through Foreign Immigration, and the Present State of the Naturalization Laws* (New York: E. B. Clayton, 1835).

The Present Attempt to Dissolve the American Union, a British Aristocratic Plot (New York: John Trow, 1862).

Moses, Montrose Jonas, *The Fabulous Forrest: The Record of an American Actor* (Boston MA: Little, Brown & Co., 1929).

Moses, Montrose Jonas, and John Mason Brown, *The American Theatre as Seen by Its Critics 1752–1934* (New York: W. W. Norton & Co., 1934).

Mott, Frank Luther, *Golden Multitudes: The Story of Best Sellers in the United States* (New York: Macmillan Co., 1947).

Murray, Charles, *Travels in North America during the Years 1834, 1835 & 1836, Including a Summer Residence with the Pawnee Tribe of Indians in the Remote Prairies of the Missouri and a Visit to Cuba and the Azore Islands* (London: Richard Bentley, 1839).

Nettle, George, *A Practical Guide for Emigrants to North America by a Seven Years Resident in North America* (London: Simpkin, Marshall & Co., 1850).

Nisbet, Richard, *Slavery Not Forbidden by Scripture. Or, A Defence of the West-India Planters, from the Aspersions Thrown out against Them* (Philadelphia, 1773).

Noah, Mordecai, *Shakespeare Illustrated, or, The Novels and Histories on Which the Plays of Shakespeare are Founded, Vol. I. Collected and Translated from the Originals, by Mrs. Lennox; with Critical Remarks and Biographical Sketches of the Writers, by M. M. Noah* (Philadelphia: Bradford & Inskeep, 1809). First published 1753.

Olson, Charles, *Call Me Ishmael* (London: Jonathan Cape, 1967).

Paine, Thomas, *Common Sense,* ed. Isaac Kramnick (Harmondsworth: Penguin, 1976).

Pascal, Roy, *Shakespeare in Germany 1740–1815* (Cambridge: Cambridge University Press, 1937).

Paterson, Thomas G., ed., *Major Problems in American Foreign Relations,* 2 vols. (Lexington KY: D. C. Heath, 1989).

Pessen, Edward, *Jacksonian America: Society, Personality, and Politics* (Homewood IL: Dorsey Press, 1969).

Pierson, George Wilson, *Tocqueville and Beaumont in America* (New York: Oxford University Press, 1938).

Poole, John F., *Ye Comedie of Errours, a Glorious, Uproarous Burlesque. Not Indecorous nor Censorous, with Many a Chorus Warranted Not To Bore Us, Now for the First Time Set before Us* (New York: Samuel French, [*c.* 1858]).

Rapin de Thoyras, Paul, *Histoire d'Angleterre* (n.p., 1727).

Rawlings, Peter, ed., *Americans on Shakespeare 1776–1914* (Aldershot: Ashgate, 1999).

Rees, James, *The Life of Edwin Forrest with Reminiscences and Personal Recollections* (Philadelphia: T. B. Peterson & Bros., 1874).

Remini, Robert V., *Andrew Jackson* (New York: Harper & Row, 1969).

Richards, William C., *The Shakspeare Calendar; or, Wit and Wisdom for Every Day in the Year* (New York: George P. Putnam, 1850).

Riddle, Rev. David Hunter, *A Sermon on Behalf of the American Home Missionary Society, Preached in the Cities of New York and Brooklyn, May 1851* (New York: American Home Missionary Society, 1851).

Roosevelt, Theodore, *American Ideals and Other Essays, Social and Political* (New York: G. P. Putnam's Sons, 1897).

　The Winning of the West, ed. Christopher Lasch (Greenwich CT: Fawcett Publications, 1964).

Rusk, Ralph Leslie, *The Literature of the Middle Western Frontier,* 2 vols. (New York: Columbia University Press, 1925).

St. Pierre, Stephanie, *Our National Anthem* (Brookfield: Millbrock Press, 1992).

Schlesinger, Arthur M., *Prelude to Independence: The Newspaper War on Britain 1764–1776* (New York: Alfred A. Knopf, 1966).

Sealts, Merton M., *Emerson on the Scholar* (Columbia: University of Missouri Press, 1992).

Sedgewick, William Ellery, *Herman Melville: The Tragedy of Mind* (Cambridge MA: Harvard University Press, 1945).

Shattuck, Charles H., *Shakespeare on the American Stage* (Washington DC: Folger Shakespeare Library, 1976).

Sheridan, Richard Brinsley, *Pizarro* (New York: Thomas Longworth, 1819).

Sherzer, Jane Belle, *American Editions of Shakespeare: 1753–1866* (Baltimore: Modern Language Association of America, 1907).

Simms, William Gilmore, *Border Beagles, a Tale of Mississippi* (New York: W. J. Widdleton, 1855).

Simon, Henry W., *The Reading of Shakespeare in American Schools and Colleges* (New York: Simon & Schuster, 1932).

Slade, William Adams, 'The Significance of the Folger Shakespeare Memorial: An Essay toward an Interpretation in *Henry C. Folger: 18 June 1857–11 June 1930* (New Haven, 1931).

Slotkin, Richard, *The Fatal Environment: The Myth of the Frontier in the Age of Industrialization 1800–1890* (Norman OK: University of Oklahoma Press, 1985).

  Regeneration through Violence: The mythology of the American Frontier, 1600–1860 (Middletown CT: Wesleyan University Press, 1973).

Smith, Elizabeth Oakes, *The Autobiography of Elizabeth Oakes Smith*, ed. Mary Alice Wyman (Lewiston ME: Lewiston Journal Co., 1924).

  Bald Eagle; or, The Last of the Ramapaughs, a Romance of Revolutionary Times (New York: Beadle & Co., 1867).

Smith, Henry Nash, *Virgin Land: The American West in Symbol and Myth* (Cambridge MA: Harvard University Press, 1950).

Smith, Robert Metcalf, *The Formation of Shakespeare Libraries in America* (New York: Shakespeare Association of America, 1929).

Smith, William Henry, *Bacon and Shakespeare: An Enquiry Touching Players, Playhouses, and Play-Writers in the Days of Elizabeth* (London: John Russell Smith, 1857).

  Was Lord Bacon the Author of Shakespeare's Plays? A Letter to Lord Ellesmere (London: William Skeffington, 1856).

Smither, Nelle, *A History of the English Theatre in New Orleans* (New York: Benjamin Blom, 1944).

Sonneck, Oscar George Theodore, *Report on The Star-Spangled Banner, Hail Columbia, America, Yankee Doodle* (Washington DC: Government Printing Office, 1909).

Sowerby, E. Millicent, *Catalogue of the Library of Thomas Jefferson* (Washington DC: Library of Congress, 1952).

Sprague, Charles, *The Poetical and Prose Writings of Charles Sprague* (Boston MA: Ticknor, Reed, & Fields, 1849).

Spiller, Robert E., *James Fenimore Cooper* (New York: American Book Co., 1936).

Stiles, Ezra, *A History of Three of the Judges of King Charles I. Major-General Whalley, Major-General Goffe, and Colonel Dixwell Who, at the Restoration, 1660, Fled to America; and Were Secreted and Concealed, in Massachusetts and Connecticut, for Near Thirty Years* (Hartford CT, 1794).

Stoddard, Elizabeth, *The Morgesons* (New York: Penguin, 1984).

Stowe, Harriet Beecher, *Sunny Memories of Foreign Lands* (London: Piper, Stephenson & Spence, 1854).

  Uncle Tom's Cabin or Life among the Lowly (New York: Penguin, 1981).

Strong, Josiah, *Our Country*, ed. Jurgen Herbst (Cambridge MA: Belknap Press, 1963).

Studing, Richard, *Shakespeare in American Painting: A Catalogue from the Late Eighteenth Century to the Present* (Rutherford NJ: Fairleigh Dickinson University Press, 1993).

Sturtevant, Rev. Julian Monson, *American Emigration* (New York: American Home Missionary Society, 1857).

Sumner, Charles, *An Oration Delivered before the Municipal Authorities of the City of Boston, July 4th, 1859* (Boston MA, 1859).
 The True Grandeur of Nations, Mr Sumner's Oration. July 4, 1845 (Boston MA: American Peace Society, 1845).
Taylor, Bayard, *Eldorado or Adventures in the Path of Empire* (Berkeley: Heyday Books, 2000). First published 1850.
Taylor, Gary, *Reinventing Shakespeare: A Cultural History from the Restoration to the Present* (London: Vintage, 1991).
Thaler, Alwin, *Shakespeare and Democracy* (Knoxville TN: University of Tennessee Press, 1941).
Thoreau, Henry, *The Portable Thoreau*, ed. Carl Bode (New York: Penguin, 1947). First published 1854.
Thorndike, Ashley Horace, *Shakespeare in America* (London: Oxford University Press, 1927).
Timrod, Henry, *The Essays of Henry Timrod*, ed. Edd Winfield Parks, (Athens GA: University of Georgia Press, 1942).
 The Poems of Henry Timrod (New York: E. J. Hale & Son, 1873).
Tocqueville, Alexis de, *Democracy in America*, ed. Phillips Bradley, 2 vols. (New York: Vintage Books, 1945).
Travers, Len, *Celebrating the Fourth: Independence Day and the Rites of Nationalism in the Early Republic* (Amherst MA: University of Massachusetts Press, 1997).
Trollope, Anthony, *North America*, ed. Donald Smalley and Bradford Allen Booth (New York: De Capo Press, 1951).
Trollope, Fanny, *The Domestic Manners of the Americans*, ed. Pamela Neville-Sington (London: Penguin, 1997). First published 1832.
Tryon, Warren S., ed., *A Mirror for Americans: Life and Manners in the United States, 1790–1870*, 3 vols. (Chicago: University of Chicago Press, 1952).
Turner, Frederick Jackson, *The Frontier in American History* (New York: Henry Holt & Co., 1920).
 The United States, 1830–1850 (New York: Henry Holt & Co., 1935).
Turner, Sharon, *The History of the Anglo-Saxons, from Their First Appearance above the Elbe, to the Death of Egbert: with a Map of Their Ancient Territory* (London: T. Cadwell & W. Davies, 1799).
Tyler, Royall, *The Contrast* (Philadelphia: Prichard & Hall, 1790).
Twain, Mark, *The Adventures of Huckleberry Finn* (London: Penguin Classics, 1985).
 Following the Equator: A Journey around the World, 2 vols. (New York, 1897).
 Life on the Mississippi (New York: Oxford University Press, 1996).
 Roughing It (London: Penguin Classics, 1985).
 1601, and Is Shakespeare Dead? (New York: Oxford University Press, 1996). First published 1909.
US Bureau of the Census, *A Century of Population Growth: From the First Census of the United States to the Twelfth, 1790–1900* (Washington DC: Government Printing Office, 1909).
Vernon, Grenville, *Yankee Doodle-Doo: A Collection of Songs of the Early American Stage* (New York: Payson & Clarke, 1927).

Wall, A. H., *A List of the Editions of Shakespeare's Works Published in America* (Stratford-upon-Avon: Shakespeare Memorial Association, 1889).

Warner, George James, *Means for the Preservation of Public Liberty, an Oration Delivered in the New Dutch Church, on the Fourth of July, 1797: Being the Twenty-First Anniversary of Our Independence, 'Ode Composed for the Occasion, by P. Freneau'* (New York, 1797).

Webster, Noah, *Dissertations on the English Language* (Boston MA, 1789).
  Effects of Slavery on Morals and Industry (Hartford CT: Hudson & Goodwin, 1793).

Wells, Stanley, *American Shakespeare Travesties (1852–1888)*, 5 vols. (London: Diploma Press, 1978).

West, Anthony James, *The Shakespeare First Folio: The History of the Book* (Oxford: Oxford University Press, 2001).

Westfall, Alfred Van Rensselaer, *American Shakespearean Criticism 1607–1865* (New York: H. W. Wilson, 1939).

Wheeler, Edward L., *Deadwood Dick's Doom; or, Calamity Jane's Last Adventure, a Tale of Death Notch* (New York: Deadwood Dick Library [Beadle and Adams], 1899).

White, Richard Grant, *Words and Their Uses, Past and Present* (New York: Sheldon & Co., 1871).

Whitman, Walt, *The Collected Writings of Walt Whitman*, ed. G. W. Allen and S. Bradley (New York: New York University Press, 1964).
  Leaves of Grass and Selected Prose, ed. Ellman Crasnow (London: Everyman, 1993).
  Prose Works 1892, vol. ii, *Collect and Other Prose*, ed. Floyd Stovall (New York: New York University Press, 1964).

Wilmeth, Don B., and Christopher Bigsby, eds., *The Cambridge History of American Theatre* (Cambridge: Cambridge University Press, 1998).

Winship, Michael, *American Literary Publishing in the Mid-Nineteenth Century: The Business of Ticknor and Fields* (Cambridge: Cambridge University Press, 1995).

Wister, Owen, *The Virginian* (New York: Macmillan & Co., 1902).

Woodward, George Washington, *Woodward on Foreigners* (Philadelphia: H. B. Ashmead, 1863).

Wyman, William Henry, *The Bibliography of the Bacon–Shakespeare Controversy, with Notes and Extracts* (Cincinnati: Cox & Co., 1884).

ARTICLES IN NEWSPAPERS AND PERIODICALS

Adams, Joseph Quincy, 'The Folger Shakespeare Memorial Dedicated April 23, 1932, Shakespeare and American Culture', *Spinning Wheel*, 12/9–10 (June–July 1932), pp. 212–15 and 229–31.

Aiken, Albert W., 'Richard Talbot of Cinnabar; or, The Brothers of the Red Hand', *Saturday Journal*, 530 (14 August 1880).

Bacon, Delia, 'William Shakespeare and His Plays: An Inquiry Concerning Them', *Putnam's Monthly*, 7 (January 1856), pp. 1–19.

'The Birthplace of Shakespeare', *The Times*, 26 October 1868.

Carrell, Jennifer Lee, 'How the Bard Won the West', *Smithsonian*, 19/5 (August 1998), pp. 99–107.

Conway, Moncure D., 'Hunting the Mythical Pall-Bearer', *Harper's New Monthly Magazine*, 72/428 (January 1886), pp. 211–17.

'The Shakspeare Tercentenary', *Harper's New Monthly Magazine*, 29/171 (August 1864), pp. 337–46.

Crawford, James, 'A Nation Divided by One Language', *Guardian*, 8 March 2001.

'Earth and Water from Bard's Homeland Is Sprinkled on Stage', *Dallas Morning News*, 3 June 1936, section 1, p. 12.

Falk, Robert, 'Shakespeare in America: An Annual Survey to 1900', *Shakespeare Survey*, 18 (1965), pp. 102–18.

Fawcett, James Waldo, 'Dedication of the Folger Shakespeare Memorial Library', *Washington Post*, 24 April 1932.

Hawthorne, Nathaniel, 'Recollections of a Gifted Woman', *Atlantic Monthly*, 11/63 (January 1863), pp. 43–58.

Higginson, T. W., Andrew Carnegie et al., 'Do Americans Hate England?', *North American Review*, 150/403 (June 1890), pp. 740–79.

'History of the United States', *United States Democratic Review*, 26/139 (January 1850), pp. 44–9.

Howells, William Dean, 'Editor's Study', *Harper's New Monthly Magazine*, 83/498 (November 1891), pp. 962–7.

'Literary Boston Thirty Years Ago', *Harper's New Monthly Magazine*, 91/546 (November 1895), pp. 865–79.

'Hung Be the Heavens with Black-Shakespeare', *New York American*, 10 January 1822.

Irving, Henry, 'The American Audience', *Fortnightly Review*, 43 (1 February 1885), pp. 197–201.

Kaufmann, Eric, 'American Exceptionalism Reconsidered: Anglo-Saxon Ethnogenesis in the "Universal" Nation, 1776–1850', *Journal of American Studies*, 33 (1999), pp. 437–57.

Loring, Frederic Wadsworth, 'In the Old Churchyard at Fredericksburg', *Atlantic Monthly*, 26/155 (September 1870), pp. 273–4.

'Major Publishers Begin Massive Distribution of Free Books to US Troops Abroad', United States Department of Defense, News Release no. 627-02.

Marovitz, Sanford E., 'America vs Shakespeare: From the Monroe Doctrine to the Civil War', *Zeitschrift für Anglistik und Amerikanistik*, 34 (1986), pp. 33–46.

Meacham, Jon, 'The New Face of Race', *Newsweek*, 18 September 2000, pp. 38–48.

Anon (J. T. Thompson), *New Englander*, 1/1 (January 1843), pp. 64–84.

'New York Riots – Law – Liberty – Order', *National Era* (Washington DC), 24 May 1849.

'Our Language Destined To Be Universal', *United States Democratic Review*, 35/4 (April 1855), pp. 306–14.

'The Philosophy of Theatrical Riots', *Public Ledger and Daily Transcript* (Philadelphia) 11 May 1849.

'Popular Amusements in New York', *National Era* (Washington DC), 15 April 1847.

'Professional Jealousy', *The Times*, 12 March 1846.

'St George's Day in New York', *Daily Picayune* (New Orleans), 9 May 1850.

Scheide, William H., 'The Earliest First Folio in America?', *Shakespeare Quarterly*, 27 (1976), pp. 332–3.

'Shakespeare', *Commercial Cincinnati*, 23 April 1877.

'Shakespeare and America', *The Times*, 18 October 1887.

'Shakespearean Study', *Daily Enquirer* (Cincinnati), 6 February 1876.

'Shakesperiana Collection', *Congressional Record*, 70th Congress, 1st session, 1928, 69, part 7, pp. 7422–3.

'Shakspeare in America', *Literary World*, 7 (July–December 1850), pp. 348–9.

Smith, Goldwin, 'The Hatred of England', *North American Review*, 150/402 (May 1890), pp. 547–63.

Taylor, Gary, 'Cry Havoc: Shakespeare Saw Henry V's Brutal Strike against the French as a Battle of Good against Evil, of "Plain Shock" and "Awe"', *Guardian*, 5 April 2003.

Timrod, Henry, 'Literature in the South', *Russell's Magazine*, 5 (August 1859), pp. 385–95.

'To the People of Pennsylvania', *Pennsylvania Gazette*, 27 March 1776.

Turnbull, Rev. Robert, 'Expensiveness of Theatres', *Colored American* (New York), 21 March 1840.

'The United States and the United Kingdom', *United States Democratic Review*, 1/5 May 1853), pp. 385–414.

Watson, Joseph, 'Shakespeare in America', *New York Herald*, 12 and 26 February 1877.

West, Anthony James, 'Provisional New Census of the Shakespeare First Folio', *Library*, 17/1 (March 1995), pp. 60–6.

Whitman, Walt, 'An English and American Poet', *American Phrenological Journal*, 22/4 (October 1855), pp. 90–1.

'Have We a National Literature?', *North American Review*, 152/412 (March 1891), pp. 332–9.

'What Lurks behind Shakspeare's Historical Plays?', *Critic*, 27 September 1884.

'Who Wrote Shickspur?', *Daily Picayune* (New Orleans), 11 June 1857.

Willoughby, Edwin Eliott, 'The Reading of Shakespeare in Colonial America', *Bibliographical Society of America*, 30/2 (1936), pp. 45–56.

Wilson, Gen. James Harrison, 'Do Americans Hate England?', *North American Review*, 150/403 (June 1890), pp. 771–5.

Index